Treasures of the Kingdom

Christ Revealed In Gifts to His People

Cho Larson

WESTBOW
P R E S S®
A DIVISION OF THOMAS NELSON
& ZONDERVAN

Contact: cho@cholarson.com
P.O. Box 1141, Cottonwood, AZ 86326

WestBow Press books may be ordered through booksellers or by contacting:
WestBow Press
A Division of Thomas Nelson & Zondervan
1663 Liberty Drive
Bloomington, IN 47403
www.westbowpress.com
1 (866) 928-1240

Cover design by Ian Loudon. Microscopic photo, copyright ©Reuben Birkholz 2015, Calcite on other minerals, Pima County, Arizona.

ISBN: 978-1-5127-3193-4 (sc)
ISBN: 978-1-5127-3195-8 (hc)
ISBN: 978-1-5127-3194-1 (e)
Library of Congress Control Number: 2016902715

Print information available on the last page.

WestBow Press rev. date: 2/24/2016

Dedicated to my sons, whom I treasure.

Brandon Gregory, Douglas Michael

Michael Lewis, Ian McKay, Andrew Stuart

"But we have this treasure in jars of clay to show that this all-surpassing power is from God and not from us."

2 Corinthians 4:7

Contents

Acknowledgements

How can I acknowledge each and every person and experience that played a part in the shaping of this study book? So many people have contributed in some way, small or major, most of all my wife Susie, who has kept me focused on what is right and most important in my life. Writing these words is not something achievable on my own apart from the gifting and empowering work of the Holy Spirit. My prayer is that the following pages will pour out an "abundant rain." May they be like the "dew of Hermon falling on Mount Zion."

It's a miracle I'm still around to write anything. On several occasions, death knocked on my door. In a fourteen-foot aluminum boat with my pregnant mom on board, twelve-foot waves should have taken our family to the bottom of the bay. At five years old a major mastoid infection tried to take me. At seven, river currents sucked me under. And I'll never forget the oversized rear tire of a farm tractor running over my chest, its lugs grazing my head. I vividly remember the panic I felt when caught in a rip tide. Later, I rolled my Austin Healey Sprite convertible, ripping off the top of the car, but not my head. Then I survived the Tet offensive in Qui Nhon, Vietnam, in spite of flying bullets, and incendiary grenades. Finally, an eighteen-wheeler came at me head on at sixty-five mph. God has preserved my life over and over again, and I am thankful that He has kept me for this day.

All of my pastors have had an impact on this message. Some because they were not teaching the whole truth, and that made me dig deeper into the Word to find out what was right. Others because of their diligent and faithful teaching of the Word that inspired and challenged me to search as for lost (hidden) treasures. I'm thankful for all the prayers and encouragement of so many godly people as this study came together.

My mom, Geraldine Elizabeth Mae (DeGroot) Larson, taught me the disciplines of self-control and determination. From my dad, Pastor Phillip Albert Larson, I inherited the gift and desire for writing. My siblings helped to shape my life also. My oldest brother Bill used boxing gloves; my sister Patricia used a flying spoon aimed my way when I tormented her; my brother Dan helped me see the humor in things; and my youngest brother Paul was just an easy going, come-what-may kind of kid.

How is it possible to be dad to five boys and Papa Cho to their children without having a major impact on my life? My oldest son Brandon inherited my love for digging in the dirt to grow beautiful things; Professor Doug is a gifted teacher, very creative and a dad to four delightful girls; Michael is the whiz-kid who really gets theology; Ian has a servant's heart, a creative mind, and a beautiful family; and Andrew thinks outside the box and challenges me. They are all an inspiration.

Our home Bible study group provided the catalyst that got me back on track with the Lord's call to teach and write on this topic. They tested and challenged my teaching, and we learned so much from each other: my dear friends, Dick and Connie Nichols, Jim and Andi O'Mara, Mark and Lorie Edwards, Glenn and Fran Pollock, Herman and Anita Mickley, and Carole and Glen Bailey.

To all who have walked with me along on this pathway, "Many Blessings in Christ Jesus, our Lord and Savior."

Cho Larson

Preface

The roots of this study on "Kingdom Treasures" may well have been seeded in me during an unplanned time of fasting, prayer, and cherished communion with the Spirit of Jesus. The seed took root and grew because many years later I was called again to earnest prayer and fasting. My prayers were for the desire of God's heart to become the desire of my heart. Then the light began to break through in a time personal distress, as if God had his hand on me, turning up the light slowly so I could absorb what He was teaching me. My eyes opened slowly, and I began to see the desire of God's heart. At this time so many Christian friends in our church, home Bible study group, and family became severely ill in a short period of time with cancers and other serious, life threatening illnesses. At every turn, friends or family were struggling and suffering. My search began in earnest. Trials touched even closer to my heart when our newly wed son became ill. We dashed off to California, hoping and praying that he would still be alive when we got there. Compassion and grief drove me to my knees to plead on his behalf, and for our dear friends as well. I became driven to search the Scripture for answers. What I found was so much better than answers.

Through reading, studying, and prayer, an awesome God revealed Himself to me, telling of His Holy Name: "I AM the God who heals you." Throughout this study, my eyes were being opened to the power and authority vested in the church. My eyes opened to the great treasures of love, compassion, and healing that flow out of God's promises. My vision slowly improved, and I began to see a clearer picture of God, who is a God of covenants. Beyond the shadow of a doubt, I learned so much more of the Great I AM, who restores, rebuilds, renews and refreshes His people, and who strengthens the fabric of Christian communities.

Surely, God has not changed. But is He ministering the grace of healing to His people today? Is He still a God of miracles? Is it possible that He would ever desire to withdraw His power and authority from the church? Why would He covenant with His church and then withdraw any part of His covenant? Questions and more questions have driven me to search as if for lost treasure. And there is treasure in abundance. Jewels of inestimable value — uncovered. Pure gold and refined silver of eternal worth — revealed. It has become clear — the brightness and beauty of fine adornments intended for the bride of Christ are held out to all who will ask and receive.

During my time of testing and searching, a regular member of our home Fellowship group asked, "Can we do a study on the Holy Spirit?" We all agreed, and a few weeks later we dug in. Where this simple question would lead our group (and me personally) was beyond anything that I could have imagined, for the Lord is accomplishing a good work.

The result was not a study on healing; rather, it was about the ministries and gifts of the Holy Spirit for the Church, the bride of Christ, to prepare all who will come for the Bridegroom's great Wedding Banquet. What I didn't expect was to find so much fear, misinformation, misleading half-truths and even lies about the Holy Spirit, whom our Lord Jesus sent to be our Comforter. It turns out that this fear was common among Christians, and unlike the "fear of the Lord" kind of fear, it was an "enslaving fear," a cowering fear that comes from the enemy of our souls. But God's perfect love for us casts out all enslaving fear.

My search for Scriptural truth led me to inquire of people in the know (Bible scholars with degrees in theology). "What is the difference between spiritual and natural gifts?" I asked. But their answers were incomplete, and didn't settle right when tested with Scripture.

One of the challenges in presenting this study is that "Holy Spirit types" are often seen as loose cannons in the church. While there is some basis for this impression, being a loose cannon is not consistent with the nature of the Holy Spirit, and we must not use the Holy Spirit as our excuse for erratic behavior. Being disruptive is unscriptural, self-focused, and does not build up the church. It creates confusion.

Another challenge is our misunderstanding of the nature and person of the Holy Spirit. As an example, this one of the most off-center popular descriptions of the Holy Spirit I've ever seen:

> *"Her nature is rather ethereal, full of dynamic shades and hues of color and motion. No wonder so many people are a*

*little unnerved at relating to her... she obviously is not a being
who is predictable... she wafted about like a playful eddying
wind, and he never quite knew which way she was blowing."[1]*

I've heard people defend the author by saying that it's just fiction.
But one of the rules of writing fiction is that it must be founded
in some reality, either present or past; otherwise, it's classified as
science fiction (future) or fantasy, where the author creates his/
her own reality. Also, if a writer is describing a real person, even in
fiction, the description should be as accurate as possible. If an author
wrote a fictional account of Abraham Lincoln, the story would not be
believable if Lincoln were inaccurately described as a round-faced,
stocky, bald man.

The truth is that although we do not have physical contact with
Jesus, we are comforted by the conscious presence of the Holy Spirit,
whom Jesus promised to give us. The Holy Spirit is not, however, an
abstract or vague power that we can barely grasp hold of or understand,
but a Presence that is as real as the once physical presence of Jesus.
We know the reality of His presence because of the power of miracles
made manifest by His divine nature in the gifts given to individual
believers, who are the Church.

Another challenge in presenting this study is that there are so
many who claim that God's only voice in the earth today is the written
Word, Scripture. Beyond a shadow of doubt, I know this is not true.
How dare we be so arrogant as to even attempt to limit how and when
God can speak to His church? "He who has an ear, let him hear what
the Spirit says to the churches" (Revelation 2:29). This is not only past
tense. This is in the here and now, the church of today. The problem is
not that God has no voice in the church today; the problem is that our
ears are stopped up and we refuse to hear. "But they refused to pay
attention; stubbornly they turned their backs and stopped up their
ears" (Zechariah 7:11). There are also some who say that God will only
speak His word (prophesies) through an ordained minister and from
a pulpit in an organized church. But the truth is that God will speak

---

[1] William Paul Young. *The Shack.*

through whom He wishes to speak, often confounding the wisdom of the wise and studied scholars of the Scripture. "For it is written: 'I will destroy the wisdom of the wise; the intelligence of the intelligent I will frustrate'" (1 Corinthians 1:19).

This study is not typical of many spiritual gift teachings, seminars, and retreats. It's is not about "self-discovery." My hope is that you will find it to be more about "Holy Spirit discovery."

The Apostle Paul describes the spiritual gift of prophecy as most valuable in building up the church.[2] This spiritual gift speaks the heart of God to His church today. Yet, as with all gifts of the Spirit, it is most powerful and effective when ministered in unison with all spiritual gifts.

Many themes and Scripture that are a part of this study are repeated in more than one chapter or section. This is for the purpose of emphasis and to be sure that when the students have completed the study, they will have these important messages imprinted in their heart of hearts.

You are welcome to disagree with some or all of what you find in this study. But let's disagree in Christian charity. Let's be good Bereans: "Now the Bereans were of more noble character — for they received the message with great eagerness and examined the Scripture every day to see if what Paul said was true" (Acts 17:11).

Pray that God will accomplish all that He desires for us, and pray earnestly for the Holy Spirit to teach you from within your heart of hearts. Yes, even instructing your heart in the night and awakening you in the morning, opening your ears and understanding.

> *In my hand is treasure of great value. Jewels from another realm — a Kingdom not of this world. It is a treasure of inestimable, eternal value — beyond measure. The Spirit of Jesus holds it out to each one of you; and yet when you receive it, His treasure is not diminished, but replenished. This treasure is offered to each of you who will receive, in the name of Jesus Christ our Savior and Messiah.*

---

[2] An in-depth study of the spiritual gift of prophecy is available in book three of the Kingdom Series: *A Jewel of the Kingdom: Christ Revealed in the Spiritual Gift of Prophecy.*

BOOK ONE

Treasures for the Bride

1

Beginning the Search

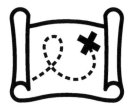

Christians from many backgrounds and denominations are searching. But they're like people who frequent garage sales. They don't know what they are searching for. Some are pursuing Christ, earnestly praying for more of what God desires for them. You, like them, may feel as if the light on your pathway could burn brighter: you were baptized; you grew up in the church; you learned all the Bible stories in Sunday school; you were confirmed; got an award for memorizing Scripture at Vacation Bible School; you receive communion regularly; you gather to worship and fellowship consistently; attend Bible studies; and the list goes on and on. You may be new to your Christian faith, wondering, "Where do I go from here?" A yearning stirs inside you, crying out for more. Every time you read your Bible you sense that there's a greater blessing available now. Every time you pray, you long to touch the heart of God.

On the other side of the coin, there are many people we rub elbows with who know they are sinners. They know there's an answer somewhere and maybe it has something to do with church and the Bible. They come searching, hear the church singing hymns or songs of praise, listen to the reading and preaching of the Word, get a few handshakes and a free coffee mug with the church logo on it as they make their exit and never return — because it felt dry and lifeless to them. Oh yes, the truths of Scripture were taught, preached and sung, but it all seemed to be such a formality and it didn't touch their heart of hearts. In all of this they found no answer to the weight of their guilt. The answer may have been proclaimed, but it didn't connect.

There is another grievous dimension that jumps out at me like a 3-D movie. If this is you, my heart breaks for you. Deep groans of prayer have gone up on your behalf. I've interceded for you, because you have you been driven away from the church. Do you love the Lord God Almighty, but literally have been forced away? Oh, yes! There are too many reasons why this can happen. Church splits, power hungry people, abusive leaders, gossip, jealousy, etc.; it would take a book to list them all. I recall a time of desperation when I cried out to God about my church, "Lord, this isn't working!" It took a while for me to appreciate His answer, "To whom will you go?" There is only one church and many, many Christians who love the Lord have literally been driven away (Isaiah 42:22). For years, the memories of church may have turned your stomach. But now something is stirring, calling you. God is preparing a way for you, for He is a God of justice and love (Jeremiah 23:2, Isaiah 49:22).

Our awakening hearts and Kingdom Treasures; what is the connection? And why do we need gifts from the Holy Spirit? Why is this important today? Some would say, "Church is just fine as it is, so why the fuss?" Others might say, "Church is broken; why should I try?"

Take a journey with me to find the answers to these questions. But first take a moment to pray, ask for the Holy Spirit to reveal truth to you, to give light to your eyes, awaken your ears, and open your understanding — to change your heart and renew your mind. Don't go on until you take this important step.

Our journey in this chapter will take us, step by step, to days in the lives of the people of Jesus' day. This is not a history lesson, but a pilgrimage that reveals Christ in all His glory, from His birth in Bethlehem to His victorious ascension to the right hand of God the Father. On this tour we will witness the earth-shaking changes that came with Jesus' birth, His ministries to the downtrodden, teaching the people, His life-giving sacrifice, His promise to send the Holy Spirit, ascending into heaven, and being seated at the right hand of the Father. We will learn truths that are important for us today so that we can grow and mature in our faith, treasuring what Jesus has done for us and then go forward. Finally, we will see how unwise it is to reject any part of what our Lord Jesus accomplished and promised for those who are called by His name. As we walk in Jesus' footsteps, we will see God's plan for His church unfold, and we will see the power and majesty of our resurrected Lord and Savior as He establishes, gifts, and empowers His church.

Board the Bible Bus with me as we travel through time. This tour is unique in that we will revisit each stop, building upon the truths we have witnessed, stone upon stone, layer upon layer.

🚌 1ˢᵗ Stop

Our journey begins as the bus comes to a stop at a simple but ancient stone well in the Village of Nazareth. We instantly recognize Mary as she draws water from the well. She will soon be the mother of Jesus by Immaculate Conception. Before we know it, we must pack up and follow Mary and Joseph to Bethlehem where Jesus was born and placed in a manger, a cow's trough, in a stinking stable. Shepherds that smelled like sheep and goats came to see what the angels proclaimed to them and they left "glorifying and praising God for all the things they had heard and seen, which were just as they had been told" (Luke 2:8-20). Later the Magi came from the East to worship Jesus, bringing "gold, incense, and myrrh."

This is the Christmas story that so many of us love and have heard every Christmas, year after year. This miraculous story has been proclaimed in children's pageants, great choral offerings, and in Christmas dramas time and again. How rapturous it is for us to hear and sing Handel's *Messiah* as we joyously celebrate the Christmas seasons.

If only we could have Christmas every day!

🚌 2ⁿᵈ Stop

Get back on the Bible Bus and travel with me on the narrow, dusty roads from Tiberius to Capernaum along the shores of the Sea of

Galilee. Scripture proclaims that "the people living in darkness have seen a great light; on those living in the land of the shadow of death a light has dawned" (Matthew 4:16). When we arrive, we see a crowd gathered on the shore and Jesus in a boat, teaching the people. We follow Jesus, and stop the bus as He sits down to teach on a mountainside, "Blessed are the poor in spirit, for theirs is the kingdom of heaven" (Matthew 5:3). Who is this man we see speaking to the crowds with unusual authority? He is Immanuel, God with us. The Word who was with God at the beginning. "Through him all things were made" (John 1:3).

He is the carpenter from Nazareth, and He is the Word who spoke everything into existence. He holds all things together. "If it were his intention and he withdrew his Spirit and breath, all mankind would perish together and man would return to the dust" (Job 34:14). This is God of the entire universe who walked among us, teaching, healing the sick, calling the sinner to repentance, prophesying, and raising the dead. Through His work and ministry, he announced, "Repent, for the kingdom of heaven is near" (Matthew 4:17). We too are privileged to walk with Him and to see Him, God with us, in the very words of Scripture manifested in our lives.

🚌 3ʳᵈ Stop

The next stop brings us to Mount Calvary outside the limestone walls surrounding the city of Jerusalem. Jesus prophesied the events of this Passover season to His disciples, even though often they did not understand. Jesus and His followers travel in triumphal procession into Jerusalem, with the crowds singing, "Blessed is the king who comes in the name of the Lord!" (Luke 19:38). Then He cleanses the temple saying, "My house will be a house of prayer, but you have made it a den of robbers" (Matthew 21:13). And then Jesus shares a Last Supper with His disciples. Judas slips out the back door determined to betray Him. A mob comes to arrest Jesus and He is put on trial before the Sanhedrin. The disciples disown Him. Peter denies Him. Jesus is brought before Pilot who proclaimed, "I find no basis for a charge against this man" (Luke 23:4), and then condemned Him to die a shameful death, with nails pounded though His hands and feet on a cruel Roman cross.

🚌 4th Stop

At this stop we witness a wondrous miracle that once again changes everything — Jesus shatters the religious status quo. At the tomb where the rich man placed Jesus' body, grieving women come to the tomb at sunrise on Sunday morning, bringing spices they had prepared. We watch as they turn to stare at each other with tears running down their cheeks and dropping to the dust at their feet. The stone has been rolled away and Jesus' body is missing. They cling together, grieving, wondering what this means. Their confusion and grief is interrupted by men dressed in clothes as bright as lightning who declare, "He is not here; he has risen!" (Luke 24:6). Jesus' resurrection from the dead, as the first fruits of many resurrections to come, changes everything, for all eternity, for all who will call on His name.

🚌 5th Stop

As we arrive in the vicinity of Bethany we join the crowd where Jesus is speaking of a great promise to all who are gathered and to all who follow Him: "And surely I will be with you always, to the very end of the age" (Matthew 28:20). After speaking to His disciples, He ascends into heaven to be seated at the right hand of God (Mark 16:19), where "all authority in heaven and on earth has been given to [Him]" (Matthew 28:18). As Jesus the Christ prepares to take His position of power and authority at the right hand of God, He continues to prepare His disciples: "Therefore go and make disciples of all nations, baptizing them in the name of the Father and of the Son and of the Holy Spirit, and teaching them to obey everything I have commanded you" (Matthew 28:19). This too will change everything — the church is commissioned.

🚌 6th Stop

At this stop, we find ourselves mixing with the disciples of Jesus who are remembering His clear instructions: "Do not leave Jerusalem, but wait for the gift my Father promised, which you have heard me speak about. For John baptized with water but in a few days you will be baptized with the Holy Spirit" (Acts 1:4-8).The Spirit of Jesus, the Spirit of Grace, the Holy Spirit of God, the Spirit of Truth, the Spirit of Life, the Spirit of Wisdom, the Holy Spirit of Fire, the Spirit of Holiness, the Spirit of Power, and the Spirit of Love would come upon them — One Spirit empowering them, inhabiting God's holy people. This changes everything — they are given gifts, empowered to accomplish the monumental task that Jesus gave them.

We've finished the first leg of our tour, becoming witnesses of Jesus' mighty work among His people, yet we must explore further to see how each of these earth-shaking miracles changes everything for us in the present time, too. I don't mean *changed* as in past tense. This is now, at this time in the age of the church. Get back on the bus with me as we revisit each point along our journey. As we reflect on what we witnessed, these truths will become ingrained in us, and we'll come to understand more of the power and might of the resurrected Jesus.

🚌 1st Stop

Have you known people who were stuck at Christmas? The only time it's important for them to be at church is during the holidays. After all, the kids are in the Christmas play. Little Johnny is singing "Little Star of Bethlehem" in his star costume and Missy is playing Mother Mary in the living manger scene.

Being stuck at Christmas is like a car spinning its wheels in the snow. That person's understanding of the gospel ends somewhere around the 25th of December. The Immaculate Conception and birth of Jesus is one of the most powerful and earth shaking events of all time. Yet God has even more for us; we must build on this miracle and go forward.

Many cults and false doctrines stop here, thinking that Jesus was born like all of us and was a great teacher, prophet, and healer; but they deny the deity of Christ Jesus. They have refused to go forward and have made for themselves a false Jesus — a great man.

I can tell you, I've looked into the manger in Bethlehem. It's empty. He is not there. Even the cows, sheep, and donkeys have left. We, like Mary, mother of Jesus, must treasure these things in our hearts and go forward, because Jesus changes everything — overturning the establishment.

🚌 2nd Stop

We can still hear the echoes of Jesus calling out to the crowds, "Repent, for the kingdom of heaven is near" (Matthew 4:17). He preaches the good news, teaches in parables, instructs His disciples, and does many miracles. The promised Messiah has come to walk among His people, demonstrating the power of His love and compassion. This carpenter from Nazareth proves again and again that He is truly Immanuel, God with us.

For over three years He leads and trains His disciples. He sends the twelve on a mission; "he gave them power and authority to drive out all demons and to cure diseases, and then he sent them out to preach the kingdom of God and to heal the sick" (Luke 9:1-2). Jesus sent them out again two by two (Luke 10:1-20). They came back with great joy, reporting, "Lord, even the demons submit to us in your name."

This was intense training at Jesus University for over three years. No Easter break. No summer vacation. No weekends off. No Christmas break. No time off for family funerals. This was twenty four hours a day, seven days a week for over three years. It was grueling and required enormous self-sacrifice. But what was the end result of it? Was it enough?

Over and over Jesus gave many signs and wonders to demonstrate that He was, without a doubt, fully God manifested in the flesh. What incredible, powerful, visible evidence He gave to all who touched Him, walked with Him and called out for Him to touch them. As He walked among us, He healed the sick, raised the dead, forgave sinners, lifted up the downtrodden, ate with sinners, and confronted the proudly religious. Jesus toppled the establishment, and everything changed. To witness all of this is awesome beyond comparison; yet He calls us to something even greater. I've traveled from Israel's Northern border with Lebanon to the Southern border with Egypt; the man, Jesus, no longer walks along their dusty roads and we too must go forward to fulfill Jesus' Great Commission.

🚌 3rd Stop

We file, one by one, off our tour bus to join those who mourn on a hill outside the walls of Jerusalem. The Passion of Christ humbles us beyond anything I can imagine. How does He love you and me so much that He died in our place, because of our sin? How is it that He would suffer such trauma to His physical body and such a humiliating death — willingly submitting to the hands of cruel oppressors? Jesus gave His body to be broken and His blood to be shed for all mankind, to take away the sin of the world?

He was tried, convicted, and sentenced to death. He was without guilt. He had committed no crime. He was not guilty of any offense. Yet He died a criminal's death. He destroyed principalities and powers, changing everything (Colossians 2:15).

We repent and fast for Lent, we sing of His glorious and precious sacrifice in songs like "O, the blood of Jesus." Some people go on pilgrimages to Israel and Palestine to walk the Stations of the Cross to remind themselves of these life-changing days. We celebrate and remember His Last Supper, His new covenant, His command to love one another, and the promise of the Passover Supper on Maundy Thursday.

We preach Christ and Christ crucified. Beyond a doubt, we must preach "Christ the power of God and the wisdom of God" (1 Corinthians 1:23). This is central to our faith and the precious promises of Scripture.

The day of His atoning work was a great and awesome day, a day when the Lord Jesus gave a precious gift of eternal value to all who will repent and call on His name. We are commanded to "remember" and live this precious promise. He has given us a great treasure, yet He has even more for us. Look and see for yourself. LOOK UP! The cross is empty. He is not there. We too must take hold of the cross and move forward. The cross changes everything.

🚌 4ᵗʰ Stop

The power of resurrection is beyond comparison. The resurrected Christ comes forth in all His power and majesty as the first fruits of many, promising that we too shall be resurrected to be with Him forever. "And if the Spirit of him who raised Jesus from the dead is living in you, he who raised Christ from the dead will also give life to your mortal bodies through his Spirit, who lives in you" (Romans 8:11). God's resurrection power changes everything, forever. What a great promise He has given to us! I invite you stoop down and look into the tomb. He is not there. He has even greater plans for us and we must go forward (Jeremiah 29:11).

🚌 5ᵗʰ Stop

The air brakes on the bus announce our next arrival and we find ourselves back near Bethany where Jesus' disciples were told to meet Him. As Jesus appears to them they begin to worship. "Then Jesus came to them and said, 'All authority in heaven and on earth has been given to me. Therefore go and make disciples of all nations, baptizing them in the name of the Father and of the Son and of the Holy Spirit'" (Matthew 28: 16-20). Jesus ascends into heaven as they stand looking intently upward. From the looks on their faces, they must be thinking, *"Now what?"* Two men dressed in white bring them to their senses saying, "Men of Galilee. Why do you stand there looking into the sky?" (Acts 1:11).

This changes everything — the powers that be are defeated and Christ's authority is established in His church.

Jesus is now seated at the right hand of God Almighty in His position of authority and power until all things are placed under His feet. Because all authority has been given to Him, Jesus says, "Therefore go." He is commanding us that with the authority of His Holy Name, and in the power of His Holy Spirit, we must "go and make disciples of all nations." By His command He confers His authority upon Christians, placing us under His authority to "go and make disciples" just as He did early in His ministry with the twelve and the seventy-two who he sent out to proclaim the kingdom of God.

The commission given to the church overwhelms us with awe. Jesus' command fills us with wonder. The Holy Spirit's power at work in us gives us confidence to fulfill the great work of the church. God reveals His awesome power and might as He takes weak and helpless people and makes them into a mighty army. We, like Jesus' disciples, are called to pray and wait. His followers went to Jerusalem and had a prayer meeting, and they waited on the Lord. Christ Jesus, who is seated at the right hand of God in all power and authority, baptized them with an empowering work of His Holy Spirit. Yes, we too must pray, ask, and wait for this empowering work, available to all who believe and become a part of the body of Christ. He is seated at the right hand of God the Father Almighty ready for us to gather and pray, to wait upon Him and ask for this precious promise to be fulfilled in us today.

What a wonderful work God has accomplished to give us right standing with Him, to bring us close to Him through His Son and His awesome sacrifice on our behalf. We who are in Christ have authority by His command to do all that He has called us to do as His church, to reach every tribe, nation, people and tongue with the Good News of Jesus Christ, proclaiming His power to save. Giving us His authority is just the beginning; He also empowers and gifts us in His Holy Spirit to accomplish this work. This changes everything — mighty soldiers of heaven's kingdom are raised up so that Jesus Christ will become the desire of all nations.

As incredible as this is, He has given us even more. And we must step out to take hold of these truths and stop gazing up into heaven like the disciples.

🚌 6ᵗʰ Stop

John the Baptist prophesied, "He will baptize you with the Holy Spirit and with fire" (Matthew 3:11). This is a cleansing fire. "And anything else that can withstand fire must be put through the fire, and then it will be clean. But it must also be purified with the water of cleansing" (Numbers 31:23; see also Malachi 3:2-3). This is an empowering fire. "But you will receive power when the Holy Spirit comes on you" (Acts 1:8). The Holy Spirit purifies by fire as we are baptized into the Holy Spirit. In water baptism we are cleansed and then sealed against the just wrath of God, and we are baptized into Christ who is seated in His position of power and authority at the right hand of God. The Father adopts us as His precious sons and daughters, giving us a new family name.

Take this to heart because this Scripture is a powerful declaration of our position in Christ:

> "But you have come³ to Mount Zion, to the heavenly Jerusalem, the city of the living God. You have come to thousands upon thousands of angels in joyful assembly, to the church of the firstborn, whose names are written in heaven. You have come to God, the judge of all men, to the spirits of righteous men made perfect, to Jesus the mediator of a new covenant, and to the sprinkled blood that speaks a better word than the blood of Abel. See to it that you do not refuse him who speaks." (Hebrews 12:22-24)

This is a declaration of our position in Christ today! This is a declaration of the kingdom of God in this present age. And we will

---

³ Like them, we are called to know Christ in the present! Today — right now. For those who are called by His Name in the age of the church, we can take hold of this truth: We have the kingdom of God, we are receiving the kingdom of God, and we shall be given the kingdom of God.

soon move forward into His fulfillment of greater promises. "This same Jesus, who has been taken from you into heaven, will come back in the same way you have seen him go into heaven" (Acts 1:11).

Now, let's zero in our focus and examine the church's commission even closer. Think about what we are called to do. How many times did Jesus rebuke the disciples because they didn't "get it?" "The disciples did not understand all of this. Its meaning was hidden from them, and they didn't know what he was talking about" (Luke 18:34). And again Jesus confronted them: "Don't you know me, Philip, even after I have been among you such a long time?" (John 14:9; see also Matthew 16:11, Luke 9:45).

Jesus was full of the Holy Spirit, without measure or limit, and yet He didn't bring the disciples to complete understanding. He taught by the power of the Holy Spirit. But His teaching did not penetrate to their heart of hearts. Their understanding was dull. Three years of Jesus University ended in the disciples' deserting and denying Jesus. They went back to fishing in the Sea of Galilee (John 21:3). They didn't understand there was a greater blessing yet to come.

When Jesus taught, it seems as if He reserved the best for later, not completely opening His followers' understanding because He was waiting until He would send His Holy Spirit — because this is the work of the Spirit. Like so many who hear the Word by listening to a sermon or teaching, the disciples only heard His words with their ears and processed them in their fisherman and tax collector minds, awaiting the day the Holy Spirit would teach them from within their heart of hearts. The truths and promises of Scripture are completely different than learning math, geography, language or even memorizing the Ten Commandments. The mysteries of the gospel can only be opened to us and applied to change our lives when this seed of truth is revealed within our heart of hearts, where the life-changing power of the Spirit accomplishes its good work.

Divine words require a divine teacher for the message to be revealed in our spirits (1 Corinthians 2:14). Without the Spirit's work of revelation among believers, the truth crumbles into facts, figures, and academic pursuits — the letter without the Spirit. But the Holy Spirit, our Divine Teacher, breaks through to the very soul of man, overcoming these limitations to teach us in our heart of hearts. Christian professors can train and equip you to teach, but you need more than Jesus University. It is the Holy Spirit who gifts and empowers a teacher with life giving Living Water flowing out from the depths of his soul. This is the work of the Holy Spirit and this can only happen by the power of the Spirit. Without the anointing and empowering work of the Holy Spirit, your ministries and service come to little more than a puff of smoke from an expiring candle.

After Jesus ascended to the right hand of the Father, He sent the promised Holy Spirit to finish the work He began. The Holy Spirit taught them from the inside out. He caused the Word to take root in them; He drenched their hearts with remembrances of what Jesus taught, and by the power of the Holy Spirit for the first time the Word came to life, poured into them like springs of Living Water. And the rivers flowed out of them by the same power of the Holy Spirit as the Spirit gifted and empowered them for the ministries in His Kingdom and the church.

Take hold of what you have, treasure it and build on it. Move forward. If your faith begins and ends with Christmas, I encourage you to treasure this miraculous time, build on it and go forward. If you're still walking with Jesus of the Gospels, I say, "Amen." You treasure Christ's redemptive work on the Cross? I say, "Hold fast." Grasp hold to what you have and go forward. If you glory in the power of the resurrected Christ, I encourage you to cherish this promise, rejoice, and be glad. Now step up to more of what Jesus calls you to. If you delight in the power and authority of our Ascended Jesus, I say, "Blessed be the name of the Lord." Yet He holds out to you even more than this, for He sends His Holy Spirit to gift and empower His people for the strengthening and building of His church, for the advancing of His kingdom one soul at a time until every tribe, nation, people, and tongue sees His glorious salvation and glorifies His Holy Name.

We cannot understand or attend to all that we are called to do, using all the good gifts the Bridegroom has for His bride, until we move forward into all that He holds out to us in His open hands. He longs for us to take hold of these precious gifts and promises by faith and move forward in Him to reach new heights. "He makes my feet like the feet of a deer; he enables me to stand on the heights. He trains my hands for battle; my arms can bend a bow of bronze" (Psalm 18:33-34).

This is the work of the Holy Spirit! This is God manifested throughout all the earth, alive and actively ministering through His people — the church — TODAY! Although we don't bump into the man who was a carpenter from Nazareth on our hometown streets, we have His Holy Spirit indwelling us, gifting us, empowering us, and demonstrating His active, living presence in real and tangible ways, in every sense as real as if Immanuel stood among us in bodily form ministering in power and might. He is as close to us as the air we breathe, the very "glue" that holds our being together.

Adam and Eve rejected the Tree of Life, the very best of God's creation. The people of Noah's day refused to walk with God. God's prophets from Abel to Zechariah were rejected, stoned, and killed. Jesus, the only Son of God, was rejected and crucified. The Holy Spirit is sent to manifest His living, active presence in and through every Christian who has saving faith (Revelation 2:29). What will you do with the Holy Spirit of Jesus? What will you do with His precious gifts? What will you do with the very best the Holy Spirit has for YOU, a living part of His church?

The religious leaders of Jesus' day rejected Jesus saying, "The only Father we have is God himself" (John 8:41). They claimed God's Holy Name, but rejected His only Son. Jesus' answer was clear: "If God were your Father, you would love me, for I came from God and now am here" (John 8:42). The teachers of the law claimed, "We are disciples of Moses! We know that God spoke to Moses, but as for this fellow, we don't even know where he comes from" (John 9:28). They called themselves the chosen people of God. They claimed to be disciples of Moses, yet they rejected the One who Moses revealed and proclaimed to them in the law.

The Holy Spirit is sent from God as promised by our Lord Jesus. The Holy Spirit is living and actively present in the earth today, manifested through God's people, the church. When we come to saving faith, the

Holy Spirit comes to take up residence in us, sealing us and adopting us as children of the Most High God (Ephesians 1:5). When we are baptized in water, the Holy Spirit makes us one with Christ, and a part of His body (1 Corinthians 12:13, Galatians 3:27-28). And we can also receive the gifting and empowering work of the Holy Spirit when we do as Jesus commanded, praying and waiting for Jesus' baptism with fire.

If we reject the Holy Spirit, His good gifts, His empowering work, or the manifestations of his ministering presence among us, we are rejecting Him. If we reject the Spirit of God, we are also rejecting the One who promised the Spirit and God the Father who has sent His Spirit. Jesus spoke of this successive chain when He said, "Very truly, I tell you, whoever receives the one whom I send receives me; and whoever receives me receives him who sent me" (John 13:20 NRSV). You cannot say, "I accept Jesus, but I don't go for this Holy Spirit stuff." It doesn't ring true to say, "I believe in the Holy Spirit, but I only want His gifts that are to my liking." Jesus sent the Holy Spirit to manifest His glory through those He has called. It's worth repeating. If we reject the Holy Spirit, we reject Jesus also. If we reject the Holy Spirit sent to us by Jesus, God's only Son, we also reject the Father. For they are One.

On our tour we witnessed the miracle of the Christ child. We walked shoulder to shoulder with Jesus, hearing His words, seeing His miracles, and experiencing His forgiveness and miracles. We looked on as He was mocked, scourged, beaten, and crucified — shedding His blood to wash us clean from the stain of our sin. We grieved to see His body being broken so that we might be made whole. We stood with the disciples and watched Jesus ascend into the heavens where He is seated at the right hand of God the Father. We visited Jerusalem to watch as Jesus' followers gathered to pray and wait for the promised Holy Spirit. We were overjoyed to see the Holy Spirit descend upon them as tongues of fire, gifting them and empowering them for the work of the church. With each stop on our tour, it's important that we delight in the truth revealed to us, treasure the miracle, and go forward, not missing the bus. It is good to cherish all of what God has given us and open our hearts to receive even more, because at each stop Jesus has something greater to offer; and we do well to receive all He has for us to receive.

We must not scorn or reject any of what Jesus holds out to us. We must not refuse the Holy Spirit, using His name, speaking of Him, acknowledging Him in our creeds but rejecting what He holds out to us, His good spiritual gifts. We must not reject the Holy Spirit by claiming that what we do or say is "of the Spirit" when in fact it is a product of our own intuition, enthusiasm, desire, tradition and personal initiative, bringing honor for ourselves (John 7:18).

May I invite you to join me in taking a step forward into greater abundance, receiving gifts from the Holy Spirit, Kingdom Treasures, which are of great and precious value with an eternal effect upon all those to whom we minister and serve. Read on, chapter by chapter, and you will come to understand the blessings of all He has ordained for us.

YOUR JOURNEY JOURNAL
Chapter 1: Beginning the Search

Take this opportunity to consider your journey with the Lord. Begin with a private time of introspection that every Christian is called to (2 Corinthians 13:5). Now think about where you find yourself on this Bible Bus tour? Is it possible that your tour bus got stuck along the way?

Use these pages as a personal journal and listen to the Spirit of Jesus speak to you to reveal your need for Christ in your heart of hearts.

Write about where you are in your Christian walk. Do you sense a yearning for more? Do you have a sense of poverty — surrounded by abundance, yet you can't take hold of it? Where are you on this tour?

1. What is revealed to you about the very nature of God in the miraculous conception and the events surrounding Jesus birth?

2. As the power of Jesus' resurrection sinks in — what do you see about the awesome nature of a Holy God? What changes does this bring about in your life?

3. What is it about the nature of God that is revealed to you in the earth-shaking events of Acts chapter two?

Your Journal Notes:

Be encouraged to take your journal and get together with a like-minded and trusted friend in a quiet place over tea or coffee (hot chocolate works too) and share what you've written in your journals. Open up your heart and soul to confess your weaknesses, your sin, your doubts and fears. You'll find that confession heals the wounded soul. Pray together, asking for your Heavenly Father to refresh you in His Holy Spirit. Commit yourselves to each other to hold each other accountable as you go forward in your walk with the Lord. Ask yourselves the hard question: Have you been content to stop at any point in the journey and not go forward? Write about where you will go from here....

If you are in a "Treasures" study group, take time to share and pray with each other at your next meeting.

2

The Tree of Life

The beauty, depth, and symbolism given to us in Eden's Tree of Life are beyond measure. The Tree of Life reveals concepts central to our study of spiritual gifts. The Tree teaches us the source of spiritual gifts, the foundation for the gifts, the power and purpose of the gifts, and the value of these gifts that were won at great cost. I feel an incredible sense of responsibility as I undertake the task of opening up the Scripture for the Spirit to reveal our Blessed Lord and Savior to all who are blessed to receive Him.

In this chapter, we'll discuss what the Tree of Life symbolizes for us. You will see battle lines clearly drawn, and the enemies' plot exposed. You'll hear the call to be part of a mighty army of saints, armored up and prepared for the battle of kingdoms. You will see two Trees, like light and darkness, standing in opposition: the Tree of Life and the Tree of the Knowledge of Good and Evil. And finally, you will see our part in the battle plan that leads to Christ's victory over the forces of darkness.

Part 1

The first book in the Bible introduces us to the Tree of Life. "And the Lord God made all kinds of trees grow out of the ground — trees that were pleasing to the eye and good for food. In the middle of the garden were the tree of life and the tree of the knowledge of good and evil" (Genesis 2:9). When you read all the way through the Bible and come to its closing words you will find the Tree of Life again in the last chapter.

"Then the angel showed me the river of the water of life, as clear as crystal, flowing from the throne of God and of the Lamb down the middle of the great street of the city. On each side of the river stood the tree of life, bearing twelve crops of fruit, yielding its fruit every month" (Revelation 22:19). We must not overlook this Scripture: "He who has an ear, let him hear what the Spirit says to the churches. To him who overcomes, I will give the right to eat from the tree of life, which is in the paradise of God" (Revelation 2:7).[4]

All of the illustrative pictures throughout the Bible overwhelm us with awe at the beautiful work God has accomplished and continues to accomplish through the power and authority of our Lord Jesus Christ. Jesus is the Tree of Life. "Jesus answered, 'I am the way and the truth and the life. No one comes to the Father except through me'" (John 14:6). The book of Proverbs is interwoven with several Scriptures regarding the Tree of Life. In chapter 3:18, "[Wisdom] is a tree of life to those who embrace her; those who lay hold of her will be blessed." And in 11:30, "The fruit of righteousness is a tree of life, and he who wins souls is wise." Again in 13:12, "Hope deferred makes the heart sick, but a longing fulfilled is a tree of life." Also in 15:4, "The tongue that brings healing is a tree of life." In Proverbs, wisdom is clearly connected with the Tree of Life. "The Lord possessed me at the beginning of his work, before his deeds of old; I was appointed from eternity, from the beginning, before the world began" (Proverbs 8:22-23). The Apostle John brings truth this together: "In the beginning was the Word, and the Word was with God, and the Word was God. He was with God in the beginning. Through him all things were made; without him nothing was made that has been made. In him was life, and that life was the light of men" (John 1:1-4). This is the Tree we ought to embrace.

The Tree of Life clearly is our Lord Jesus who is the Way, the Truth, and the Life. After Adam and Eve sinned against God and were expelled from the garden, a holy angel with a flashing sword guarded the way to the Tree of Life. Jesus became the Way, and He is the Tree of Life. He is the narrow gate. "Enter through the narrow gate. For wide is the

---

[4] The Tree of Life is the "Narrow Gate" through which we enter into God's rest. See Hebrews 4:9-11.

gate and broad is the road that leads to destruction and many enter through it. But small is the gate and narrow the road that leads to life, and only a few find it" (Matthew 7:13-14).

Consider that the Tree of Life was likely **not** the most beautiful tree in the garden — it may not have been most pleasing to the eyes of man. It was partly the beauty of the other Tree, the Tree of the Knowledge of Good and Evil that attracted Eve: "When the woman saw that the fruit of the tree was good for food and **pleasing to the eye,** and also desirable for gaining wisdom, she took some and ate it" (Genesis 3:6, emphasis added). This is another link between the Tree of Life and Jesus: "He grew up before him like a tender shoot, and like a root out of dry ground. He had no beauty or majesty to attract us to him, nothing in his appearance that we should desire him" (Isaiah 53:2).

In contrast to "no beauty or majesty," look at what is said in allegorical prose regarding the "King of Tyre":

> "*You were the model of perfection, full of wisdom, and perfect in beauty. You were in Eden, the garden of God; every precious stone adorned you: ruby, topaz and emerald, chrysolite, onyx and jasper, sapphire, turquoise and beryl. Your settings and mounting were made of gold; on the day you were created they were prepared. You were anointed as a guardian cherub, for so I ordained you. You were on the holy mount of God; you walked among the fiery stones.*" (Ezekiel 28:11-13)

Here is the created angel Lucifer, the most beautiful of angels, right there in the Garden of Eden; but when wickedness was found in his heart, this guardian cherub was expelled from the garden of God.[5]

Few of us need to be reminded that sin is often more attractive to the natural man, to our eyes and to our sensibilities, than what is right and good. But it is a deceptively thin veneer, beautiful on the surface and rotten underneath. Sin can be likened to a beautiful red apple that we find to be foul, decayed, and worm infested to the core. The world's attractions satisfy much more in the moment than those

---

[5] The earthly king of the ancient city of Tyre was not ever in the Garden of Eden.

things of eternal value (see Romans 8:5). But what is most pleasing to our eyes is like a sparkling, candy-coated poison pill.

My greatest sins, my most disastrous failings in life — too many to count — have been just like this. In times of temptation, it's as if my Lord Jesus were standing there, holding out His arms and whispering, "Will you come to me?" But I deafened my ears and the siren song of the tempter overwhelmed Jesus' whisper and stood between us holding out beautiful, lustrous fruit that was beautiful to my eyes. At the time it didn't appear to be a simple black or white, light or darkness kind of choice, because I had deceived myself and my eyes were blinded by the glittering attraction of sin. I justified my choice, at times making it sound so spiritual and good. But it was bitter to the core.[6]

Consider some more mundane examples: It's always more fun to go four wheeling than to sit and stand through an hour of worship. Reading *Self* magazine might be more interesting than searching the Bible. And we often think a tailgate party would be a lot more exciting than a prayer meeting.

The concept of the natural seeming more attractive than the Heavenly can affect us even in how we choose to serve and minister in the church, such as whether we use our natural gifts or our spiritual ones. Is it possible that ministering in our natural gift is more attractive to us because it is more self-satisfying and a greater boost to our self-esteem than ministering in a spiritual gift? Look what John the Baptist said of Jesus: "He must become greater; and I must become less" (John 3:30). It's painful to become less because it requires pruning; it requires finishing work like that of sandpaper. It goes against our grain to become less significant. Our human nature drives us to seek our moment of fame, our opportunity for notoriety. Our American culture presses us into joining that deceptive cult of

---

[6] Typically, I don't divulge the nature of my past sins because I do not believe it is useful for Christians to go around telling all, wearing them on their chest as if they were some kind of battle ribbons or war medals. We testify of God's redeeming grace, but need not display our past sin as a trophy for all to see. At the same time, it is good to have a trusted confessor to whom we admit our sins and not attempt to keep them hidden.

celebrity. But ministering in a spiritual gift makes you less noticeable and illuminates Christ.

The natural person is in a constant battle against the spiritual person who is born of the Spirit (see Ephesians 6:12). The natural self, the flesh, battles constantly to rule over the soul: "Abstain from the desires of the flesh that wage war against the soul" (1 Peter 2:11 NRSV). What determines which part of you will rule over your life? The part you feed makes a big difference. Your flesh desires things that are pleasing to the eyes and the senses. Feed it and it will grow stronger. The spirit desires the things of the Spirit. Feed your spirit with spiritual food and it will grow stronger to overcome your flesh (Romans 8:4). What nourishes the "flesh" always comes easier than what strengthens the spirit. A. W. Tozer offers another, more critical view of this challenge:[7]

> "Self is the opaque veil that hides the face of God from us. It can be removed only in spiritual experience,[8] never by mere instruction. We may as well try to instruct leprosy out of our system. There must be a work of God in destruction before we are free. We must invite the cross to do its deadly work within us. We must bring our self-sins to the cross for judgment. We must prepare ourselves for an ordeal of suffering in some measure like that through which our Savior passed when He suffered under Pontius Pilate."

Tozer is saying that sacrificing our body is the work of the cross that we must bear, submitting ourselves to the destruction of the flesh just as Christ offered His body to be nailed onto a cruel Roman cross (Luke 9:23). And our bodies will not submit by any lesser means than to be offered up as a living sacrifice every moment of every day of our lives (Romans 12:1). A living sacrifice rejects what is pleasing to the eye, the Tree of Knowledge of Good and Evil. Those who live a

---

[7] A.W. Tozer. *The Pursuit of God*, page 43.

[8] Spiritual experience is proof that the instruction we have received is right, true, and rooted in Scripture.

sacrificial life embrace the Tree of Life, the Giver of the precious gifts, treasures of God's kingdom.

Part 2

Remember the beginning recorded in Genesis? "In the middle of the garden stood the Tree of Life and the Tree of the Knowledge of Good and Evil" (Genesis 2:9). Here we see representations of two opposing kingdoms set to battle for dominion over all God created in six days. The light and darkness are at odds over God's creation. "The light shines in the darkness, but the darkness has not understood it" (John 1:5). The kingdom of darkness offers a beautiful, yet deceptive representation of itself in the Garden of Eden as the Tree of Knowledge of Good and Evil. The fruit is pleasing to the eye, but the substance is a deadly poison. Scripture does not say that God planted the Tree of Knowledge of Good and Evil — we don't know how it got there. Yet, this tree drew God's created beings into rebellion against what God had established in His creation. "The mind of sinful man is death, but the mind controlled by the Spirit is life and peace; the sinful mind is hostile to God. It does not submit to God's law, nor can it do so" (Romans 8:6-7). Death or Life, light or darkness: choose today which kingdom you will serve.

We must be reminded that sin is an act of violence against the kingdom of God. This is because in our sin we are despising and rejecting the Tree of Life, and we are complicit in Satan's purpose to overthrow the Kingdom of Light and all of God's creation. The devil's purpose is to enslave and tear down all of God's creation and all of God's created beings. Why would we knowingly cooperate in this war of darkness against the Light? Why would we not pray earnestly for God to open our eyes to our unknown sins? The destructive nature of Satan's warfare is clear: "Before them the land is like the garden of Eden, behind them, a desert waste — nothing escapes them" (Joel 2:3). But Satan isn't satisfied with turning the creation into a desert wasteland; he wants to destroy the very foundation of God's creation:

"They have neither knowledge nor understanding, they walk around in darkness; all the foundations of the earth are shaken." (Psalm 82:5 NRSV)

"When the foundations are being destroyed, what can the righteous do?" (Psalm 11:3)

"Let us destroy the tree and its fruit." (Jeremiah 11:19)

Adam and Eve rejected the Tree of Life for a moment of pleasure that was pleasing to the eye. They would have been blessed to hear the words of Joshua as they stood before these two trees in the middle of the Garden of Eden: "But if serving the Lord seems undesirable to you, then choose for yourselves this day whom you will serve" (Joshua 24:15). We see this same kind of scene taking place in Deuteronomy, chapter 27, where God instructed that the tribes of Israel were to be divided between Mount Ebal and Mount Gerizim. The tribes standing on Mount Ebal proclaimed warnings about the curse of sin. The tribes on Mount Gerazim pronounced God's blessings that come with obedience. They were to choose which kingdom they would serve: The kingdom of darkness or the Kingdom of Light. Would they serve a kingdom of death or a Kingdom of Life?

Could it be that spreading branches of the two trees covered the crests of each mountain? We find a hint in this Scripture: "It may be that there is among you a root sprouting poisonous and bitter growth" (Deuteronomy 29:18 NRSV).

This very same battle rages right before our eyes every day of our lives. These Scriptures paint a picture of this conflict.

"Wisdom has built her house; she has hewn out its seven pillars. She has prepared her meat and mixed her wine; she has also set her table. She has sent out her maids, and she calls from the highest point of the city. 'Let all who are simple come in here!' she says to those who lack judgment. 'Come, eat my food and drink the wine I have mixed.'" (Proverbs 9:1-5)

Not to be outdone, the kingdom of darkness raises its dark head and takes its stand.

> *"The woman Folly is loud; she is undisciplined and without knowledge. She sits at the door of her house, on a seat at the highest point of the city, calling out to those who pass by, who go straight on their way. 'Let all who are simple come in here!' she says to those who lack judgment. 'Stolen water is sweet; food eaten in secret is delicious!' But little do they know that the dead are there, that her guests are in the depths of the grave."* (Proverbs 9:13-18)

We must also heed God's warning to Cain: "But if you do not do what is right, sin is crouching at your door; it desires to have you, but you must master it." (Genesis 4:7). That is, the reborn spirit of man must rule over the natural man that is bent on rebellion. In today's high-tech, media culture we hear the tempting shouts of folly every time we click our remote control, each time we stream a movie, when we click on what pops up on our laptop, and when we choose a magazine or book to read. What will you choose? Will you hear the voice of Wisdom calling out to you? Or will you serve the kingdom of darkness, furthering the enemy's destructive purpose under every spreading tree (Jeremiah 3:13)?

A similar battle scene takes place on Mount Calvary, shedding light on the conflict. Two thieves were bound to crosses cut from trees, placed on either side of Jesus. It was as if their crosses were set to face Jesus' cross between them. They were confronted with Jesus Christ, the Messiah, the Son of God, King of the Jews. One thief's heart filled with rebellion and hardened — he would die serving the kingdom of darkness, hurling insults at our Lord and Savior. The other thief's heart turned away from those insults and his heart melted with repentance. He entered the Kingdom of Life and Light as he hung, bound to a cross.

With Adam and Eve's act of rebellion they sold all their descendants as slaves to sin (Romans 7:14). Satan began his reign of death. Satan's kingdom established roots in man's dominion — the roots of death and decay permeated the earth like invasive roots of a tree. But have hope! "The creation itself will be liberated from its bondage to decay" (Romans 8:21). Destruction and decay were not God's intention, purpose, or plan. His desire was for Adam and his seed to prosper and multiply. "God blessed them and said to them, 'Be fruitful and increase in number; fill the earth and subdue it. Rule over the fish of the sea and the birds of the air and over every living creature that moves on the ground'" (Genesis 1:28). Can there be any doubt of God's intent for them to fill the earth with godly offspring, establish a just and righteous reign over God's creation, and, in so doing, subdue the earth?

But what is the end of this battle between the Kingdom of Light and the kingdom of darkness?

As we see in Genesis 1:28 (quoted above) and in Isaiah 45:18, God formed the earth to be inhabited. But inhabited with what? Here we see what God did **not** intend for the earth. "We were with child, we writhed in pain, but we gave birth to wind. We have not brought salvation to the earth; we have not given birth to people of the world" (Isaiah 26:18). Adam and his seed were meant to bring the Tree of Life to all the people who would fill the earth and subdue it. But Adam and Eve rejected this for a tree that was pleasing to the eyes. They rejected the work God ordained for them: "The highest heavens belong to the Lord, but the earth he has given to man" (Psalm 115:16).

Adam lost this great gift given to him by the Creator of all good things. "We have done nothing to rescue the world; no one has been born to populate the earth" (Isaiah 26:18 NLT). Is this a call to populate the earth with children, any children, no matter what? Certainly not! There is more to this call of God: "He was seeking godly offspring" (Malachi 2:15). God's intent was for Adam and his seed to fill and subdue the earth with righteousness — with a people who established nations and kingdoms under the rule and authority of our Creator God. But what have we done instead? "They committed adultery with their idols; they even sacrificed their children, whom they bore to me, as food for them" (Ezekiel 23:37). Today it is uncommon to offer children as human sacrifices to idols; but we still fail in raising them, for we do not present them before a Living God as children of righteousness.

Too often, in our armchair, padded-pew kind of walking with

the Lord, we are not diligent to bring our children up to walk in the Light. Maybe we feel that we have fulfilled our duty if our infants are baptized or dedicated to the Lord, brought up in Sunday school, dropped off at church for Vacation Bible School and confirmation classes and offered their first communion. Job done! Whew! Woohoo! Next Sunday we take the boat and camper to the lake. God's prophet indicts us with this charge: "For they have betrayed the honor of the Lord, bearing children that aren't his" (Hosea 5:7 NLT; see also Deuteronomy 6:7).

We have a greater call than to lukewarm mediocrity and complacency: "Enlarge the place of your tent, stretch your tent curtains wide, do not hold back; lengthen your cords, strengthen your stakes. For you will spread out to the right and to the left; your descendants will dispossess nations and settle in their desolate cities" (Isaiah 54:2-3). This is a call to advance the kingdom of heaven into all the earth.

We must also consider Jesus' words: "You are the salt of the earth. But if the salt loses its saltiness, how can it be made salty again? It is no longer good for anything, except to be thrown out and trampled by men. You are the light of the world. A city on a hill cannot be hidden" (Matthew 5:13-14). You and I are called to be overcomers in Christ, to be the light of the world, reflecting the light of Christ Jesus. Jesus overcame the world on our behalf so the work of the kingdom of God, being the salt of the earth and light of the world, is now possible in the power, strength, and authority given us in Jesus Christ, the Tree of Life.

Part 3

Can there be any doubt that the kingdom of darkness exposed Satan's plan in the Tree of Knowledge of Good and Evil? He is hell-bent on ruling over God's creation and destroying every last trace of life and light. The prophets uncovered his deception:

> "I looked, and there before me stood a tree in the middle of
> the land. Its height was enormous. The tree grew large and

strong and its top touched the sky; it was visible to the ends of the earth. Its leaves were beautiful, its fruit abundant, and on it was food for all. Under it the beasts of the field found shelter, and the birds of the air lived in its branches; from it every creature was fed." (Daniel 4:10)[9]

"Consider Assyria, once a cedar in Lebanon, with beautiful branches overshadowing the forests; it towered on high its top above the thick foliage." (Ezekiel 31:3)[10]

"The cedars in the garden of God could not rival it, nor could the pine trees equal its boughs, nor could the plane trees compare with its branches — no tree in the garden of God could match its beauty. I made it beautiful with abundant branches, the envy of all the trees of Eden in the garden of God." (Ezekiel 31:8)[11]

Satan boasted of a kingdom[12] as he tempted our Lord Jesus. "The devil led him up to a high place and showed him in an instant all the kingdoms of the world. And he said to him, 'I will give you all their authority and splendor, for it has been given to me, and I can give it to anyone I want to. So if you worship me, it will all be yours'" (Luke 4:5). Man's earthly dominion was surrendered to Satan by Adam as he ate from the Tree of Knowledge of Good and Evil rather than from the Tree of Life. The kings, princes, lords, and rulers of this world also give power and honor to Satan, the prince and power of the air as they

---

[9] This Scripture must be read in context: The tree in the king's dream represented Nebuchadnezzar's kingdom that became a source of pride, leading to his downfall. ""Is not this the great Babylon I have built as the royal residence, by my mighty power and for the glory of my majesty?" (Daniel 4:30).

[10] In context, these Scriptures are clearly referring to earthly kingdoms: ""Son of man, say to Pharaoh king of Egypt and to his hordes" (Ezekiel 31:2).

[11] To the eyes of man the beauty of the kingdoms of this earth are far more enticing than the trees in the garden of God.

[12] We must be clear. Satan lied at this moment, boasting of a kingdom that was not his. Adam did surrender a part of his domain to Satan by his sin, but Satan did not take over any part of God's sovereign rule over all of creation.

choose to serve him.[13] But we do not despair because we know which kingdom will prevail. "For the nation or kingdom that will not serve you will perish; it will be utterly ruined. The glory of Lebanon will come to you, the pine, the fir and the cypress together, to adorn the place of my sanctuary; and I will glorify the place of my feet" (Isaiah 60:12-13).

The kingdoms are locked in a battle for all creation. The war rages on to this very day and will continue until all things are subjected under the feet of the Son of God who is seated in His position of power and authority at the right hand of God. Jesus opened our eyes to this war in the spiritual realm on His way to the cross on Mount Calvary: "For if men do these things when the tree is green, what will happen when it is dry?" (Luke 23:31).

By the finished work of the cross, Jesus crushed His enemies, as the prophets proclaimed: "Surely, as I have planned, so it will be, and as I have purposed, so it will stand. I will crush the Assyrian in my land; on my mountains I will trample him down. His yoke will be taken from my people, and his burden removed from their shoulders" (Isaiah 14:24). And in 14:5, "The Lord has broken the rod of the wicked, the scepter of the rulers." In verse 12, "How you have fallen from heaven, O morning star, son of the dawn! You have been cast down to the earth, you who once laid low the nations!"

John the Baptist prophesies the end of Satan's kingdom and of all who are in league him, "The ax is already at the root of the trees, and every tree that does not produce good fruit will be cut down and thrown into the fire" (Luke 3:9). Christ's victory is our victory, yet, like a babe in a manger, this victory has humble beginnings. But "who despises the day of small things" (Zechariah 4:10)?

Christ's triumph is proclaimed by the prophets. "All the trees of the field will know that I the Lord bring down the tall tree and make the low tree grow tall. I dry up the green tree and make the dry tree

---

[13] I recall watching the Parade of Nations at the 2012 Olympic opening ceremony in London. Each nation's athletes followed the flag bearer for their nation and then every nation's flag was planted beneath the tree on a "mountain." The branches of the tree were spread over the flags of the nations. The symbolism struck me as significant for these last days.

flourish. I the Lord have spoken, and I will do it" (Ezekiel 17:24). The prophets agree on this. "A shoot will come up from the stump of Jesse; from his roots a Branch will bear fruit" (Isaiah 11:1).

From this unlovely Tree in the Garden, God has won a mighty victory:

> *"He told them another parable, 'The kingdom of heaven is like a mustard seed, which a man took and planted in his field. Though it is the smallest of all your seeds, yet when it grows, it is the largest of garden plants and becomes a tree, so that the birds of the air come and perch in its branches.'"* (Matthew 13:31)

Digging further, we see the power in these lowly beginnings. "I tell you the truth, unless a kernel of wheat falls to the ground and dies, it remains only a single seed. But if it dies, it produces many seeds" (John 12:24). Jesus is the "seed" that died; and as we are submersed in the waters of baptism we die with Him. He is the seed of Adam, the seed of Abraham, the seed of David, the seed of Truth, the seed of life that conquers death. The "many seeds" are New Covenant Christians: "It is sown in dishonor, it is raised in glory; it is sown in weakness, it is raised in power; it is sown a natural body, it is raised a spiritual body" (1 Corinthians 15:43). By His death on the cross, Jesus made a way for us to be transformed from dishonor to glory, from weakness to power, from natural to spiritual. "My grace is sufficient for you, for my power is made perfect in weakness" (2 Corinthians 12:9). In the weakness of the flesh, by means of water baptism, we are buried with Christ and raised in the power of the resurrected Christ. "For to be sure, he was crucified in weakness, yet he lives by God's power. Likewise, we are weak in him, yet by God's power we will live with him to serve you" (2 Corinthians 13:4 NSRV). Jesus prophesies the final victory: "Now the ruler of this world will be driven out" (John 12:31).

From the most humble beginnings, our Lord Christ Jesus gains the victory in the battle of kingdoms and finally, all His enemies will be placed under His feet. "Then the end will come, when he hands over the kingdom to God the Father after he has destroyed all dominion, authority and power. For he must reign until he has put all his enemies under his feet. The last enemy to be destroyed is death. For he 'has put everything under his feet'" (1 Corinthians 15: 24-27). We share in His victory, because we are sons of the Most High God, soldiers of the cross, and overcomers by the power of the resurrected Christ.

Part 4

Like the mustard seed, the smallest, most insignificant-looking seed is planted in the soil to flourish like a tree in the garden (Matthew 13:31-32). Is it important to understand where Jesus' body was buried? "At the place where Jesus was crucified, there was a garden, and in the garden a new tomb, in which no one had ever been laid" (John 19:41).

Jesus was rejected by His own kind and buried in a garden. The Tree of Life was at the center of the Garden of Eden. Jesus humbled Himself because of His love for us and became like this seed. His own people rejected Him, screamed out for Him to be crucified, and then planted Him in a garden. What will come of this Seed whose body was buried and sealed in the ground with a stone?

In this time of upheaval and uproar in the world, we need a mustard seed of faith to step into what God has for this kingdom whose King was wrapped in strips of linen and planted in the ground — in a garden. "I tell you the truth, if you have faith as small as a mustard seed, you can say to this mountain, 'Move from here to there' and it will move. Nothing will be impossible for you" (Matthew 17:20). This is Kingdom faith. It is resurrection faith. It is faith that can only come by truly hearing the Word of God.

This smallest of seeds is planted in the ground and becomes like a tree that grows to be the largest in the garden. Jesus is Victorious over death and the grave and is raised to life as the First Fruits of many people in His resurrection body. He has conquered the grave. He told His disciples, "I am the vine; you are the branches" (John 15:5). He has called us to fulfill His purpose and plan, for we are the branches that are grafted into the True Vine, and we are to spread over the whole garden and with Him become the largest in the garden.

As His branches, we are called to "armor up" and join this battle between Light and darkness. We are enlisted in the fight for the kingdom of heaven against the kingdom of death and decay. We are called and commissioned to go forth to conquer on behalf of the kingdom of heaven. God's kingdom cannot be brought to every tribe, nation, people, and tongue by human effort or by human design. This is the work of the Spirit that is accomplished in weak vessels by the power of the Spirit.

We are called to arms to defeat the evil serpent that is opposed to all of God's good creation. "The last enemy to be destroyed is death. For he 'has put everything under his feet'" (1 Corinthians 15:26). Our Lord Jesus paid the price with His broken body and the shedding of His blood and now we must take this kingdom into all the earth. This is **not** "Kingdom Now" theology.[14] I am not advocating that we conquer cities, states, and nations, because "Jesus said, 'My kingdom is not of this world'" (John 18:36). This is a call to battle and a call for Christians to be gifted and empowered by the Holy Spirit so that we may win the battle to fulfill the Great Commission: "Therefore go and make disciples of all nations, baptizing them in the name of the Father and of the Son and of the Holy Spirit, and teaching them to obey everything I have commanded you" (Matthew 28:19-20). You have a unique and special place in the battle to advance the kingdom of God. God has given you a job to do as He fills the earth with righteousness, taking back God's creation one soul at a time — driving back the forces of darkness.

With your battle gear in hand, press on to be prepared for battle.

Part 5

Armor up! Just as Pharaoh gave the authority of his name to Joseph by giving his signet ring, just as Zerubbabel is made to be like the signet

---

[14] Kingdom Now theology teaches that God lost control of the world when Adam sinned. God has since been trying to reestablish control over the world by seeking a "covenant people." Through these people, world governments and laws will be brought under God's authority. They teach that since the Holy Spirit indwells believers just as He indwelled Jesus, we have all authority in heaven and on the earth, and by faith, we have the power to believe for and speak into existence things that are not, and in this way bring about the Kingdom Age.

ring of the Lord Almighty (Haggai 2:23), and in the same way that King Xerxes presented his signet ring to Mordecai (Esther 8:2), we too, by Christ Jesus' command, are given the authority of His name and by His Holy Spirit we are given power to carry out His great commission. Advancing the Kingdom of Light is not accomplished by the wisdom of man, by great civic or religious organizations, or by naturally talented men and women.[15] "Not by might nor by power, but by my Spirit says the Lord" (Zechariah 4:6). We must choose which side we are on — we must choose the Tree of Life or the Tree of the Knowledge of Good and Evil. When we choose Life, how are we prepared for this great task in the Kingdom of Light? What is needed to make us ready to go into all the world (Matthew 28:19)? Learn with me how the authority of our Lord Jesus Christ is conferred upon Christians who will receive and act under His authority to do all He has commissioned the church to do in this present age.

For the work of the church, education is excellent. Schooling in the skills of language, cultures, and the work of missions is good and necessary. A quick wit is helpful. But in this battle of kingdoms, in the application of our battle skills, these good things are not enough. All these things fall desperately short of what is needed. We are left vulnerable and weak at our very educated best when we face the forces of darkness. We must armor up with the whole armor of God.

Think of it this way: education, training, mentoring, and schooling are like building a sailing ship with its timbers and decking, fastening masts and rigging for the sails, and finally unfurling the sail cloth. The ship goes nowhere until the wind blows. The ship drifts with the currents until the wind fills the canvas sails and drives the ship forward. The Holy Spirit of Jesus is the empowering wind that drives the ship and the rudder that gives it direction. The Spirit of the Lord is the "rain" that waters the earth, like God's Word that will not return void. In fact, the "showers" of God's Word cause the mountains and the hills to burst forth in song and "all the trees of the field will clap their hands" (Isaiah 55:12).

---

[15] I am not saying that there is anything wrong with the wisdom of man, great civic or religious organizations, or naturally talented people; but they are not the means by which we carry out the Great Commission.

> *"Finally, be strong in the Lord and in his mighty power. Put on the whole armor of God so that you can take your stand against the devil's schemes. For our struggle is not against flesh and blood, but against the rulers, against the authorities, against the powers of this dark world and against the spiritual forces of evil in the heavenly realms. Therefore put on the full armor of God, so that when the day of evil comes, you may be able to stand your ground and after you have done everything, to stand."* (Ephesians 6:10)

I've heard Christians say, "Yeah, I've got my armor on, but it has a few chinks and holes in it." Excuse me, but the real stuff, the genuine article is **God's** armor not our own. Certainly, if you are depending solely upon your charisma, skills, education, and human wisdom, you are armored with your own armor. You are a fine sailing a ship without the wind to drive it. But the battle calls for God's armor. We must put on the whole armor **of God.**

The shepherd boy, David, declared that he would fight Goliath. King Saul thought David should wear his battle armor, but it didn't fit. David was uncomfortable in it and knew it would hinder him in the fight. He took it off and gave it back to King Saul. But did he go without armor? Not in the least. He went with the full armor of God and it fit perfectly.[16] Surely David appeared to be wearing a shepherd's tunic, but he was covered with God's armor. He defeated the giant Goliath, the champion of the Philistines who didn't have a chance (1 Samuel 17). The whole armor of God is more than just a New Testament concept (Isaiah 59:17).

We see in 1 Samuel 18:3-4 that the giving of armor and a robe is the sign of a covenant between David and Jonathan. In the same way, when God gives us His armor to wear in battle and when Christ Jesus gives us his robes of righteousness, this is a "sign" of His covenant with

---

[16] If you're in doubt, consider this: did David go with faith as a shield? Did David go against Goliath, holding onto God's Word as a sword? Did David advance boldly, with a helmet of God's salvation? Did David put on the breastplate of righteousness and the belt of truth? Certainly. Without a doubt.

us. He makes us ready for battle. We are ready to go forth and conquer, to spread His righteousness throughout all the earth.

Another way to illustrate this is to look at the days of Noah. "As it was in the days of Noah, so it will be at the coming of the Son of Man" (Matthew 24:37). Offenses against a Holy God were rampant throughout all of the earth, infecting all people, nations, and tribes. The people were in rebellion against a Holy God, so God commissioned Noah to build an ark out of cypress wood to save a remnant of people unto God. Our commission is similar to Noah's. We are to spread the Good News of Jesus Christ throughout all the earth, inviting people to come into the "ark" to be saved from the coming just wrath of a Holy God. The "ark" we are compelled to enter into by faith is Jesus Christ who alone can save us — for He is the Tree of Life from which we are to partake. In Jesus Christ we will rise above, protected against the just and holy wrath of our Lord God Almighty.

Jesus sent out the twelve disciples to proclaim the kingdom of God. He sent out the seventy-two to announce the Kingdom is near. We too are protected, sealed, armored and then commissioned, gifted, and given authority to proclaim the Kingdom and announce the saving graces of our Lord and Savior Jesus Christ, who is the Way to the Tree of Life.

Like the shepherd boy David going out to fight Goliath, we must not go out in our human strength, but in the power and authority of the Name of an Almighty God, Maker of heaven and earth. If we go in the flesh, we go out in weakness, without armor, without the mighty weapons given to us to fight the fight.

Our Lord Jesus struggled, carrying a wooden cross up the road to Mount Calvary, His body beaten and bloodied, a crown of thorns on His head, His back torn with a whip, spit of soldiers in His face, and His beard ripped from His cheeks. In this moment He saw the "daughters of Jerusalem" weeping for Him. He told them, better to weep for themselves. Then Jesus concluded, "For if men do these things when the tree is green, what will happen when it is dry?" (Luke 23:31). The most applicable understanding of this statement is that when the tree, which is likened to the branches of the Vine, is dry and lifeless, they are in danger of suffering a greater wrath of men than what Christ suffered. This dry tree could be described as Christianity without Christ. These withered branches are a church that is not receiving its sustenance from the Vine. These shrunken offshoots hold to a form of godliness, but deny the power and are in danger of being cut off and burned. They are trying to please men rather than God and are not serving under the authority of Christ (Galatians 1: 10). They have abandoned the Spring of Living Water for a well they have dug by their own effort.

Christians are the branches of the Tree of Life, branches of the Vine, and we are to receive power given by the Holy Spirit, to take this Good News of Jesus Christ to every nation. We are to enlarge the Kingdom just as the tiny mustard seed grew and spread out to be the largest plant in the garden.

> *"Sing, O barren woman, you who never bore a child; burst into song, shout for joy, you who were never in labor; because more are the children of the desolate woman than of her who has a husband,' says the Lord. 'Enlarge the place of your tent, stretch your tent curtains wide, do not hold back; lengthen your cords, strengthen your stakes. For you will spread out to the right and to the left; your descendants will dispossess nations and settle in their desolate cities." (Isaiah 54:1-3)*

We are the branches grafted into the Tree of Life and we must draw from the Vine and bear fruit in Christ. We are called to arms in winning this war of the kingdoms, one soul at a time and we *cannot* accomplish this in our own strength, by our own methods, through earthbound organizations, or by human means. "Yet he will be destroyed, but not by human power" (Daniel 8:25b). "So he said to me, "This is the word of the LORD to Zerubbabel: 'Not by might[17] nor by power, but by my Spirit,' says the LORD Almighty" (Zechariah 4:6).

Let's look at the Tree of Life and the Tree of the Knowledge of Good and Evil side by side to grasp the stark realities of light and darkness to illustrate where the battle lines are drawn.

---

[17] The original meaning of the Hebrew implies that it is not by human might or earthbound power, or by the strength of man.

Tree of Life		Tree of Knowledge of Good and Evil	
1. Life	Romans 8:6	1. Death	Romans 6:23
2. Renewal, Restoration	Joel 2:25	2. Decay	Romans 8:21
3. Liberty	John 8:36	3. Bondage	Romans 8:5
4. Blessings	Psalm 65:9	4. Curses	Galatians 3:10
5. Light	Psalm 27:1	5. Darkness	Job 12:25
6. Truth	John 8:2, 17:17	6. Deception, Lies	Revelation 12:9
7. Love	1 John 4:16	7. Hatred	Proverbs 10:12
8. Hope	Romans 5:5	8. Despair	Joel 1:11
9. Refreshing	Jeremiah 31:25	9. Weariness	Lamentations 5:5
10. Bond of Peace	Ephesians 4:3	10. Divided	1 Corinthians 3:3
11. Security	Psalm 18:2	11. Insecurity	Proverbs 27:24
12. Submission	Ephesians 5:21	12. Rebellion	Romans 8:7
13. Flourishing	Psalm 92:12	13. Desolation	Isaiah 24:4
14. Growing	Psalm 92:12	14. Wasting Away	Psalm 112:10
15. Wisdom	Proverbs 14:1	15. Foolishness	1 Corinthians 1:18
16. Community	Psalm 68:6	16. Isolation	Psalm 68:6
17. Peace	Isaiah 9:6	17. Distress	Isaiah 8:22
18. Bread of Life	John 6:48	18. Bread of Wickedness	Proverbs 4:17
19. Cup of Covenant	Luke 22:20	19. Wine of Violence	Proverbs 4:17
20. Protection	Job 1:10	20. Abandonment	Jeremiah 12:7
21. Fulfillment	Psalm 20:4	21. Emptiness	Jeremiah 4:23
22. Strength	Psalm 84:7	22. Helpless	Psalm 10:9
23. Healing	Malachi 4:2	23. Disease	Psalm 106:15
24. Treasure	Proverbs 15:6	24. Great loss	Proverbs 6:15
25. Provision	Deut. 11:15	25. Lack, Poverty	Amos 4:6
26. Plenty	Philippians 4:19	26. Want	Matthew 13:25
27. Good Fruit	Luke 6:43-45	27. Bad Fruit	Luke 6:43
28. Beauty	Isaiah 61:3	28. Ashes	Isaiah 61:3
29. Oil of Gladness	Isaiah 61:3	29. Mourning	Isaiah 61: 3
30. Garment of Praise	Isaiah 61:3	30. Spirit of Despair	Isaiah 61:3
31. Fruit of the Spirit	Galatians 5:22	31. Fruit of Death	Romans 7:5
32. Mind of Christ	1 Cor. 2:16	32. Selfish Ambition	James 3:16
33. Forgiveness	Mathew 26:28	33. Condemnation	Psalm 34:21
34. Mercy	Psalm 28:6	34. Malice	Psalm 41:5
35. Dominion of Light	Colossians 1:12	35. Dominion of Darkness	Colossians 1:13
36. Life and Prosperity	Deut. 30:15	36. Death and Adversity	Deut. 30:15
37. Feasting	Isaiah 65:13-14	37. Hunger	Isaiah 65:13-14
38. Quenched Thirst	Isaiah 65:13-14	38. Thirst	Isaiah 65:13-14
39. Rejoicing	Isaiah 65:13-14	39. Shame	Isaiah 65:13-14
40. Singing	Isaiah 65:13-14	40. Crying in Anguish	Isaiah 65:13-14

Reviewing all the above Scripture has made exceedingly clear to me that the enemy of our souls, Satan, has no power over Christians that we do not give him. When we surrender to him, walking upon his broad, easy pathway, we leave the gate wide open to destruction (Matthew 7:13). We become "plunder" for the enemy of our souls (Isaiah 42:22). Even in our unknown sins, we motor along on "Easy Street." C.S. Lewis puts it like this: "Indeed the safest road to hell is the gradual one — the gentle slope, soft underfoot, without sudden turnings, without milestones, without signposts."[18]

We are vulnerable to the deceit of the enemy when we deceive ourselves. Too often we choose to believe a lie because a lie will not warn us of our sin. We would do well to pray earnestly for the Holy Spirit to convince us and convict us of our sin. But we do not despair for we are a people with an eternal hope: "If we confess our sins, he is faithful and just and will forgive us our sins and purify us from all unrighteousness" (1 John 1:9).

Be encouraged to buy gold: "I counsel you to buy from me gold refined in the fire, so that you can become rich; and white clothes to wear, so you can cover your shameful nakedness; and salve to put on your eyes, so you can see" (Revelation 3:18).

Cable news channels bombard viewers with messages crying, "Buy Gold!" But this gold is yellow with impurities, corrupted. It is not pure. "Your gold and silver are corroded" (James 5:3). The Apostle John encourages us to buy gold that has passed through the refining fire, "...for our God is a consuming fire" (Hebrews 12:29). Any corrupted gold you buy will be consumed and burned up. Store up Kingdom Gold instead. This gold is given to the bride of Christ as gifts, a precious gift for enriching the church, strengthening the church and beautifying the bride of Christ. You have become a witness to the battle of the kingdoms. Will you serve the kingdom of heaven in resurrection power or the kingdom of darkness? Will you receive the blessings of the Tree of Life? When you join forces with the kingdom of heaven, you are issued God's personal battle armor. My encouragement to you is to armor up and serve under Jesus' authority to accomplish all that God has purposed and planned for you.

Stand back and observe for just a moment. You will see a solid

---

[18] C. S. Lewis. *Screwtape Letters.*

foundation being built for the ministries and service of spiritual gifts that strengthen the church and further God's kingdom. Each one who is called by the Name of our Lord Jesus Christ has precious gifts awaiting them right now, and the power of the Holy Spirit is given to them for works of service and ministry (Ephesians 2:10). You have chosen the Kingdom of Light. As you are gifted and empowered by the Holy Spirit, armored in God's armor, you are fully prepared to fulfill the great commission, in His strength, in His power manifested in the ministries and service of spiritual gifts, our defenses are mighty and our weapons powerful. Our Fortress is a mighty Rock, and we will prevail in this mighty battle of the kingdoms.

YOUR JOURNEY JOURNAL
Chapter 2: Tree of Life

Part 1:

1. What tree in the Garden of Eden was likely the most pleasing to the natural eye? What does this teach you about your weaknesses and the temptations you face every day?

2. Describe your personal soul and spirit battle. How will you win this battle?

Part 2:

1. Compare the response of the two thieves hanging on crosses at Jesus' right and left on Mount Golgotha as they were confronted with the suffering Christ. What is the significance of their polar opposite responses to Jesus?

2. How do your choices in life contribute to the battle of the kingdom of darkness and the Kingdom of Light?

Part 3:

1. God's power is manifested or made perfect in weakness. What is the significance of this truth in your life?

2. What is the truth revealed in the "Seed" that is sown in weakness?

Part 4:

1. Describe resurrection faith. How is this significant in your daily communion with the Lord God?

2. How will it be possible that God's kingdom will advance and take root in every tribe, nation, people, and tongue before He returns in His glory?

Part 5:

1. What does it mean to be "armored up"?

2. How is it possible for the Great Commission to be fulfilled when there are only weak and fallible human beings to fulfill this Great Commission?

3. Write a short paragraph comparing the kingdom of darkness and the Kingdom of Light.

Your Journal Notes:

3

Body, Soul, and Spirit

The concept that spiritual and natural gifts are distinct in characteristics and purpose is foreign to many Christians, making it difficult to grasp hold of. You will read the terms "natural" and "spiritual" many times in this study. Defining the three parts of our make up will open your understanding to the importance of distinguishing between the natural and spiritual, between what is common and what is holy. Making this distinction is of crucial importance in the ministries and service of spiritual gifts.

My hope is that as you advance through this study, you are getting hungrier for the Word and will chew on it, test it, prove it, and then embrace it and walk in it. In this chapter we will draw a picture of the being that God has created each of us to be, a tripartite person made in God's image. We study this concept to have a greater understanding of the workings of spiritual gifts in the church. As we comprehend this principle, we will be able to distinguish between what is holy and what is common, what is natural and what is spiritual.

There is confusion about gifts of the Spirit because of a misunderstanding about our make up as human beings. Many people think that we consist of two parts — soul and body. This belief leads us to think of the soul as the invisible part, and the body as the visible outward part of us. While there is some truth to this, it is incomplete. This two-part concept comes from human reasoning and does not stand the test of Scripture; when we arrive at a belief based on human reason, it is fallible and does not hold up to the proofs of God's Word.

The Scripture does not confuse spirit and soul even though it is often difficult to distinguish one from the other (Hebrews 4:12). The body, soul, and spirit are each distinct and unique, and must not be confused or blended together. This tripartite concept of man is consistent with the nature of God who created us, who is the triune God; our one God consists of three distinct persons — the Father, and the Son, and Holy Spirit. He created us in His image.

The Apostle Paul wrote a letter to expand on this truth: "May God himself, the God of peace, sanctify you through and through. May your whole spirit, soul, and body be kept blameless at the coming of our Lord Jesus Christ" (1 Thessalonians 5:23). This verse clearly shows that we are made up of three distinct parts, not two as is commonly taught.

Our Creator God formed man out of the dust of the ground, and breathed into him the breath of life, "and man became a living soul" (Genesis 2:7 KJV). First God formed a body for Adam from the dust of the ground. Then God breathed into Adam's flesh the breath of life that became his spirit. As God brought together the body and breath of life in Adam, he became a living soul — a tripartite being made in the image of God.

The truths regarding our three part being come alive in this Scripture, revealing the value of a person's spirit and the value of a person's body: "The Spirit gives life" (John 6:63). This same verse makes clear the value of the flesh: "the flesh counts for nothing." It doesn't say the body is not useful, but that it counts for nothing — nothing of eternal value. The original Hebrew word for "life" in Genesis 2:7 is חַיָּה (chavah, pronounced khä·yä'). חַיָּה is plural and refers to the Spirit's inbreathing that creates the soul by joining together spirit and body.

We cannot exist on this earth without a body. We cannot lift hands to praise a Holy God without these working extremities. We cannot bend our knees to worship God Almighty unless we have knees. We cannot proclaim the Good News of Jesus Christ without a mouth. This body, a working, healthy body, is incredibly important while we walk about on terra firma, but we must offer it up to God as a living sacrifice (Romans 12:1).

We all know what the body is. We can pinch it, we feel pain when something goes wrong, and it gives other people a first impression of us. Our bodies are the outward, visible part of us. The Apostle Paul refers to the body as a tent. This is the earthbound part. Our soul is our individuality, our personality, and the source of our emotions. The spirit of a man is the part of us that is able to commune with God and by our spirit we truly worship God who is Spirit. This is the God-conscious part of us.

Watchman Nee helps us understand these truths:[19] "If man's soul wills to obey God, it will allow the spirit to rule over the man as ordered by God." But the soul, when bound up in the flesh, may overpower the spirit and all that is truly spiritual in a man. Spiritual gifts belong with the spirit of man and natural gifts are for the good of the body, the flesh and the temporal wellbeing of humankind. The soul will manifest influence upon body or spirit, and the soul's effect will be reflected in how we use and apply both natural and spiritual gifts. Remember, the natural man is constantly at war with your spirit to rule over your soul, and can become hostile to all that is spiritual[20] (Romans 8:5-7, 1 Peter 2:11). This hostility must be torn from the soul by force, just as Christ threw the moneychangers out of the temple (Matthew 12:12). Jesus is the "force" who will strengthen you in this battle.

Take some time to study and meditate on Romans chapter 8 and

---

[19] Watchman Nee. *The Spiritual Man*, page 25.
[20] Recommended reading: Chapter One, "Spirit, Soul and Body," *The Spiritual Man*.

it will change your perspective. In verse 7, you will see that the flesh is hostile toward God. The flesh, if given reign, will lead the soul into rebellion against God. In verse 6 we see that the mind — or soul — can align with either our flesh (natural man) or with the Spirit of God. "For the sinful nature desires what is contrary to the Spirit, and the Spirit what is contrary to the sinful nature" (Galatians 5:17).

How does this battle play out in our lives? If the mind is fixed on the flesh, then when hardship comes, the mind accuses the spirit saying, "Where is your God when you really need Him?" Our anguish shakes its finger in our faces and demands an answer. "If God really cared, He wouldn't have allowed this, would He?" In persecution, the natural man says, "You don't deserve to be treated like this." In our want, whether from famine or for clothes to keep us warm, the mortal man reminds us over and over how hopeless is our want, reminding us of unanswered prayers. We can overcome these temptations with an awesome weapon, the sword of the Spirit, which is the Word of God (Ephesians 6:17).

This is an important truth to grasp. If you want your flesh (natural man), to rule over your soul, all you need to do is feed the flesh with things that are pleasing to the eye and self-satisfying. The Apostle Peter refers to feeding the flesh as encouraging "sinful desires, which war against your soul." Satisfying sinful desires is nothing but a temporary satisfaction that creates a craving for more. Sinful self-gratification can lead to addictions of all kinds.)[21] But if your desire is for the Holy Spirit to rule your spirit and for the Spirit of Christ to be exalted in your soul and body (Philippians 1:20), you must feed the spirit continually with spiritual food. This feeding comes by hearing the preaching of the Word, meditating on the Word, fellowship with Christians who will hold you accountable to the Word, and faithfully digging into the Scripture, which is your spiritual food.

---

[21] Chains that bind us are the result of sin. Today we call this addiction, and certainly all sin is addictive. "Some sat in darkness and the deepest gloom, prisoners suffering in iron chains, for they rebelled against the words of God and despised the counsel of the Most High" (Psalm 107:10-11). How can we help but love our Heavenly Father and delight in His Word, for He does not leave us without hope in our sinful, dark prison. In verse 14, we find this hope. "He brought them out of darkness and the deepest gloom and broke away their chains."

Will you have the temporal, natural man rule over you or will you have the Spirit of Christ reign over your whole being? Will you do the work of the church and the kingdom of heaven by natural, temporal means or by the power and might of your spirit, under the authority and power of the Holy Spirit of Jesus? When you begin to think with an eternal perspective, and when your worldview is Biblically based, your answer to these questions becomes obvious.

Remember, the challenge is this: the natural man is born into rebellion against a Holy God, because we are born of Adam, the original rebel. We are not "born free." In the ministry of spiritual gifts we must have courage so that Christ is exalted and ruling over our natural man, overcoming the rebellion by the blood of the Lamb. Our natural tendency is for our natural man, born of Adam, to lord over soul and spirit and to do everything by physical means rather than by spiritual means.

But the gifts of the Spirit are for those who live and walk according to the Spirit, whose minds are fixed on the unseen eternal things. As you gain an understanding of the spiritual realm and as the kingdom of heaven comes closer to you, truths of eternal consequence will be revealed to you, powerfully affecting your ministries and service in the kingdom of heaven.

As our understanding is opened, it becomes evident that we are dealing with two distinct realities in this world. The spiritual realm is the greater reality because it is lasting and eternal. The natural realm is a lesser reality because it is temporary; it will all go away at the end of time. The natural man's longing is in the here and now — in the immediate gratification of the needs and desires of the flesh. But temporal things count for nothing and in fact when we pursue them beyond God's intended purpose, they bring us into bondage, death, and destruction. We must instead subject the natural man, the body, the flesh, to the Spirit of Jesus and produce fruit that is of eternal value. This is the true and lasting reality.

So what is reality? Our earthly existence is described in Scripture as a shadow, a breath, a vanishing vapor, swift, and a mere handbreadth. Our present state is but a shadow. Is a shadow real? Or is what casts the shadow real? Think on it!

Jesus is our example. He ruled over His appetite (John 4:32). He ruled over his emotions (Luke 23:34, Matthew 26:39, 53). He ruled over anxious thoughts (Luke 22:42). We too must earnestly desire what is spiritual and eternal, overcoming the rebellion of the flesh so that Christ may be exalted in our bodies as we minister by the gifting and empowering work of the Holy Spirit. Anything less serves no eternal purpose. "And [God] is not served by human hands, as if he needed anything" (Acts 17:25). There is no lack in God's kingdom that human hands can fulfill. The work of the kingdom is accomplished in the power of the spirit that is empowered in the Spirit.

Meditate on the Scriptures in this chapter to fix in your mind and your spirit on God's purpose in creating you as a three-part being in His image. Apply this truth to see the beautiful and unique creation God has made when He "knit you together" and breathed into you the breath of life (Psalm 139:13). Now with a clear understanding of how you were created, you are better equipped for the ministries and service of spiritual gifts, for the work and mission of the church. With your feet on the ground and your spirit communing in the eternal Spirit of Jesus, you are powerfully equipped to fulfill Christ's great commission.

Our prayer: *"Lord, may I become less and less and You become more and more."*

YOUR JOURNEY JOURNAL
Chapter 3: Body, Soul, and Spirit

1. We are tripartite beings, created in the image of God. What are the three parts? Why three?

2. Describe the tension or battle between the natural man (flesh) and the spiritual man.

3. The spiritual realm and the natural realm are both real. Which is the greater reality? Why?

Your Journal Notes:

4

Treasures Plundered —
Treasures Recaptured

The prophet Hosea declared, "They will come trembling in awe to the Lord, and they will receive his good gifts in the last days" (Hosea 3:5). He was speaking of you, the church, in this day! Beyond a doubt, we live in the last days. And yet, Hosea's life serves as a warning sign for us too, of treasures plundered by the enemy. His wayward wife left him for another. In the same way, the church has too often left the very best that God holds out to His bride, adornments given to prepare His bride. And we have settled for far less.

Ezekiel's message, like Hosea's, was lived out in his life experience. His wife, the delight of his eyes, the object of his affection, was taken from him to dramatically illustrate that the Lord would take His Presence in the sanctuary away from His people; then Jerusalem would fall, and the temple would be destroyed.

Hosea and Ezekiel's messages are recorded to help us, to teach us, and to warn us against following the same destructive path.[22] We should not despise God's good gifts, because in rejecting them, it is as if the enemy plunders us too. We must treasure the gifts that Our Lord Jesus offers to us so that they may be restored to His bride to adorn her in preparation for the Bridegroom.

Is it even possible in our day that God's good treasures could be taken from those He loves? God has given the church an abundance of good gifts. His heart overflows to us with treasures and blessings

---

[22] "These things happened to them as examples for us. They were written down to warn us who live at the end of the age" (1 Corinthians 10:11 NLT).

beyond our imagination. These gifts He has given are the desire of His heart for His people. So how is it possible for the enemy of our souls plunder those who call on the name of the Lord?

Consider the beauty and splendor of the Garden of Eden. The garden was God's blessing for Adam and Eve to enjoy. They happily walked with their Creator God. I imagine that they were like two young lovers on a honeymoon in paradise. Imagine them exploring their paradise hand in hand as they fell in love. They must have frolicked about, discovering all God had given them. Yet the enemy stole this treasure and they were driven out of their paradise.

Think about some other examples. Cain lost the right to dwell among his family, becoming a fugitive and wanderer (Genesis 4:12). The people of Noah's day despised their Creator and lost everything, yet God saved a remnant (Genesis 7:23). Lot chose the fertile plains surrounding Sodom and Gomorrah and later he ended up hiding in the mountains and living in a cave (Genesis 19:30). King Saul went against Samuel's instructions, going his own way, and lost his kingdom and his life (1 Samuel 15:23). Eleven sons of Jacob despised their brother Joseph and sold him into slavery. They lived in dread the rest of their lives (Genesis 42:21). King David despised God's call in a pleasure seeking moment, yielding to what delighted his eyes. He took what was not his, and the peace that prevailed over Israel was taken away (2 Samuel 12:11). The northern kingdom of Israel shunned the God who had given them a land flowing with milk and honey. The southern kingdom of Judah also turned away and God called a foreign army to march against them and plunder them. The land that once flowed with abundance was subjected to ruin (Jeremiah 25:11).

The religious leaders and the people of Jesus' day rejected and crucified the Son of God, as Jesus predicted, and in AD 70 the Romans burned Jerusalem, tore down the temple and burned the nation's orchards, fields, and forests, leaving behind only a barren wilderness of charred remains.

We, like our predecessors, do not serve God in all His fullness and majesty, but a lesser god of our own making. A designer god — a god we have created to serve our own purpose. Certainly, we worship one we call Jehovah God, Creator of heaven and earth, but we have left behind some of His most awesome attributes (2 Corinthians 11:4). We serve God buffet style, choosing what we prefer and rejecting what we don't like — in this way we have created our own lesser god.

Who is Almighty God? We must know Him in order to serve Him with due reverence and awe, with worshipful fear. Look at what we can know of God, as revealed in Exodus 34:5:

- His name is "The Lord."
- He is compassionate and gracious.
- He is slow to anger.
- He abounds in love and faithfulness.
- He maintains love to thousands.
- He forgives wickedness, rebellion, and sin.
- He punishes the guilty.

This is a thumbnail glimpse of the true God who is worthy of our worship.

The book of Revelation offers a description of the church that applies to this day: "Yet this I hold against you: You have forsaken your first love. Remember the height from which you have fallen! Repent and do the things you did at first. If you do not repent, I will come to you and remove your lampstand from its place" (Revelation 2:4). And again: "Wake up! Strengthen what remains and is about to die, for I have not found your deeds complete in the sight of my God. Remember, therefore, what you have received and heard; obey it, and repent" (Revelation 3:2). This is a good description of what is amiss in today's church. We do not know God. We do not desire or seek revelation knowledge of God. We do not strive to learn more of who God is. We don't search after God as we would for lost treasure and as a result there is a very grievous lack of His "gifts in the last days."

You say, "I am rich; I have acquired wealth and do not need a thing." Certainly we have rich and meaningful traditions, and beautiful forms of worship that enrich us. Our worship services and gatherings abound in excellent music, fellowship, learning, mingling and networking. We have everything we want and desire no more. But we have denied the power of Christ. We have abandoned the Spring of Living Water.

Yes, we believe in repentance, forgiveness, salvation, baptism, and communion, but we do not see that we are "wretched, pitiful, poor, blind and naked" (Revelation 3:17).

Maybe we don't want to know God in this depth because when we start to inch closer to God, we begin to tremble with awe; we tremble at our own depravity before a Holy God. And we don't like to tremble. But remember, we may stand before a Righteous God in Jesus Christ who is our righteous covering. When we come before God, He sees the righteousness of Jesus Christ our Lord and Savior because we are "in Him," wrapped in His robe of righteousness. In Christ we come boldly into God's presence and in this there is no fear of harm.

Have we remade a Holy God into an American god who is 100% love and whose judgment only applies to other people? Have we made our god into a sugar daddy that requires little of us? He did all the work for us. We can put our money in the slot, punch the big vending machine button in the sky and the promises we want pour into our cup. Does the American church worship a god who is the product of our willing ignorance? Do we attempt to operate our churches in a void of spiritual gifts and offices because our custom designed "god" is not able to give them to us? Or is it because of the hardness of our hearts?

What god do we serve? So often we act like King David on his first attempt to move the Arc of the Covenant on an ox cart (1 Chronicles 13). He did not take care to learn what God required for moving the Arc and it cost David the life of one of his valued men. At first, David was angry with God. Then he repented and searched the Scripture to know what was required of him. We too, like the people the prophet Jeremiah spoke to, refuse to know the requirements of the Lord.

> *"I thought, 'These are only the poor; they are foolish, for they do not know the way of the Lord, the requirements of their God. So I will go to the leaders and speak to them; surely they know the way of the Lord, the requirements of their God.' But with one accord they too had broken off the yoke and torn off the bonds." (Jeremiah 5:4-5)*

This was a yoke of blessing and a bond of fellowship, and they refused it as an unlovely, entangling vine.

Join me in my prayer: *"Lord, help me to know what You require of me. Give me a hunger and thirst for more of You. Give my heart of hearts the willingness to absorb more of who You are. Help me to press in and learn to know You. Help me to be like that much-loved servant who closely watches and observes his Master to meet his every desire. O God, teach me to walk in the 'fear of the Lord.'"*

The engine in your car typically has four, six, or eight cylinders. Have you ever had one spark plug that didn't spark, causing the cylinder to misfire and stop working in sync with the others? Your car begins to lope along, shaking, vibrating as you drive down the road. In this same way, is the church operating minus one or more cylinders (so to speak) because we do not have that trembling awe of the Lord that drives us to know what He desires of us? Is the church operating without all of the Offices (Ephesians 4) and spiritual gifts because we are serving a god of our own making (design)? Is the church operating without all the serving gifts because we have created a god who is a mere shadow of the Creator God of the Universe?

Please pray with me: *"Lord, break our hearts with a grieving repentance over our complacency and for accepting less than all of what You desire for us."*

After coming before the Lord with repentant hearts, let's diligently seek the Lord with all our hearts, minds, and souls. "But if from there you seek the LORD your God, you will find him if you look for him with all your heart and with all your soul" (Deuteronomy 4:29). Note: Those who diligently seek God's face and find favor with Him must continually be refreshed in the Spirit through a) seeking Him; b) asking for revelation knowledge of God; c) coveting a bond of fellowship with Him; d) desiring to be made right with Him in Jesus Christ; e) setting your love and delight in Him; and f) fervently searching the Scripture asking the Holy Spirit to be your Teacher.

Too many churches have tossed away (in whole or in part) three good things:

1. Kingdom authority: The authority of the saints who are in Jesus Christ who is seated at the right hand of God in all power

and authority where all things are made to be under His feet. "And God placed all things under his feet and appointed him to be head over everything for the church, which is his body, the fullness of him who fills everything in every way" (Ephesians 1:22).

Our prayer: *"Show me, Lord, how we have forgotten and put aside our first love."*

2. The community of saints: Saints are the body of Christ Jesus, strengthening every ligament and going out to "make disciples" among every tribe, nation, people and tongue "and baptizing them in the name of the Father and of the Son and of the Holy Spirit" (Matthew 28:19). Each of us is called to be a strengthening fiber in the fabric of our church community, to be disciple makers; but too often we leave this for others to do.

Our prayer: *"Show me, Lord, how we have left You."*

3. The sanctuary: True and real worship and service is proven in our daily deeds, in our words, work, and ministries.

Our prayer: *"Show me, Lord, how we have abandoned Your house."*

Think about the two kingdoms in the last chapter. No other kingdoms exist beyond the Kingdom of Light and the kingdom of darkness. There are no free agents. No one escapes this reality. You can't ride the fence. When Satan won the battle and made Adam subject to sin and death, we too were plundered. We were taken captive and lost so much of what God had given to us in His creation. Because of the fall, all of Adam's progeny are born into slavery. We too are subject to sin. All men and women since Adam naturally love darkness rather than light. Access to the kingdom of darkness is easy; it's a wide downward slope and we only have to coast. We can slide freely, right through the wide-open gates of the kingdom of darkness.

But you have been called out of darkness into His glorious light. When you step into the light a narrow gate and a narrow path come into view. This way is not an appealing alternative at first blush, until the Lord opens your eyes to see and partake in the bountiful treasure He holds out to you. When the eyes of your understanding are open, you will see a bountiful table et before you.

Imagine the branches of the palm trees waving in celebration under a gentle mid-summer ocean breeze on the day two firstborn sons came into this world. The first mother, Annaleah Isabelle Rothfeller Goldson, having contractions exactly one minute and thirty-two seconds apart, arrived at the hospital in a 40 foot white limousine after a twenty-minute ride from their California beach house. The uniformed chauffeur jumped out of the car, opened the back door, and held out his hand for the struggling mom. The family doctor was waiting for them at the curb with a gurney and his medical team.

Within two hours their son was born and they bequeathed their strapping 8 lb. 10 oz. boy with the name William Thornton Goldson the Third. He howled in protest at the bright lights and the cold delivery room, and everyone laughed with delight as they counted his fingers and toes. A perfect Goldson firstborn son. Annaleah shed tears of delight as she held her newborn son to her chest, cuddling him close for his first taste of the outside world. Flowers and gifts filled Annaleah's room. Uncle Richard brought a sterling silver cup engraved with "William Thornton Goldson III."

On the other side of town, Ann Lee Lowson, cried out to her husband, George, to call their family friend and midwife, Sherry, to let her know the contractions were about two minutes apart. Within five minutes, Sherry burst through the front door with her arms full of the tools of her trade. They began the long struggle to deliver Ann's first. Ann cried, screamed, pushed and then squeezed George's hand for dear life through the worse moments of pain. After pushing and sweating for twelve-hours they finally heard the first squall of their red headed baby boy. The scale weighed him in at 6 lb. 5 oz. and he measured 20 inches long. Their dog, Skipper, was shooed away when he tried to sneak in the door to share in the excitement. Billy's yellowish skin was an indication of jaundice. Sherry assured them it was not abnormal, but he would need to see a doctor right away. George winced, thinking about the cost. They had no insurance and only forty-seven dollars in their savings account.

They named him Billy B Lowson. He would have no middle name — just an initial, because they couldn't think of a good one and liked the sound of the name "Billy-b." Ann held him close and glowed with delight in spite of her exhaustion. She smiled at her husband, "The Good Lord has given you a strong, healthy son, George."

Two families from opposite ends of the economic spectrum are welcoming sons into diametrically opposite worlds. One son will live in a family of means, and the other in a struggling household. One will attend private schools and universities and the other will fight his way through public school, battling tough guys and gang members for survival every day. If he's smart enough and works real hard, he might get a scholarship for college. They live on opposite sides of the track, so to speak, literally worlds apart.

It is important to remember Jesus' words: "Blessed [happy] are the poor in spirit, for theirs is the kingdom of heaven" (Matthew 5:3). I'm inclined to think that Billy will carry into this world fewer impediments to receiving this precious gift of salvation. He carries less of this world's baggage into a life full of cares and woes.[23] And that is the greater blessing.

The two boys are completely equal in this: As descendants of Adam, they are born in bondage to sin and in need of redemption by a Living Savior. There is no escaping this reality. As each one responds to the call of our Savior and Lord Jesus, they will stand equal before a loving God. And the Holy Spirit holds out to them equally the treasures of the Kingdom. God is no respecter of persons (Acts 10:34).

It is much the same with Christians and churches today. Monumental Cathedrals, grand facilities, stained glass, luxurious carpeting, computer controlled lighting, sound systems that rival the best theaters, and mortgages to match. None of these are wrong in themselves, but those who are of lesser means have fewer impediments, less baggage to keep them from receiving from the Lord all that He holds out to them.

The writer of Hebrews admonishes us to throw off all that hinders

---

[23] As I write this I'm being reminded that our Lord is God of the impossible; in fact, He specializes in the impossible.

us: "Therefore, since we are surrounded by so great a cloud of witnesses, let us also lay aside every weight and the sin that clings so closely, and let us run with perseverance the race that is set before us, looking to Jesus the pioneer and perfecter of our faith" (Hebrews 12:1 NRSV). If the burdens of this world hold you back, throw them off. If they keep you from God's eternal best for you, get rid of them. If burdens are weighing you down so you can't run the race, lighten the load.

For God's church to find its way back, we must return and seek all of God's covenant promises. Remember that it is not only the Lord and His greatness that we are to fear, but the Lord and His goodness — not only His majesty, but His mercy. We must fear God's goodness; that is, we must admire it and stand amazed at it, we must adore it and worship as Moses did at the proclaiming of His Holy name (Exodus 34:6). We must fear offending His goodness, being ungrateful for it, and so forfeiting it. "But with you there is forgiveness, so that we can, with reverence, serve you" (Ps. 130:4). We must rejoice with trembling in the goodness of God; we must not be self-righteous but walk in the fear of the Lord. We ought to, like our Lord Jesus, delight in the fear of the Lord, repent of going our own way and allow God to give us the very best that He desires for us.

Because of our apostasy, is the American Church experiencing a spiritual famine (Amos 8:11)? Or is that just that other church down the street? No, the famine threatens all of us. But in reality, when the famine overtakes us, this famine of not "hearing God's Word,"[24] would we care? Would it make a difference in most Christian's lives? The spiritual consequences, the impact on the kingdom of heaven and the church would be traumatic, the spiritual drought would be devastating — but would we care? Would it change anything we are doing? Would it matter all that much?

During this famine, sermons will not be heard (and there will be fewer messages with roots deep in God's Word). There will be sermons

---

[24] This is a most unusual famine, not of food, but a famine of the hearing of God's Word. This Scripture doesn't say that God's Word will not be preached, taught or proclaimed, but the Word will not be heard. No matter how long, and hard we search, the Word will not be heard because we are lukewarm apostates (Revelation 3:16).

about life's issues and cares. Our Bible Study groups will be about caring about each other and sharing our personal lives and needs and go no further. Radio and T.V. preachers will still preach about God's blessings. But a good solid, well-rounded feast on God's Word will be hard to find. And when we do perchance come across one, the Spirit will not be present to open our ears and stir our hearts to repentance. These are the effects of a famine of hearing God's Word, and today's church is standing at the precipice of this famine.

Is it possible that we wouldn't much care about this famine? Will we still carry on with our forms of godliness (2 Timothy 3:5), our beautiful traditions of worship that delight us, Sunday after Sunday? Some might drift away because they find no spiritual connection, and some will find more interesting things to do on Sunday morning. But maybe it wouldn't make much difference in our church lives. We will still refer to Easter sunrise service as a beautiful spiritual moment. The Christmas pageant will still bring tears to our eyes. The music and congregation singing will lift our spirits.

Yet the famine will eat away at us, leaving us to become like moth eaten rags. We will be like people walking across a beautiful bridge, not knowing it is rusted and rotting at every rivet and seam. Unknown to us, each footfall causes the rusty iron and rotted timbers to crumble and fall away until the day when final destruction comes (Isaiah 64:11).

There is so much evidence that today's churches have put out the Holy Spirit's fire (1 Thessalonians 5:19). Too many churches have abandoned the Spring of Living Water and dug their own wells (Jeremiah 2:13). At what price are these precious treasures restored to us? What battles must be fought? Indeed, the price has already been paid and the battle is won.

Take a few minutes to look at some Scriptural parallels that may help you see a very great truth and the foundation of this truth regarding spiritual gifts:

"Lot _looked up_ and _saw_ that the whole plain of the Jordan was well watered, like the garden of the Lord, like the land of Egypt, toward Zoar" (Genesis 13:10, emphasis added). Verse 11 continues, "The two men parted company." Then verse 12, "Lot lived among the cities of the plain and pitched his tents near Sodom."

Next: Read Genesis 14:8-24
Key points and phrases:

- V. 4, "But in the thirteenth year they rebelled."
- V. 11, The four kings seized all the people, goods, and property.
- V. 16, Abram recovered everything and brought back his relative Lot with his possessions.
- V. 20, God delivered his enemies into his hand.
- V. 20, Then Abram gave a tenth of everything.
- V. 23, Abram restored the king's possessions to them. Abram gave gifts from what he had rightfully captured as spoils of war. He gave: a) to Melchizedek a king's tithe; b) to the kings, the property they lost; c) to his allies, the spoils of war; d) to the men who fought with him, what they had used in their conquest.
- Melchizedek offered Abram bread and wine. These were confirmations of a covenant. Abram gave Melchizedek material goods of earthly value and received in return a blessing of eternal value.

This record of Abraham's battle presents a great picture of treasures being recaptured and gifts being given from the spoils. Lot and his family were recaptured, released from their chains and given gifts from what was plundered from the invading kings. Abraham's victory foreshadowed Christ's victory on the cross and the triumph of resurrection. Like Abraham, Jesus overcame the enemy, plundered the enemy, recaptured us from the bondage of sin, and set us free. Our Lord Jesus has redeemed us by His precious blood. By faith, He has given us a new name. But His goodness has no boundaries and He holds out to us even more good gifts for the good of His church, the bride — spiritual gifts given by the Spirit of Jesus.

But why is it that so often, Christians reject these good spiritual gifts? It is because they do not appeal to the natural man. The gifts don't have that "eye appeal," so to speak. This is what brought about original sin and the fall of man and once again, it is our downfall. "When the woman *saw* that the fruit of the tree was *good and pleasing to the eye*, and also desirable for gaining wisdom, she took and ate it" (Genesis 3:6). Eve allowed her natural eye to rule over her spirit and she accepted a lie. Now compare Eve's actions to Lot's choice in Genesis 13:10. Lot also chose what was pleasing to the eye.

It was by what was pleasing to the eye that Satan stole from Adam's treasure and carried away the very best gifts God had given to those created in His likeness. Is it possible that Satan carried off the "jewels of the Kingdom" as his own precious possessions in a gloating victory parade accompanied by his fallen angels?

But Satan's victory would not stand. The destroyer's destruction was set in place. "And I will put enmity between you and the woman, and between your offspring and hers; he will crush your head, and you will strike his heel" (Genesis 3:15). In fact, not only did God plan to crush the enemy, but He also planned a victory celebration with a parade. "Oh clap your hands, all ye peoples; Shout unto God with the voice of triumph" (Psalm 47:1).

The custom in ancient cultures was for a conquering army to return with its captives and the spoils of war. Gold, silver precious stones, jewelry, valuable artifacts, and the list goes on. The victor would parade through town followed by his victorious soldiers, the captives in chains and captured treasures carried along with them.

Have you been to a parade? Where do you suppose the custom comes from for people who parade down the street to throw candy and trinkets to the crowd? It goes back many centuries. Victorious armies would throw gifts to the cheering crowds.

Look at the glorious victory of our Lord and Savior Jesus Christ as He restored to His people, by means of grace, the precious gifts of the kingdom of heaven. "But to each one of us grace has been given as Christ apportioned it. This is why it says: 'When he ascended on high, he took many captives and gave gifts to his people'" (Ephesians 4:7-8). Take note of the power of Christ's victory that this Scripture proclaims:

- He ascended on high: (Christ's victorious parade).
- He led captives in his train: What did Jesus take captive? Death and the grave, the curse of the law, darkness, sickness, poverty, depravity, confusion, ignorance, darkness.

- He plundered the enemy: "He descended."
- He gave gifts to men: These are the gifts both immediate and promised, the treasures and jewels of the Kingdom (Exodus 28:20, & 39:13, Song of Songs 5:14, Ezekiel 1:16 & 28:13, Daniel 10:6, Revelation 1:20). In the context of these Scriptures, the gifts are for the efficient and effective ministries of His church. God's gifts to His created ones are being restored to those who receive Him as Lord and Savior, His church. The gifts are rightfully returned to strengthen the body of Christ so they will reach every tribe nation, people, and tongue.
- The gifts will continue, beautifying His bride until the perfecting of the saints as they prepare for the return of Christ the Bridegroom.

"But thanks be to God, who made us his captives and leads us along in Christ's triumphal procession." (2 Corinthians 2:14). Look at the parallels with Abram's nephew Lot: a) We were captives of sin; b) Jesus set us free from this captivity and we followed Him in His triumphal procession — He captured us, heart and soul; c) He first gave us the gift of freedom and restored us to a right relationship with God the Father; d) He gave us gifts, power, and the authority of His Holy Name to make us a working part of His kingdom that will reign over all.

The enemy was defeated on a barren hill called Golgotha. The Destroyer was destroyed even as nails were driven into Jesus' hands and feet. As the tree was hewn into a Roman cross, the enemy surely gloated, but in the end he was thrown down and plundered. In death, Jesus defeated death. In shedding His blood He has remitted our sin, washing us clean. As His body was broken, He made our body, soul, and spirit whole. By the power of His resurrection, He gave us new life in Christ. He sent His Holy Spirit to establish His church and He is now preparing a bride for Himself. It is His desire to give His bride good gifts and to adorn her with the precious jewels of the kingdom of heaven. At great cost, He has recaptured gifts and treasures and now uses them to adorn His bride for His coming, for the great wedding supper.

By faith in Jesus Christ, you are the bride of Christ being prepared for His coming and for the great wedding banquet. Will you receive all the good gifts He holds out to you in His nail scarred hands?

YOUR JOURNEY JOURNAL
Chapter 4: Treasures Lost — Treasures Recaptured

1. Repentance lays a foundation for renewing, restoring, and rebuilding. Begin writing your prayer of repentance for the church.

2. What did it cost for our Lord Jesus to take back what was stolen by the enemy of our souls in the Garden of Eden?

3. When God gives His sons and daughters a gift, a treasure, a bridal adornment, is it even possible for this precious gift to be lost? What examples do you find in Scripture?

Your Journal Notes:

5

Natural Gifts

This chapter offers an overview of God-given natural gifts, contrasting them with spiritual gifts to help us discern between what is holy and what is common. Distinguishing between spiritual and natural gifts is vital because when we minister to people for an eternal effect, we can only do so by means of spiritual gifts.

Natural, temporal gifts (we could call them earthbound gifts), are given to individuals by our Creator God for the good of **all** people, to help them earn their way and to provide for them in this present, temporal world. "He causes his sun to rise on the evil and the good, and sends rain on the righteous and the unrighteous" (Matthew 5:45). James adds, "Every good and perfect gift is from above, coming down from the Father of heavenly lights, who does not change with the shifting shadows" (James 1:17).

Natural gifts are exercised through human might, power, and effort. In the world of commerce, a man or woman is apprenticed, trained, schooled, or mentored and thereby gains experience, knowledge, and skill in a trade or profession. This work exercises and provides for the nourishment of the body with daily bread that God provides, so the workers will have the strength and energy to perform their daily tasks. Our careers and our daily tasks require various levels of reasoning ability, skills, strength, and dexterity. These natural gifts, when enhanced through training and education, are applied for the good of families and communities and may be distinguished by referring to them as "civil righteousness." Typically we use our natural gifts to minister to people's temporal needs.[25] In the exercise of these gifts and talents, we honor God who created us and gave us the abilities to do our work.

What motivates us in the use of our natural gifts? Some motives are good and godly, while others are not. For example, the need to fatten an already fat bank account, because "money is power," is an example of a selfish motive. A desire to provide and care for our families is an obvious example of a godly motive; and indeed the ability to care for the physical needs of one's spouse and children is a natural gift from God and may be accomplished as a form of worship.

We must consider that people use natural gifts for the purpose of injustice and tyranny as well as for law and liberty, for corruption as well as godly virtue. The exercise of natural gifts is too often for one's own benefit alone, because we are not naturally altruistic. That is why the Bible says, "A righteous man cares for the needs of his animal, but the kindest acts of the wicked are cruel" (Proverbs 12:10). They are cruel in that his motives are earthbound and self-centered.

While using our natural gifts, we are subject to our abilities and good fortune. We are not all of the same age, gender, size, strength, stature, energy, courage, health, industry, patience, ingenuity, wealth, knowledge, fame, ego, temperance, perseverance, education, or intelligence. Therefore in the use of natural gifts, people are not equal. And we can use our natural gifts to exalt ourselves above others.

John Adams, second president of the United States, offered words of wisdom to caution us regarding man's natural gifts. "Human appetites, passions, prejudices, and self-love," he writes to Samuel Adams, "will never be conquered by benevolence and knowledge alone, introduced by human means." He also wrote in a letter to John Taylor that there never was or will be a society of equals "in natural and acquired qualities."[26] He held that every natural society possessed a hierarchy of "superiors and inferiors."

---

[25] When ministering to temporal needs like clothing the poor and feeding the hungry as Jesus taught, (Matthew 25:35-36 & 40) there is a blending of spiritual and natural gifts. We meet a temporal need for an eternal purpose.

[26] John Adams. *The Works of John Adams Second President of the United States*, vol. 6, pg 416.

What Adams says rings true because clearly, natural gifts are bound together with the natural man, while spiritual gifts are given to those who live by the Spirit. In the use of natural gifts, there is a great disparity among people. Your circumstances, family name, good fortune, being in the right place at the right time, a supersized ego, personal ambitions, and so many other factors affect the use of our natural gifts and talents. But in the ministries and service of spiritual gifts, we all have equal standing before God. The field is leveled in gifts of the Spirit because all we accomplish is by the power and anointing of the Holy Spirit who ministers through us — even the weakest among us.

> *"If anyone builds on this foundation using gold, silver, costly stones, wood, hay or straw, their work will be shown for what it is, because the Day will bring it to light. It will be revealed with fire, and the fire will test the quality of each person's work. If what has been built survives, the builder will receive a reward. If it is burned up, the builder will suffer loss but yet will be saved — even though only as one escaping through the flames." (1 Corinthians 3:12-15)*

A part of what this Bible passage is saying is that when the "works" or "building" we do is accomplished by human effort alone and not in the Spirit, it will not stand in that Day when it will be tested by fire. Our eternal "work" or "building" must be accomplished under the authority of and in the Name of our Lord Jesus Christ, by the power of the Holy Spirit, through the gifting of the Holy Spirit, and in the strength of the Holy Spirit. This building is what will be proven by fire. But what is accomplished by natural gifts alone will not stand this test of fire.

So we must conclude what is self-evident, that natural gifts and talents are given to all people, but in the use of these gifts, all people are not equal. Mankind may use the "rain" for good, as God intended, or may use it for evil, contrary to God's desire. But in the ministries of spiritual gifts, the Spirit works through the believer to accomplish God's good purpose and plan. Anything contrary to this will not stand the test of fire. The distinction between the eternal and the temporal, the tares and the wheat, the good and bad fish, the wheat and the chaff are not immediately obvious because of the weakness of the saints and the skilled duplicity of the unbeliever. We must see through the weakness and duplicity to get to the truth of the matter.

A distinct difference exists between spiritual and natural gifts in that we can discover what natural gifts we are born with by taking skill and personality tests. Every college and trade school offers this service. Most recruits take a test as they enter the military. After I took the test, the Army told me I'd be a great mechanic. (I bucked the tide and became a good computer technician.) But the church has no written test or questionnaire that will impart a spiritual gift.

Examples of God Given Natural Gifts:

(This is not a comprehensive list.)

1. Teaching: The ability to help learners assimilate knowledge, facts, figures, theories, information, reasoning skills, life skills, and professional skills for the purpose of self-fulfillment of the learner, earning a living, or the good of society.
2. Healing practices: The ability to diagnose and treat the physical body or the emotional wounds from an injury, trauma, or illness using learned treatments and medicines.
3. Oratorical gifts: The ability to entertain, inform, and influence an audience.
4. Debating: The ability to articulate your viewpoint and persuade others to accept your opinion while refuting the statements of another. (Most teenagers have this gift.)
5. Hospitality: The ability to bring people together to entertain and offer comfortable, welcoming accommodations according the guest's desire or need.
6. Generosity, philanthropy: The ability to serve a charitable cause. These actions are typically beneficial to society, and often motivated by a personal interest; to honor a family

member, to be socially responsible, to pursue a cause, or to leave a legacy.

7. Caregiving: The ability to care for and nurture those who are weak or in need of physical care.

8. Leadership: The ability to inspire people into action and to follow where you lead and direct.

9. Musicianship: The ability to create and or perform music for the purpose of entertaining people or to send a message carried along by a memorable score.

10. Entertaining: The ability to make people laugh, feel warm and fuzzy inside and help them forget life's difficulties as a comedian, musician, actor, etc.

11. Tradesman/craftsmanship: The ability to build, create, or construct and fill a need for a structural or material requirement in service to a business or customer, providing useful necessities of life.

12. Poetry: The ability to express thoughts, emotions, and agendas with special words in a rhythmic manner.

13. Writing: The ability to tell or relate a story to entertain, moralize, convey a message or take people, in their imagination, into another space and time. An author may retell historic events in interesting ways.

14. Artistry: The ability to create artistic images, both two and three dimensional, to convey a message, create an impression or provide decorative works to enhance a home or office.

Comparing a spiritual and natural gift may be useful to see how they are as different as night and day:

Natural Gift of Teaching: The ability to convey knowledge, facts, figures, theories, information, reasoning skills, life skills, and professional skills to learners for the purpose of self-fulfillment of the learner and for the good of commerce and society. A naturally gifted teacher may teach from the Bible, but the lesson will come across as facts and information with no change of heart in the learner.

Spiritual Gift of Teaching: By means of the gifting and empowering work of the Spirit, the ability to open the Word of God to the hearer, revealing the cross of Jesus Christ and the resurrected Christ so that hearts are brought to repentance, out of darkness into spiritual maturity and to good works (read Ephesians 2:10). The ability to teach doctrine, faith disciplines and the truths of Scripture by means of the Spirit for an eternal effect — to bring the learners' hearts to repentance before Christ.

A God-given natural gift or talent is like getting a box of Legos. You have to dig in and make something out of it. A spiritual gift may be like getting an Xbox. It must be connected to the power source and must continue to be connected to effectively minister.

The result of using a spiritual gift is clearly eternal and not temporal. In the use of a teaching gift, we bring the learner to a place where the Holy Spirit may teach them within their heart of hearts. Teaching **about** Biblical facts, characters, history, doctrines and the Ten Commandments does not by itself lead the learner to Christ. A Christian with a spiritual gift teaches spiritual truths in spiritual words (1 Corinthians 2:13), and this teaching changes lives forever.

In the ministries and service of a spiritual gift, something is accomplished that you could not do using a natural gift. For example, when teaching by means of a spiritual gift, you prepare under the anointing of the Spirit, you present your topic by the strength of the Spirit, and the message is heard and understood by the means and work of the Holy Spirit in the student. Your learners may say, "I finally understand that. You made it so clear." The understanding and clarity comes by means of your Spirit empowered preparation, your anointed delivery of the topic and by means of the Holy Spirit at work in the hearts of the hearer. There is no natural gift that accomplishes this eternal purpose.

Which is better, a match that flares for a moment or an eternal flame? Which is of greater consequence, a plastic ring from a gum machine or a gold wedding band that declares, "Till death do us part"? Which is of greater benefit, giving a poor man a burger in a bag or teaching him skills that give him a lifetime of opportunity? These simple comparisons illustrate the difference between spiritual and natural gifts.

God has given each and every person He has created natural gifts for the good of all earthly communities. Jesus gives even greater gifts, sending His Holy Spirit to gift and empower His church to minister and serve for people's eternal good. This is not a matter of choosing one or the other, but a matter of not rejecting the very best Jesus holds out to you.

Be diligent in the use of the natural gifts God has given you to provide for your family and to work for the good of your community. But the Spirit of Jesus offers even more for Christians who desire His precious gifts. Get out your treasure pouch and search for God's unending treasures in His excellent spiritual gifts for the church. The Apostle Paul said it well: "Although I am less than the least of all the Lord's people, this grace was given me: to preach to the Gentiles the boundless riches of Christ" (Ephesians 3:8).

YOUR JOURNEY JOURNAL
Chapter 5: Natural Gifts

1. What is necessary for the use of natural gifts?

2. What is necessary for the ministries of spiritual gifts?

3. What motivates you to use your natural gifts?

4. What motivates you to minister in your spiritual gifts?

Your Journal Notes:

6

Spiritual and Natural Gifts

Scripture reveals the nature and purpose of the gifts of the Holy Spirit. "God also testified to [great salvation] by signs, wonders and various miracles,[27] and gifts of the Holy Spirit distributed according to His will" (Hebrews 2:4). The gifts of the Spirit are God's testimony among us, and a confirmation of the message proclaimed by those who are witnesses of the resurrected Christ. They are both proof and pledge of our covenant. Proof that the gospel we have received for our salvation is true and genuine, and a pledge of greater, eternal blessings to come. Spiritual gifts are supernatural empowerments from the Holy Spirit, given to those who are called by His Name. These precious gifts are not offered to those who are "unspiritual" (1 Corinthians 2:14 NRSV). That is, the gifts are not available apart from Christ.

By means of resurrection power, our Lord Jesus spoke the Word, appointing the church to fulfill His Great Commission. Christ Jesus, in His position of power and authority at the right hand of the Father, sent His Holy Spirit to gift and empower the believer so they might accomplish this good work. As we peel through the layers like an onion, we will see how interconnected spiritual gifts are with Christ's work of salvation and His commission to the church. These treasures are defined as spiritual gifts, a spiritual talent or ability that is given and empowered in the Holy Spirit and used in ministry for the good of the church — for an eternal purpose.

Please be encouraged to dig into God's Word, meditate on the

---

[27] God's signs, wonders, and miracles are a wonderful part of who God is, but the focus in this study is the gifts of the Spirit.

Scripture, weigh what is taught, and test this teaching among well-taught men and women, in the fear of the Lord. Our Lord God will use this means to open your understanding and connect you to the wisdom of the Teacher, the Holy Spirit, who will instruct you from within your heart of hearts. "I will praise the LORD, who counsels me; even at night my heart instructs me" (Psalm 16:7). Please keep in mind that even though I've made an effort to do in-depth study, I only "know in part." My understanding is not complete (1 Corinthians 13:9). But I know who holds the key to truth and understanding.

On this journey through the Scriptures you will see the living, active presence of our Lord Jesus who is the Key to unlocking God's precious treasures. In this trek through the Bible you will be equipped for battle in the strength of the Spirit and by the authority of Christ; to boldly and confidently go forth into battle. God's abundant grace is revealed as He empowers us for ministry and service within His established order for the church. We are prepared, our spiritual power is stirred up, we put aside what is weak and powerless, and we take up what is mighty. The church is built up as all God's people are equipped for the tasks ordained for them. When Christians ask and receive what God desires for us, they are prepared to go where the Spirit leads, extending our hands where God extends His hand to all those in need.

God's Purpose for Spiritual Gifts

In Ephesians the Apostle Paul writes to teach us about these great gifts to the church, gifts that "prepare God's people for works of service" and proclaim of our glorious salvation in the resurrected Jesus Christ.

Paul primes our thoughts in Ephesians 3:10-11, so we can understand spiritual gifts in chapter four. Chapter three offers a snapshot of the church: "[God's] intent was that now, through the church, the manifold wisdom of God should be made known to the rulers and authorities in the heavenly realms, according to his eternal purpose that he accomplished in Christ Jesus our Lord." Take special note of Paul's words: "NOW, THROUGH THE CHURCH." Think on it because God is revealing a great mystery of His kingdom. The holy angels, who dwell in the heavens and hold sway over the principalities and governments of this world, are commanded to serve and assist as God manifests His power and authority through His people — the church — in order to accomplish His good purpose and plan for all eternity. We work side by side with the holy angels who are commanded to back us up in this sacred mission.

Gifts of the Spirit serve many purposes within the church and the greatest is to testify, offering proof of God's great salvation through His Son Jesus Christ; this testimony is accompanied with signs, wonders, and various miracles. Spiritual gifts are a powerful witness, proof of God's saving grace at work among his people, and they are notable and noticeable as God's people minister in these gifts. Spiritual gifts are not silent witnesses; they announce to the world, "Listen up, people." They serve as a warning to people to pay attention to His message, the gospel of Jesus Christ. As we minister in the gifts of the Spirit, we proclaim to the world, "This salvation is for real. The Spirit of the resurrected Jesus lives in us." The "frosting on the cake" is that the gifts, though imperfectly manifested in Christians, give us a foretaste of the full work of the Holy Spirit in the perfect age to come when the imperfect will disappear.

Spiritual Gifts Manifest Jesus' Presence

The gifts of the Spirit are the manifestations of resurrection power in Christ Jesus through His body, the church. Watchman Nee says it well:

> "The Church and Christ are not only the same in nature, they are the same in power. Otherwise, the Church is empty. The way by which God broke through all limitations in the Lord is the same way God will enable the Church to break through all barriers.
>
> "Therefore, the Church today should reach out with this same power and enjoy the same liberty, uninhibited by anything, just as the risen Lord himself. Otherwise, it cannot be considered the Church. The exceedingly great power of God

works not just in Christ, it continues to work today also in the Church. The Church is the reservoir of power of resurrection today. This is the Church. Nothing less is acceptable. The Church is the body of Christ; under the authority of Christ and accordingly it should not fall short of this exceedingly great power of Christ."[28]

This "witness," or evidence of resurrection power, is especially needed today in our post-Christian American culture and in nations around the world that are hostile to the gospel of Jesus Christ. This power is necessary today, as much as it was in the Greco-Roman culture of the Apostle Paul's time, to manifest the living, active presence of Jesus. Is it any less important for today's people to get the message, urging them to pay attention to this great and glorious gospel of salvation? Because of our great calling, our abounding faith, eternal hope, and love beyond compare, we ought to "eagerly desire spiritual gifts" (1 Corinthians 14:1). When we desire, ask, and receive spiritual gifts, we are equipped to reveal Jesus' living, active presence to all in need.

Unlocking the Treasure

There is a sure foundation for all wisdom and knowledge, a key to treasures of inestimable value. The One who is the Cornerstone is the KEY, for He is the KEY of David. "I will place on his shoulder the key to the house of David; what he opens no one can shut, and what he shuts no one can open" (Isaiah 22: 22).[29] He is the key for all who are called by His Name, and in His Name we open this treasure. "He will be the sure foundation for your times, a rich store of salvation and wisdom and knowledge; the fear of the Lord is the key to this treasure" (Isaiah 33:6, emphasis added).[30]

---

[28] Watchman Nee. *The Communion of the Holy Spirit*, page 15.
[29] There is a rich depth of meaning in this Scripture; wisdom and knowledge are just the beginning.
[30] See chapter "In the Fear of God We are Fearless" in this book.

The Scripture Guides us through Spiritual Gifts

Please consider the following Scriptures as a foundational guide as we continue this study of spiritual gifts:

- "The Spirit gives life; the flesh counts for nothing." (John 6:63)
- "But we have this treasure in clay jars, so that it may be made clear that this extraordinary power belongs to God and does not come from us." (2 Corinthians 4:7 NRSV)
- "'Not by might nor by power but by my Spirit,' says the Lord Almighty." (Zechariah 4:6)
- "For prophecy never had its origin in the will of man, but men spoke from God as they were carried along by the Holy Spirit." (2 Peter 1:21)
- "We have not received the spirit of the world but the Spirit who is from God, that we may understand what God has freely given us." (1 Corinthians 2:12)
- "Now there are varieties of gifts, but the same Spirit; and there are varieties of service, but the same Lord; and there are varieties of activities, but it is the same God who empowers them all in everyone." (1 Corinthians 12:4-6 ESV)
- "With <u>my authority</u>, take this message of repentance to all the nations, beginning in Jerusalem: 'There is forgiveness of sins for all who turn to me.' You are witnesses of all these things. And now I will send the Holy Spirit, just as the Father promised. But stay here in the city until the Holy Spirit comes and fills you with power from heaven." (Luke 24:47-49 NLT, emphasis added)
- "<u>All authority</u> in heaven and on earth has been given to me." (Matthew 28:18, emphasis added)
- "Those who are unspiritual do not receive the gifts of God's Spirit." (1 Corinthians 2:14)

Equipped for Battle

We must be prepared for spiritual warfare when we minister and serve in the Spirit, by the Spirit, and through the Spirit. In this battle we must take the offensive against the kingdom of darkness — through the power of the Holy Spirit. This war raging in the spiritual realm is not a battle we can win by human strength and earth-bound abilities. This becomes clear when we hold spiritual gifts and natural gifts up to the light; we find that ministry and service in our natural abilities and strength alone does not measure up. Why would we limit ourselves to the same resources as the local Rotary and Kiwanis clubs when we have so much more to offer?

Jesus intended for all Christians to be equipped for battle. This includes not only the leaders, but all Christians. Each one does not mean only the apostles: "Now to each one the manifestation of the Spirit is given for the common good" (1Corinthians 12:7). Jim Cymbala in his book *Spirit Rising* says of this Scripture: "To water that down to mean human talent is unbelief in God the Holy Spirit."[31] He also says this of us: "Yet so many of us live with faint trickles and shallow pools of the Spirit, rather than the promised rivers of living water."[32] The Holy Spirit will come over us like a flood. But will we be satisfied with getting only our toes wet?

Apart from God's grace and power, as revealed in the crucified and resurrected Christ and communicated to us by the Holy Spirit through the gift of faith, the church would be no better and fulfill no greater purpose than our local Elks Club, Kiwanis Club or Rotary Club. While the good service offered to our communities through service clubs is excellent and beneficial, it is but a wisp of smoke from an extinguished candle compared to what God has called His church to accomplish. When you and I, as Christians, serve and minister in the gifts given to us by the Holy Spirit, we can and we must work under the empowering authority that comes in Jesus's name, for we are and we must continually be a people under His authority in all things. Today,

---

[31] Page 32
[32] Page 28

Christ Jesus, in His position of power and authority, calls us who are the church into battle. He has given us His command and entrusted us with affecting the world around us, beginning in our neighborhoods, communities, and throughout all the earth (Matthew 28:19-20). All who are in Christ are called to this campaign, for Christ is seated at the right hand of God, His rightful position of authority, and we are in Christ — a part of his church, the body of Christ. Because of His position and our position in Him, we go forth into the battlefield by the authority of His Holy Name and through the power of His Holy Spirit.

Christ's Authority to Minister and Serve

When the resurrected Jesus spoke the Word to His Church calling us to fulfill His great commission, it was as if He, the King of all kings and Lord of all lords, Creator of heaven and earth, took His signet ring and placed it on the hands of each and every believer present and future. We see a picture of this as the Lord gave His authority to Jerusalem's Governor Zerubbabel: "And I will make you like my signet ring, for I have chosen you, declares the Lord Almighty" (Haggai 2:23). His "signet ring" confers power to believers in the work of His great commission, just as Pharaoh gave his signet ring to Joseph. "Then Pharaoh took his signet ring from his finger and put it on Joseph's finger" (Genesis 41:42). Verse 43 makes Pharaoh's intent clear: "Thus he put him in charge of the whole land of Egypt." Joseph had all the authority and power of the name of the king of Egypt. And because of Christ's command, because Christ has ascended to the right hand of the Father, we now minister by His authority, in His name, and under His authority.[33]

We must be clear in our understanding of conferred authority. Did Pharaoh give up his sovereignty over Egypt when he gave his signet ring to Joseph? Did the Creator God pass on any part of His sovereignty over all of creation when He commissioned Adam and his progeny to

---

[33] We see more examples of this delegated authority in Esther 8:8-10, Esther 3:12, and Luke 10:3, 17.

subdue the earth? Did God Almighty bestow any part or portion of His sovereignty when He ordained the priests of Israel, giving them the priestly breastplate as a signet to lead people in worship before a Holy God? Not in the least! Pharaoh remained the earthly sovereign over Egypt. Joseph exercised Pharaoh's authority, but remained a man under authority. The priests of Israel were completely under God's authority in leading the people. Governor Zerubbabel was a man who exercised authority under the power and will of a Sovereign God. God does not compromise or give away any part of His sovereignty. All who serve Him and minister in His name must remain completely under His sovereign authority.

But what do we do instead? We want to be the authority and present our impressive ministry résumés to demonstrate our personal skills, experience, and education. But too often we're educated in the way of the world and not in the wisdom and power of God. Our natural learning and knowledge sometimes makes us dangerously self-confident. But in fact, if we rest in the Holy Spirit as we minister and serve in His church, our education, degrees, and schooling (while of great value) become secondary — they must be offered up as a sacrifice before the Lord.

May I encourage you to ask for wisdom that only comes from heaven (James 1:5, 3:17)? God will give you unwavering wisdom when you ask. Don't vacillate in your expectations, and you will receive abundantly. Ask for God's excellent gifts given to His church for the good of the church and then minister and serve by the power of the Spirit in the authority of Christ.

Confident Ministry

As the Apostle Paul wrote to the Philippians, he made this message very clear: "For it is we who are the circumcision, we who worship by the Spirit of God, who glory in Christ Jesus, and who put no confidence in the flesh — though I myself have reasons for such confidence" (Philippians 3:3). Paul goes on to tell why he may well have reason for confidence in his natural abilities and his spiritual pedigree. He was a true-blooded Hebrew of Hebrews. His education. His zeal. His faultless life. But all this He considered a big zero, a loss for the sake of Christ in order to be one who worships and serves by the Spirit of God — without confidence in the flesh.

May I encourage you to offer up your natural talents and gifts as a living sacrifice before God (Romans 12:1)? Considered them "rubbish" that you may gain Christ and the good gifts He gives to His church through His Holy Spirit. When it comes to ministering the Great Commission of the church, we must put no confidence in our own abilities, our outgoing personalities, our training or education, or in our family heritage as we accomplish His eternal work.

The gifts of the Spirit are not sanctified natural gifts. They are not given to the natural man, but they are the power of God working through those who are born of the Spirit to accomplish what the flesh can never accomplish. We must be aware that our natural gifts belong to the natural man, and when we minister or serve in the strength of our flesh, we too easily fall into serving our "selfish ambitions" rather than the kingdom of our Lord (Philippians 2:3). As you witness the Spirit accomplishing through you what you would otherwise be unable to do, your confidence will grow exponentially.

My experience has taught me that people are often reluctant to serve in the church because they lack confidence that they have the abilities necessary to do the job. But they are thinking of their natural abilities, unaware of the possibility of being empowered for ministry in a spiritual gift. One might believe that they received all they will ever get of the Holy Spirit when they were redeemed, justified by our Lord, and baptized into Jesus Christ. They say, "I'm certainly no teacher. Never will be." But they have gifts and talents waiting for them and refuse to even ask because "From everyone who has been given much, much will be demanded; and from the one who has been entrusted with much, much more will be asked" (Luke 12:48). Be encouraged to ask, because when you receive that touch of the Holy Spirit, ministered to you by God's appointed servant by laying on of hands, this is cause for great joy and confidence in your appointed work in God's kingdom.

We need the gifts of the Holy Spirit and the empowering renewal of God's Spirit in our lives to propel us forward as we face the challenges of serving in the church. The power in spiritual gifts enables us to be God's instruments as He brings people to repentance and draws people to Christ for their salvation as we obey His command to go into the world proclaiming the risen Christ and the kingdom of God. We do all of this under and by the authority given to us in Christ — all to the glory of His name.

Abundant grace revealed in Spiritual Gifts: God is good in every way in His creation of and provision for all His creatures (Genesis 1:31). His saving grace poured out to us through Christ Jesus overwhelms us with awe at His goodness. But our loving God does not stop giving to us when He justifies us by faith and His Holy Spirit seals us (Ephesians 1:13, 2 Corinthians 1:22). The Spirit of Jesus will continue pouring into Christians His constant grace every hour of their lives; this is a part of how we participate in His goodness. He who has redeemed us and brought us to faith by the Spirit will continue to bless us with more wonderful, unmerited gifts. God gives the gifts of the Holy Spirit to those who have received the grace of God in Christ Jesus. All those who come in faith to receive may be equipped for service in Christ's church that they might strengthen others. Like the rest of God's gifts, these are undeserved blessings that are not based on our merit or worthiness. In fact, God may use Christians who in their own natural ability could never accomplish the same work — so that He may be glorified: "My power is made perfect in weakness" (2 Corinthians 12:9).

What an awesome God we serve. In the manifestation of spiritual gifts He is glorified and through us, His abundant grace is made known, like light shining through to dissipate the darkness.

The Value of the Gift is in the Giver of the Gift

The spiritual gifts are referred to as "graces" to help us recognize the Holy Spirit as the source and to remind us that they are undeserved. We ought to acknowledge and rejoice in God's good gifts, but we should not confuse ourselves by blending them together with the gift of salvation itself. "These are continued blessings for those who live in the grace of the Lord Jesus."[34] We don't seek the gift for the sake of the gift but for the good of the whole church of Christ. Chuck Swindoll states it clearly: "Often we are more enamored with the gifts God gives us than with the Giver himself."[35]

This is a common error we make with gifts of the Spirit — seeking the gift rather than the Giver of the gift. Our focus must not be on the gift alone, our ministries through the gifts, a spiritual experience, or the feeling of hyper spirituality that we think may come with the gift. We must be centered on the One who is the Giver of all good gifts. Jesus reminds us of what our priorities ought to be: "But seek first his kingdom and his righteousness, and all these things will be given to you as well" (Matthew 6:33).

The gifts of the Spirit, and especially the gift of prophecy, "level the field" so to speak for men, women, boys and girls. "Now to each one the manifestation of the Spirit is given for the common good" (1 Corinthians 12:7). Yes, for the good of the Body of Christ in its entirety and for advancing His kingdom.

Seek first the Father, the Son, and the Holy Spirit and then ask and receive what is His perfect will for you — spiritual gifts for the good of the church.

God's Established Order

For the good of all Christians, God has established an order in the gifts for the church. "And in the church God has appointed first of all apostles, second prophets, third teachers, then workers of miracles" (1 Corinthians 12:28). While there must be established authority within the church for the purpose of order, we are all equal in the sight of God. "But you are not to be called "Rabbi,' for you have only one Master and you are all brothers" (Matthew 23:8). Paul echoes this in His letters to the church. "There is neither Jew nor Greek, slave nor free, male nor female, for you are all one in Christ Jesus" (Galatians 3:28).

---

[34] Steven P. Mueller. *Believe, Teach and Confess*, page 171.
[35] Charles R. Swindoll. *Elijah*, page 121.

Keep in mind this word of caution; the gifts of the Spirit are at times imitated and counterfeited. Even in the church there are some who will prophesy lies (Mark 13:22). We do not discard the gift because we have heard about someone somewhere counterfeiting a gift. What we need is to know the genuine article and to have the gift of spiritual discernment at work in each local body of believers (1 Thessalonians 5:21). Genuine spiritual gifts are only truly and powerfully exercised by the power and might of the Holy Spirit of God Almighty and always by His command and under His authority. Watchman Nee makes this clear in his book *The Spiritual Man*.[36] He interprets 1 Corinthians 2:14 as follows: "The natural (soulish) man does not receive the gifts of the Spirit of God, for they are folly to him, and he is not able to understand them because they are spiritually discerned." The NRSV translation of the same verse says, "Those who are unspiritual do not receive the gifts of God's Spirit, for they are foolishness to them, and they are unable to understand them because they are spiritually discerned."

When you are gifted and empowered in the Spirit for the service and ministries of the church, your work will be most effective and powerful when manifested within God's established order of authority.

By Faith, not by Human Strength

The operation of these gifts must be the result of faith, motivated by God's love at work in a person born of the Spirit. If the church is built by a "gift" apart from faith and love, we are but "clanging symbols" (1 Corinthians 13:1). Our work is but "wood, hay and straw" (1 Corinthians 3:11-13). We are not given spiritual gifts as a complement to our natural gifts, nor are natural gifts just a lower level of spiritual gifts. Clearly their purposes are very different and distinct. They are worlds apart.

We must also be aware that when we become self-confident in the exercise of our spiritual gift we are in danger of stealing away from the Power within the gift. A spiritual gift can easily slip into aplomb

---

[36] Watchman Nee, *The Spiritual Man*, page 53.

that diminishes the power of the cross, just as the Galatians were slipping backwards into self-driven works. "Are you so foolish? After beginning with the Spirit, are you now trying to attain your goal by human effort?" (Galatians 3:3). The goal of the kingdom of heaven cannot be attained by human power and strength, but only by faith in a resurrected Savior. Offer up your human weakness to Christ and He will certainly manifest His power and might through you — His willing ambassador.

Like power tools to a carpenter, spiritual gifts are God's tools to help us complete this good work. The mission is accomplished by the power of the Holy Spirit who gives us the gifts, empowering us to do what we otherwise cannot do.

Stir up the Gift

We may also become lax in the use of our gift and it will need to be stirred up. By the work of the Holy Spirit, the fire is rekindled to once again become powerful and effective. Paul admonished Timothy about this: "Do not neglect your gift, which was given you through a prophetic message when the body of elders laid their hands on you" (1 Timothy 4:14).[37] When we become indifferent to our gift or self-confident in the use of our Holy Spirit-given gifts, we must turn from this attitude and once again ask the Holy Spirit to refresh us and stir the fire of our spiritual gift given to us to serve the body of Christ.

Remember what you were before Christ

Because of our human nature, quite often we need to be reminded of where we came from to keep us from prideful stumbling. Ezekiel paints a graphic, yet beautiful metaphor of the work of the Savior in

---

[37] This is the ministry of Presbytery referenced in 1 Timothy 4:14, πρεσβυτέριον *presbyterion*. The church Presbyter's ministry is, by the power and leading of the Holy Spirit, to impart spiritual gifts to God's people by laying on of hands, empowering Christians for the ministries of the church.

the lives of those He has called out of bondage to sin. Included are pictures of 1) Christ's bride, 2) water baptism, 3) the pouring out of the Holy Spirit, 4) the bride being clothed in His righteousness, and then 5) the bride being adorned with bridal gifts.

> *"Then I passed by and saw you kicking about in your blood, and as you lay there in your blood I said to you, "Live!" I made you grow like a plant of the field. You grew and developed and entered puberty. Your breasts had formed and your hair had grown, yet you were stark naked.*
>
> *"Later I passed by, and when I looked at you and saw that you were old enough for love, I spread the corner of my garment over you and covered your naked body. I gave you my solemn oath and entered into a covenant with you, declares the Sovereign Lord, and you became mine.*
>
> *"I bathed you with water and washed the blood from you and put ointments on you. I clothed you with an embroidered dress and put sandals of fine leather on you. I dressed you in fine linen and covered you with costly garments. I adorned you with jewelry: I put bracelets on your arms and a necklace around your neck, and I put a ring on your nose, earrings on your ears and a beautiful crown on your head. So you were adorned with gold and silver; your clothes were of fine linen and costly fabric and embroidered cloth. Your food was honey, olive oil and the finest flour. You became very beautiful and rose to be a queen. And your fame spread among the nations on account of your beauty, because the splendor I had given you made your beauty perfect, declares the Sovereign Lord."* (Ezekiel 16:6-14)

God finds us like an abandoned infant, discarded in a field. He cleans us up and gives us beautiful gifts to adorn us, His bride. Read on in the chapter and be reminded that when self-confidence replaces confidence in God, when self-esteem replaces esteeming God, or when natural gifts are used to replace of spiritual gifts, there is a danger that selfish ambition and many other evils will creep in. Ezekiel 16:15 warns: "But you trusted in your beauty and used your fame to become a prostitute." The consequences of selling out are severe: "They will strip you of your clothes and take your fine jewelry and leave you naked and bare" (Ezekiel 16:39). When self-worth (rather than rooting our worth in Father God) takes over we become like a clanging symbol, an irritating noise.

What happened to these precious Spiritual Gifts? Too often, the church is looking in all the wrong places, redefining spiritual gifts as they search for these treasures from the Holy Spirit. If you do a Scripture search, you'll find no references encouraging Christians to "discover" or "find" their spiritual gift. Yet there are many excellent teachers in the Christian church who teach, preach, and do weekend seminars for this very purpose. It's not like you can turn over a rock and there it is. Spiritual gifts are not about "self discovery,"[38] nor are they about your personal journey. Spiritual gifts have nothing to do with astrological signs. The answer does not come by filling out a personality/talent survey. You cannot receive the Holy Spirit given gifts by discovering them, doing a "spiritual gift" treasure hunt, or by getting to know yourself.

ASK AND RECEIVE!

The Apostle Paul encourages us to "earnestly desire" spiritual gifts, especially prophecy (1 Corinthians 14:1). After desire comes asking. Ask for the desire of your heart — the desire God has put in your heart. "How much more will your Father in heaven give good gifts to those who ask him" (Matthew 7:11). God Almighty is your loving Father. His goodness is beyond anything you can imagine. Ask for the spiritual gift He has planned for you, and His Holy Spirit will give you the gift and empower you in the ministries and service of your gift.

What has happened to Spiritual Gifts?

Why do we see so little evidence of them today? It is as if today's church is searching in the basement's darkness when the treasure is

---

[38] The "journey of self-discovery" is an ungodly myth. We cannot not know God by first knowing ourselves.

to be found in the steeple, in the light of the Son. Too many churches have made finding spiritual gifts about self-discovery, finding who you are, and confusing what is common (natural gifts) with what is holy (spiritual gifts.) We have lost our desire for this precious treasure of the church, replacing them with lesser gifts. Some have gone to the extreme of despising or forbidding spiritual gifts in the church, and God will not give His good gifts if we despise or forbid them.

"So I say to you: Ask and it will be given to you; seek and you will find; knock and the door will be opened to you. For everyone who asks receives; the one who seeks finds; and to the one who knocks, the door will be opened" (Luke 11:9). What is now hidden away will be revealed to you. What is held back because of neglect will be released to you. Come out of the darkness of the church basement, into the Light of Christ, to receive all He holds out to you so that He may be glorified.

Are spiritual gifts still needed for building up the church?

"Enlarge the place of your tent, stretch your tent curtains wide, do not hold back; lengthen your cords, strengthen your stakes. For you will spread out to the right and to the left; your descendants will dispossess nations and settle in their desolate cities" (Isaiah 54:2). God's intention is for the church to spread the gospel to every corner of the globe, to every tribe, nation, people, and language group. He has declared it by His Word and His Word will be fulfilled. "'I will shake all nations, and what is desired by all nations will come, and I will fill this house with glory,' says the Lord Almighty" (Haggai 2:7). When Jesus is the desire of every tribe and nation, desiring the Lord's salvation, the growing church will be complete. Until that day, we have work to do. We know the mission is not yet accomplished because the end has not come. "And this gospel of the kingdom will be preached in the whole world as a testimony to all nations, and then the end will come" (Matthew 14:14).

There is so much work to do. The mission is not yet accomplished. There are many battles to be fought and won. Because of this, we need the gifting and empowering work of the Holy Spirit to prepare us to accomplish God's purpose and plan.

Were Spiritual Gifts only for the "Master Builders" of the Early Church?

The gifting and empowering work of the Holy Spirit, equipping people to serve, is not reserved for kings, prophets, priests, bishops, pastors, ordained ministers, elders and "builders of the church" alone. The gifts are not the exclusive territory for the upper echelons of the church. In 1 Corinthians chapter 12, the Apostle Paul uses the word "each one" twice and he uses "another" eight times, leaving no doubt this is all-inclusive and for all those who are "the church." Some claim that spiritual gifts were a special dispensation for the early church, empowering them to build the church as it stands today. But there is much building left for us to accomplish *today* and this work is not to be relegated to pastors, priests, bishops and Christian missionaries.

Beyond a doubt, we must not exclude any Christian from this blessing or we will be like wicked shepherds. "It is not enough for you to feed on the good pasture? Must you also trample the rest of your pasture with your feet?" (Ezekiel 34:18). Jesus warns religious leaders against stealing away from the people what God has given. "Woe to you experts in the law, because you have taken away the key to knowledge. You yourselves have not entered, and you have hindered those who were entering" (Luke 11:52). Too many pastors in the Christian Church have thrown away the key to the treasures of the kingdom of heaven given to adorn the bride of Christ. They either refuse the gifts or open the door for themselves and forbid others the key to unlock the storehouse.

These precious gifts are for all who are the "bride of Christ," for we are called of God to be a kingdom of priests. "But you are a chosen people, a royal priesthood, a holy nation, a people belonging to God, that you may declare the praises of him who called you out of darkness into his wonderful light" (1 Peter 2:9). Paul emphasizes this truth:

> *"I always thank my God for you and for the gracious gifts he*
> *has given you, now that you belong to Christ Jesus. Through*
> *him, God has enriched your church in every way — with all of*
> *your eloquent words and all of your knowledge. This confirms*

that what I told you about Christ is true. Now you have every
spiritual gift you need as you eagerly wait for the return of
our Lord Jesus Christ. He will keep you strong to the end so
that you will be free from all blame on the day when our Lord
Jesus Christ returns." (1 Corinthians 1:4-8 NLT)

Whom do we wait for? The Bridegroom. Who are we? The Bride. We learn several things from this Scripture that makes it clear that spiritual gifts are intended to be abundant in the church: 1) The gifts are spiritual gifts. 2) The gifts are given because you belong to Jesus Christ. 3) The gifts are given for the enrichment, comfort, and strengthening of the church. 4) The gifts are witnesses, proof that Paul preached the truth of the gospel of Jesus Christ, and that this gospel was living and working among them. 5) The gifts strengthen and build up Christians as they eagerly wait for the return of our Lord Jesus Christ. 6) As we wait, we must be prepared for ministry and service with spiritual gifts.

Christ's Great commission to His disciples extends to the church today. "Therefore go and make disciples of all nations, baptizing them in the name of the Father and of the Son and of the Holy Spirit, and teaching them to obey everything I have commanded you. And surely I am with you always, to the very end of the age" (Matthew 28:19-20).

How do you know if you are serving in spiritual or natural gifts?

Is it possible that any God-given natural gift or talent could accomplish miraculous works in the church? Not in the least! We must not confuse the common with that which God has given as holy. This was a common error even among the Old Covenant priests. Ezekiel 22:26 says, "Her priests do violence to my law and profane my holy things; they do not distinguish between the holy and the common; they teach that there is no difference between the unclean and the clean..."

Here is an example of distinguishing what is holy and what is common.

> *"The Lord said to Moses: 'Bring me seventy of Israel's elders who are known to you as leaders and officials among the people. Have them come to the Tent of Meeting, that they may stand there with you. I will come down and speak with you there, and I will take of the Spirit that is on you and put the Spirit on[39] them. They will help you carry the burden of the people so that you will not have to carry it alone.'*
> *"Then the Lord came down in the cloud and spoke with him, and he took of the Spirit that was on him and put the Spirit on the seventy elders. When the Spirit rested on them, they prophesied, but they did not do so again." (Numbers 11:16, 25)*

God asked for seventy men who were natural leaders. But God does not want leaders who are only naturally gifted to serve before the Most Holy God who made heaven and earth. He requires leaders who are singled out, dedicated, anointed, and empowered by the Spirit of God. Only then are they fit for service in His kingdom. God sanctified those who were naturally gifted with supernatural power to minister and serve. He set them apart. The work of their appointed positions of leadership and service could not be accomplished apart from the anointing and empowering work of the Spirit.

We see an example of this when the early church chose seven Deacons. "So the disciples said, 'Brothers,[40] choose seven men from among you who are known to be full the Spirit and wisdom.'... They presented these men to the apostles, who prayed and laid their hands on them" (Acts 6:3, 6).

The laying on of hands by an elder or minister under the authority of Christ is extending the very hand of our Lord Jesus, and it is a powerful impartation of the Spirit of God. This ministry is for dedicating men

---

[39] Here we see a clear difference between Old Covenant people and the New Covenant Christians. For O.T. Covenant followers the Holy Spirit was "on" them and "with" them and dwelled in a temple made by human hands. Now, the Holy Spirit inhabits the "temple" of a Holy God. 1 Corinthians 6:19, "Do you not know that your body is a temple of the Holy Spirit, who is in you, whom you have received from God?"

[40] Some translations say: "Brothers and sisters." ἀδελφός *adelphos*. Including all who were present.

and women to specific calls and ministries, giving to them the gifts of service, authority to minister and the power of ministry by the Holy Spirit. Many times after the ministry of presbytery by laying on of hands, the spiritual gift of prophecy will confirm the call.[41]

Ken Blue reveals our flawed thinking about spiritual gifts with this statement: "In general, the church in the West functions more or less like other secular institutions — we rely on human effort."[42]

When I was learning carpentry skills, my instructor would set me to a task and then keep an eye on me. Quite often I heard him saying, "Let the tool do the work." I would be trying to muscle through (typical Swedish trait), cutting a board using a power saw or using a plane on a door edge when I would hear him remind me, "Let the tool do the work." It's somewhat the same with our service in the church. The Holy Spirit gives us "power tools" (spiritual gifts), and we must allow the Holy Spirit to empower us in in our ministries and service. We don't need to "muscle" through it in our own strength.

The laying on of hands was a rite of the early Christian Church expressly associated with the gifts of the Holy Spirit. The Holy Spirit was also imparted within the church by laying hands on the believer.

> "The laying on of hands represented a prayer, and this prayer was specifically for the imparting of the gifts of the Spirit (Acts 8:18). Augustine listed the water, oil, Eucharist, and laying on of hands (in reconciliation of penitents) as occasions of sacramental prayer. Augustine's reference to the stamp (characterem) with which the neophytes were sealed may refer to baptism, the post baptismal anointing and imposition of hands, or all the rite."[43]

---

[41] Can we serve in a spiritual gift without the ministry of presbytery? When this ministry is not available, God will accomplish His purpose and plan in another way. The ministry of presbytery is a vital ministry of the church and must not be neglected, because this is the best possible way to receive a spiritual gift and minister in that gift, fully confident of what you have received.

[42] Ken Blue. *Authority to Heal*, pg 60.

[43] Everett Ferguson. *Baptism in the Early Church*, page 786.

"Laying on of Hands" was part of ancient orthodox church practice of the Christian faith. At this point in our study, let's review and meditate on the different translations of John 6:63:

- NIV: "The Spirit gives life; the flesh counts for nothing."
- NLT: "The Spirit alone gives eternal life. Human effort accomplishes nothing."
- ESV: "It is the Spirit who gives life; the flesh is no help at all."
- NASB: "It is the Spirit who gives life; the flesh profits nothing."
- NRSV: "It is the spirit that gives life, the flesh is useless."
- TR: "τὸ πνεῦμά ἐστιν τὸ ζῳοποιοῦν ἡ σὰρξ οὐκ ὠφελεῖ οὐδέν τὰ ῥήματα ἃ ἐγὼ λαλῶ ὑμῖν πνεῦμά ἐστιν καὶ ζωή ἐστιν"

We can all venture out and serve in whatever capacity we are able even if we do not know what spiritual gift the Holy Spirit has for us. As we serve and show our servant's heart, the Holy Spirit will reveal to us or to our church leaders the gift He has for us for the strengthening and building of His church. For some the "call" will come in that still small voice from within. For others the call to service will come when the phone rings and a church leader asks them to serve. Some will ask for a spiritual gift according to the desire God has put in their heart and the presbyters will lay hands on them to impart and empower the gift — and this is a most excellent way, bestowing great confidence for effective ministry.

A note from personal experience: We do a great disservice to Christians, especially to new believers, when we ask them to fill positions of service in the church and then turn them loose without any **spiritual** equipping. We give them a teacher's book, a box of crayons, a bag of cotton balls, a bottle of glue and stuff them in a classroom full of ADHD kids who stuffed themselves with Doritos or Sugar Pops for breakfast. We breathe a quick prayer and just let them sweat it out together for an hour. Even if they have a natural gift for teaching, even if the Christian worker is a teacher by profession, they are not equipped to minister the saving power and grace of our Lord Jesus Christ to students who are hungry and thirsty for the Good News.

How might we compare human strength to the Light and power of the Spirit? Is the sun greater than a candle? How does one raindrop compare to all the rivers, seas, and oceans? What is the difference between the arctic ice caps and a snowflake? These comparisons fall short because the difference between the temporal and eternal is as vast as the universe God has created.

Three things are vital in the use and application of Spiritual Gifts to distinguish them from "civil righteousness:" 1) The work will conform to His will as revealed by the Word of God and be used for the good of the church (Romans 12:2); 2) The ministries will be done according to the Word and in faith and according to God's will, purpose and plan (Romans 14:23); and 3) Our service will proceed from and be rooted in the love and power of God (Romans 13:10, 1 John 5:3). It is important to understand that spiritual and natural gifts operating in the church are at times as difficult to differentiate as is soul and spirit, but they clearly are not one and the same because the natural man cannot receive what is Holy (1 Corinthians 2:14 NRSV, Hebrews 4:12).

We must not settle for a substitute and steal away the power of the cross. But is it even possible to steal the power of the cross? Listen to the words of Paul: "Lest the cross of Christ be emptied of its power" (1 Corinthians 1:17). What Paul tells us in this verse is that he speaks "not with the words of human wisdom" for fear that people will be attracted to another message, another person. He avoided flourishing oratory, intellectual interrogatives and philosophical orations for fear that the miracle of the message would be reduced to the force of his words rather than the truth and power of the gospel. He preached a resurrected Christ in plain language, getting himself out of the way so the Holy Spirit could carry the message by divine authority into the hearts of those who would hear. (Note: The style or manner of preaching, whether powerful or mellow, loud, plain or soft, does not give the message its power. The power of the message comes by the work of the Holy Spirit through His chosen and anointed messenger.) This Scripture makes clear that natural oratorical skill, philosophical human reasoning, or an artistic, entertaining speaking style, if it becomes the focus in ministering the gospel, empties the cross of the power that makes the truth clear.[44]

---

[44] Dwight L. Moody was a powerful example of this principle. He was not a trained speaker, he butchered the English language and expressed himself poorly, but God used him in mighty ways. God manifested His power in Moody's weaknesses.

1 Corinthians 12:1-3 instructs us in these uncommon gifts. Verse one speaks of "spiritual gifts." The original Greek word is *pneumatikos*, meaning spiritualities or belonging to the Divine Spirit, serving as His empowered instrument. This is serving, grafted into Christ in a way that is uncommon, as the Holy Spirit manifests Himself through us for the glory of the resurrected Christ. This is clearly referring to ministries that are not possible in our natural abilities and strength. What is accomplished is not possible apart from the Spirit of Christ.

When you carry out the ministries and service of the church, and you see the Spirit of a Holy God accomplishing through you what would otherwise be impossible, you know your work is of the Spirit and by the Spirit. It's like a carpenter using a power saw. She can't cut the board without the saw and the power. Ask the Lord for His good gifts and He will show you His power at work through you to accomplish His good purpose and plan.

How do we know if our work is "Wood, Hay or Stubble?"

"All your children shall be taught by the Lord, and great shall be the prosperity of your children" (Isaiah 54:13 NRSV). Teachers can accomplish no eternal purpose in the lives of their students even if they have earned a Master's degree in education from Harvard. "Not many of you should presume to be teachers" (James 3:1). When we **assume** a place in the church without being called, gifted, and empowered by the Holy Spirit, we are on a presumptuous path, which the Greek interprets as shameless and irreverent. 1 Corinthians 2:13 makes this point clear, saying that you cannot express (*interpret or teach*) spiritual truths and spiritual words by means of the natural gift and training as a teacher.[45] Instead, we must bring the children before the Lord to be taught by the Lord. This is not possible by means of our natural gifts and talents alone.

The Scriptures offer a perfect picture of the Holy Spirit's gifting

---

[45] Without the gifting and empowering work of the Holy Spirit working in and through a teacher, the story of Daniel and the Lion's Den comes across with no more life than "Jack and the Beanstalk."

and empowering work. "So Samuel took the horn of oil and anointed him (David) in the presence of his brothers, and from that day on the Spirit of the Lord came upon David in power" (1 Samuel 16:13). By the Lord's command, Samuel had the authority to anoint David with oil,[46] imparting to him gifts for kingship. As king, David would shepherd God's people, just as the Lord would have cared for them Himself. God took a shepherd boy from the fields and anointed him with oil to give him power in the Spirit to do all God called him to do. Only David's sin would ever disrupt this powerful anointing.

Will all the hard work you do end up in the ash pile? The answer is quite simple. Take an inventory of yourself and your Christian service. You are the only one who can do this checkup. No one else can do it for you. Here are some suggested questions you may want to ask of yourself: Are you getting tired, exhausted, weary of heart, bored with it, unenthusiastic, dreading your next time of service? Do you give a big sigh of relief when you get a break from it? Do you require a pat on the back, public recognition, an award, and an engraved plaque for your den to motivate you to serve? Are you offended when things don't go your way, when your ideas are ignored? While the downside of Christian service happens to even to the best of us at times, if this is a growing pattern in your ministry, these are red flag warnings and you may be serving in your natural abilities and strength. Too often we deplete our physical strength and energy because we are no longer depending on, leaning upon, drawing on the power of the Holy Spirit to strengthen us in our work. More than this, we will know we are in the danger zone when people glorify us rather than giving glory to God (Mark 2:12).

Maybe the best test of our ministries, service, and church programs would be to ask this question: If you gave the Rotary club a cross and a Bible, some Vacation Bible School lesson plans, and craft materials, could they do VBS as well or better than your church? Would they accomplish the same purpose? Your pride says, "no." But are you so sure?

---

[46] Oil symbolizes the Holy Spirit throughout all Scripture. Here we see as if in a mirror reflection, the natural elements reveal what was being accomplished in the spiritual realm.

Keep in mind that when you are exercising your spiritual gift in the power of the Holy Spirit and you see God at work doing what you or the whole church together cannot do on your own, you are clearly serving in your spiritual gifts. This is a good Scripture to memorize: "'Not by might nor by power, but by my Spirit,' says the Lord Almighty" (Zechariah 4:6). When you look at the Hebrew words for might and power, it becomes clear that this means "not by human might nor by the power of the flesh." Of course, our body serves a very useful purpose. Without it, we cannot remain here on the earth and function in a useful manner. It's our earth suit, and God's instrument. (The Apostle Paul refers to the body as our tent.)

The best question to ask of yourself is this: Do you find that you are surprised at what God accomplishes through you? Paul gives us an example of what will happen to those who hear true words of prophetic ministry: "So he will fall down and worship God, exclaiming, 'God is really among you!'" (1 Corinthians 14:25). When you see God opening the kingdom of heaven to someone who is lost and desperate, when Jesus extends His hands through you, a supernatural joy will overflow from your heart. Accomplishing what is humanly impossible is what I refer to as the "Eleazar effect." He was a man who was mighty in battle, by the hand of God working through him. "He stood his ground and struck down the Philistines till his hand grew tired and froze to the sword. The Lord brought about a great victory that day" (2 Samuel 23:9-10). This was not possible in his human strength, or in his own natural abilities.

We see another example of the Eleazar effect in Exodus 35:30-35. God selected Bezalel son of Uri, son of Hur, of the tribe of Judah, and "He filled him with the Spirit of God, with skill, ability and knowledge in all kinds of crafts — to make artistic designs for work in gold, silver and bronze, to cut and set stones, to work in wood and to engage in all kinds of artistic craftsmanship." The Holy Spirit does not scatter His good gifts abroad like seed, hoping that someone will discover or find a gift. He doesn't plant a gift in you, hoping someday it will take root and grow. Because He knows each of us by name, because He knows the seasons of our lives, and because our names are written in His Book of Life — He gives us good gifts as His Spirit determines.

"'For I know the plans I have for you,' declares the LORD, 'plans to prosper you and not to harm you, plans to give you hope and a future'" (Jeremiah 29:11).

God works in different ways with different people. With David He took a simple shepherd and made him a wise ruler of His people. But with Bezalel God took a master craftsman and anointed him to create gold, silver and bronze articles of worship? What is clear is that God chose Bezalel and "filled him with the Spirit of God" so that he could skillfully make what he could not make in his own strength, skill, or natural ability. It is quite certain that when Bezalel finished each article to be used in temple worship, he would stand back in awe and praise God for what was accomplished through him, creating beautiful articles of worship for the glory of God.

At the same time we must not minimize the importance of more common tasks that are accomplished by "everyone who is willing" (Exodus 35:21). There is no need for a special "call" of God to set up chairs and tables for the church potluck, but it is a much-needed task. Yet, even in humble duties of service to the church, we see the spiritual gift of serving at work in the believer (Romans 12:7).

Always keep in mind, it is always good to offer as a living sacrifice our natural talents, abilities, education, and knowledge and thereby make way for ministry through the gifts of the Spirit, and in the power of the Holy Spirit. The gospel message of Christ dying on the cross and then being resurrected to life is to be ministered to a lost and dying world, not by the strength or words of a man, but only by demonstration of the Holy Spirit. We can attempt to accomplish God's work by the strength of our flesh alone — but we build with wood, hay and stubble (1 Corinthians 3:1-15). Jesus makes this clear:

> *"This is the verdict: Light has come into the world but men loved darkness instead of light because their deeds were evil. Everyone who does evil hates the light, and will not come into the light for fear that his deeds will be exposed. But whoever lives by the truth comes into the light, <u>so that it may be seen plainly that what he has done has been done through God."</u>*
> *(John 3:19-21, emphasis added)*

Our deeds ought to be done "through God," in the authority of the Name of Jesus Christ and in the empowering work and anointing of the Holy Spirit so that it may be plainly visible to all that "God is really among you" (1 Corinthians 14:25). We work, minister, and serve in His power, by His power, through His power so that the Almighty God, our Lord and Savior receives all the glory and honor — so that His name will be glorified in all the earth.

Take time to meditate on Isaiah 53:2-4 and 1 Corinthians 3:12 while asking the Holy Spirit to confirm this insight. The church was given birth by the fire of the presence of the Holy Spirit on the day of Pentecost. The church is being built through intensifying fires of affliction and persecution throughout the centuries. Each man and woman who is the church, on that "Day" when Christ is revealed, must pass through purifying fires in the final test of their work — is it wood, hay and straw? Or have they built on a foundation of gold, silver and precious stones? Will the work you are doing stand the test of fire? We must constantly remind ourselves that we serve under a covenant of blood and fire.

Now consider this: Our churches may be doctrinally sound, have good organizations, have a good business model, excellent homiletics and even good, friendly people, but without the power of the Spirit and the authority of Name of Christ Jesus, we accomplish little of eternal kingdom value.

Is it possible that too many seminary graduates have sound doctrine, volumes of knowledge, excellent exegetical and hermeneutical skills but lack the refining work of the Spirit of Christ to empower and gift them? Is it possible some refuse to place themselves under the authority of Christ and then offer their scholarly achievements as a sacrifice before the Lord, and are therefore ill equipped to serve the church?[47]

---

[47] It would be useful for those who receive their "sheep skin" in theology or in ministries of the church to also be prepared just as King David and Moses by tending sheep in the wilderness for a while. We all need a "wilderness" encounter with a Holy God, a revelation of God.

Count the Cost

The topic of spiritual gifts is of considerable importance at this time in church history. The gifts of the Spirit come at great cost, for Christ died on a cruel Roman cross and then in victory arose from the grave and plundered the enemy. "But to each one of us grace has been given as Christ apportioned it. That is why it says, 'When he ascended on high, he led captives in his train and gave gifts to men'" (Ephesians 4:7-8). Our Lord Jesus paid the price of our redemption in blood, making us His captives, and then making us free in Him. His ministry of grace continues as He gives us good gifts from the spoils He has captured. "Or again, how can anyone enter a strong man's house and carry off his possessions unless he first ties up the strong man?" (Matthew 12:29). The "strong man" is defeated. We are victorious in Christ. All authority is Christ's alone, and He gives us the power to serve and minister in His authority. "I saw Satan fall like lightning from heaven. I have given you authority to trample on snakes and scorpions [48] and to overcome all the power of the enemy; nothing will harm you" (Luke 10:18-19). In Christ we overcome by the power of the cross. As Christians, we share in Christ's death and resurrection and in His glorious triumph. "And having disarmed the powers and authorities, he made a public spectacle of them, triumphing over them by the cross" (Colossians 2:15).

The gifts of the Spirit are available to us because our Lord Jesus Christ gave His life, offered His blood to be shed, and allowed His body to be broken and then hung on a cross at Mount Calvary, and in this great sacrifice he won a might victory and plundered the enemy.[49] We see a preview of this in Genesis 14. Abram defeated five kings, and then his men plundered the enemy. Abram gave a tenth[50] of the plunder to Melchizedek, King of Jerusalem, and returned the rest to the kings he was defending.

---

[48] The enemies of the cross of Jesus Christ, the opponents of the kingdom of heaven.
[49] See *A Jewel of the Kingdom*, Chapter 3: "Gifts Plundered, Gifts Recovered."
[50] Scripture leads me to believe this was a customary king's tithe (that preceded the law). Giving a tithe is acknowledging submission to God's authority and rule.

Because our spiritual gifts come at such great cost to our Lord Jesus Christ, how can we bury, neglect, or reject them? We must not!

Separating the holy from what is common in the church is vital to effective and powerful ministries of the church in a world that is torn apart by the throes of sin. God-given common gifts are useful and necessary, but they do not effect an eternal purpose. God's plan is not accomplished by human strength, nor by man's power, but by the power or the Holy Spirit at work in weak vessels.

God made this plan clear in Ezekiel's day when He took him to the holy mountain of Israel to reveal this truth to him: "On that very day the hand of the Lord was on me and he took me there" (Ezekiel 40:1). With clear purpose the Lord's own hand measured the temple. "So he measured the area on all four sides. It had a wall around it, five hundred cubits long and five hundred cubits wide, to separate the holy from the common" (Ezekiel 42:20).

We too must measure up and separate what is common from what is holy. Our God-given natural gifts help us to serve for the good of our families, civic organizations, communities and churches (temporal things); but the Holy Spirit-gifted and empowered spiritual gifts give us the power and strength to minister and serve as Christ's church with eternal effect.

Where there is darkness, He will shine His light through us. Where there are storms, He will minister peace and calm through us. When people are wandering and lost, He will minister His salvation through us. When God extends His hand to show love and compassion to restore a soul, our hands will be extended to the same soul who has gone astray. God will accomplish all this by means of the Holy Spirit's gifting and empowering work in all those who follow Christ. Not by human might or by the strength of man, but by the Spirit at work through God's people.

YOUR JOURNEY JOURNAL
Chapter 6: Spiritual and Natural Gifts

1. What purpose is served in the ministries of spiritual gifts?

2. What is the connection between the operation of spiritual gifts in a church gathering and true and real worship?

3. Is God's sovereignty diminished when He confers authority or makes a covenant?

4. Why is it important to distinguish the common from what is holy?

Your Journal Notes:

7

Kingdom Treasures in Spiritual Gifts

Because Spirit-gifted ministries are too often misunderstood, rejected, redefined, and restricted from use by all the people in church, spiritual gifts are a topic of great importance for Christians today. We do God's people great harm when we minimize these awesome treasures, the gifts of the Spirit; we limit the mission of the church, taking away what is "supernatural" and unchanging from the beginning of the church until today. But spiritual gifts are not given to everyone; only to those who are "in Christ" and who desire these good gifts. A lack of desire for God's precious gifts is lamentable, a grievous wrong in present day churches.

Spiritual gifts include special abilities, roles, offices, functions, and a number of areas of Christian ministries and service. Scripture does not offer an exhaustive list. Whatever your spiritual gift or calling might be, it is given by the grace of God, through the Holy Spirit for use in His church (Romans 11:29). The gifts are intended for all believers (1 Peter 4:10) for the good of Christ's church, as proof and confirmation of the power of the gospel (Romans 15:19, 1 Corinthians 1:6-7, Hebrews 2:4), and to advance the kingdom of heaven against the kingdom of darkness. When we minister and serve according to our spiritual gifts and by the empowering work of the Holy Spirit, we are administering God's grace in its various forms. Christians are empowered by the Holy Spirit to use these gifts. Some gifts are thought of as supernatural and others as more ordinary; but they are of the same Spirit. We must use our gifts in the name of and under the authority of Jesus Christ.

Like walking on stepping-stones across a bubbling brook, in this chapter we'll walk step-by-step through a complete outline of spiritual gifts beckoning the church. The purpose is clear: The Great Commission cannot be fulfilled by human means alone. Jesus has sent His Holy Spirit to gift and empower His people to complete this mission in these last days. For the mission to be completed, we need the offices of the church, all the ministries of the church, and all the work of serving to be active and noticeably present in this great mission to which we have been called.

Ministry Gifts for the Church

One of the great leadership challenges in the church today is that the entire burden of ministry is laid at the pastor's feet. "You do it. That's what we pay you for," the pastor is told. This attitude is as much the doing of pastors as people, because the pastor is put on a pedestal or the pastor enjoys being at the man at the top. Like fabric that is made strong as the threads are woven together, we are called to work as one body to do what Jesus commanded before ascending into heaven.

> *"Then Jesus came to them and said, 'All authority in heaven and on earth has been given to me. Therefore go and make disciples of all nations, baptizing them in the name of the Father and of the Son and of the Holy Spirit, and teaching them to obey everything I have commanded you. And surely I am with you always, to the very end of the age.'"* (Matthew 28:18-20)

Is it possible to complete the mission when so many of the gifts and offices for today's church are combined into one office, the office of Pastor? But too many congregants prefer it that way. Various church and denominational leaders over the centuries have diminished the offices given as gifts to the church and have combined them, placing all the offices into one. This is a departure from the historic, orthodox Christian Church and is worth examining. We should also consider that it is possible for churches to lose gifts and offices through apostasy. Is this part of a "famine" of hearing God's Word, as mentioned in Amos 8:11?

Another part of the challenge we face regarding spiritual gifts is that, too often, those who choose to be pew sitters are all too anxious to have *all* the gifts of the Spirit manifested in just a few people — the pastor or elders. "It's written in their job description," they say. This attitude may be similar to what happened in 1 Samuel 8:5, when the people came to Samuel and said, "Now appoint a king to lead us." The people of Israel abdicated their responsibilities before God their King to an earthly king who they thought would lead them, defend them, and provide for them. Jeremiah warns us against those who would presume upon the authority of an office: "...the priests rule by their own authority, and my people love it this way" (Jeremiah 5:31). They were not leading the sheep of God's pasture by conferred authority, but by presumptive authority.

The Apostle Paul made it clear that spiritual gifts are not for the few, but for all believers. Gifts of the Spirit are intended to be common among God's people: "Now to each one the manifestation of the Spirit is given for the common good" (1 Corinthians 12:7). God's wisdom does not give any one person all the necessary gifts for the church to function as He has intended. We must all depend upon each other, working together. The church must not be run like a corporation with a CEO and all the employees working under one man.

Offices for the Church

God has given five ministry offices to build the church:

> *"So Christ himself gave the apostles, the prophets, the evangelists, the pastors and teachers, to equip his people for works of service, so that the body of Christ may be built up until we all reach unity in the faith and in the knowledge of the Son of God and become mature, attaining to the whole measure of the fullness of Christ." (Ephesians 4:11-13)*

These ministry offices are gifts of grace to the church; they are powerful abilities from the Holy Spirit and are empowered in the Spirit to prepare the saints to accomplish Christ's Great Commission.

The offices for the church are unique to the church, quite unlike any earthly organization.

1. Apostle: 1 Corinthians 12:28, Ephesians 4:11. Apostles are first in importance and authority because of their work to establish and build up the church. This is a foundational office of the church, to found, teach, train, organize, and build a functioning local church body. There are three witnesses to testify to apostleship: 1) Signs, 2) Wonders, and 3) Miracles (2 Corinthians 12:12). The apostles, with great perseverance, compassion, patience, and sacrificial love, ministered these three witnesses among the people. An Apostle gives birth to a local church as in the very pains of childbirth (Galatians 4:19). He also ministers under the call and authority given to him in Christ. "This is why I write these things when I am absent, that when I come I may not have to be harsh in my use of authority — the authority the Lord gave me for building you up, not for tearing you down" (2 Corinthians 13:10).

We encounter few, if any, who meet all the qualifications of apostleship today, and yet experience is not the arbiter of truth. God's Word is the foundation of all truth and light. What the Scriptures reveal is that the work of an apostle is still necessary in the church. Church planting without apostleship is like a cake half-baked. Missionaries who blaze new frontiers absent of the ministries of an apostle must leave the job unfinished. The obvious Biblical conclusion is that there is a great need for the work of apostleship in the church today.

Jesus was the first apostle and the foundation of all apostleship, and of their work and ministries (Galatians 1). Our Lord Jesus and God the Father are the Ones through whom all apostleship originated. This office is not of human ordination, but commissioned by Christ. Jesus sends them out with a specific calling and authority.

Jesus started out with twelve disciples, taught them at Jesus University for over three years, and then sent his Holy Spirit to indwell them, empowering them and anointing them for serving in the church. The apostles laid hands on Paul, Barnabus, and others, anointing them as apostles and sending them out as witnesses of the resurrected Christ. Paul was possibly the first to be empowered as an apostle for a specific purpose, i.e. an apostle to the Gentiles.

An apostle was unique in that he was gifted with the ministries necessary to establish a living, dynamic, functioning local church. He served in these gifts because it was his ministry to establish local bodies of believers and (serving as presbyter) to appoint elders. By the will of the Holy Spirit, the ministry gifts are passed on to the local disciples for the orderly serving in all the ministries of the local church.

Apostles are always ready to patiently do signs, wonders, and miracles among the local church in order to provide a witness to his testimony about Jesus Christ and to confirm the truth of the Word he was teaching the people. The signs and wonders were to make the people wake up and realize, "God is truly among you." This is one great purpose of the signs and wonders performed by the apostles.

One of the primary requirements of the first apostles is that they were to be eyewitnesses of the resurrected Jesus who commissioned them. On resurrection morning Jesus sent Mary Magdalene to do the work of an apostle, as the first witness of the resurrection. "Mary Magdalene went to the disciples with the news: 'I have seen the Lord!' And she told them that he had said these things to her" (John 20:18). Paul came face to face with the resurrected Jesus and was commissioned on the road to Damascus. The twelve disciples are referred to as super apostles. They were with Jesus from the beginning and were present at His death and after His resurrection witnessed Him walking among them in His glorified body. Thomas became an eyewitness when he placed his hand in His side and saw the nail prints in Jesus' hands. Note that Barnabus' personal encounter is not recorded, yet he is referred to as an apostle (Acts 14:14).

Today, an apostle's message comes by revelation of the Holy Spirit. This revelation is not apart from the Word but in fact is confirmed and illuminated by the truth of the Word. The Apostle Paul offers an example. He was exceptionally well educated in the Scripture and this kind of education was of great value to him. But consider the powerful change, taking Paul from prideful persecutions of the church to humble ministries and service within the church. His work as an apostle helps us understand the work of this office in the church:

- The Apostle Paul was not sent to baptize (1 Corinthians 1:17).
- The calling of all apostles is to plant the seed (1 Corinthians 3:6).
- An apostle lays a foundation as an expert builder (1 Corinthians 3:10).
- An apostle explains and reveals God's mysteries, a prophetic gift (Colossians 2:2).
- The proof of apostleship is teaching truth with confirming signs, wonders that are given for the purpose of proclaiming to the hearer, "Listen up." Also, spiritual gifts given to the local church were confirmations that the apostles were giving true testimony of the resurrected Christ (1 Corinthians 1:6-7).

Today, some church denominations claim to be "Apostolic." Other churches claim apostolic succession for their bishops. There is no need for confusing claims. Without a doubt, the Apostle Paul makes clear the foundation of the church. He regards the temple as God's dwelling place, i.e. the saints — the church, as "built on the foundation of the apostles and prophets, with Christ Jesus himself as the chief cornerstone" (Ephesians 2:20). We all agree that our Lord Jesus Christ, the first Apostle, is still the Living Cornerstone of the church. Look at the question in this light. What happens when the foundation of a building is removed or sinks into shifting sand? The building crumbles. It can no longer stand. Clearly, today's church, as it grows and expands throughout all nations, peoples, tribes, and language groups still needs this *living* foundation built by the apostles and prophets. We cannot be a church without this foundation. We have a solid foundation they built by the authority of the Holy Scriptures. And it continues as a living foundation for the church as it grows and builds in our day.

Paul writes, "In reading this, then, you will be able to understand my insight into the mystery of Christ, which was not made known to people in other generations as it has now been revealed by the Spirit to God's holy apostles and prophets" (Ephesians 3:4-5). This is NOW! We have what the Spirit revealed to the Apostle Paul written in the Holy Scripture and it stands to this very day as God's holy Word. This was not some time in the past when God gave a onetime revelation.

God continues revealing the mystery of Jesus Christ through the Holy Spirit by the living Word.[51] No one is able to grasp the truth of the gospel apart from the Spirit's revelation power. The church is built upon a Living Cornerstone and upon this living foundation. Is the ministry of an Apostle for the church today? The answer comes in two parts: 1) Because the canon of Scripture is complete, today's church is not given people who are gifted to speak or write with the authority of Scripture. This was the work of the first super apostles. 2) The office, ministries, and mission of an apostle — to plant the seed of God's Word, to lay a foundation for ministries and services of the local church, to reveal the mysteries of God, to teach the truth of the Scriptures with confirming signs and wonders — all this is still needed in the church today. The ministries and work of apostleship still ought to be an integral part of the church today and we suffer a great loss without this office at work among us.

Additional Scripture relating to the office of Apostle: Romans 1:1, 1 Corinthians 1:1, 2 Corinthians 1:1, Galatians 1:1, Ephesians 1:1, Colossians 1:1, 1 Timothy 1:1, 2 Timothy 1:1, Titus 1:1, 1 Peter 1:1, 2 Peter 1:1.

2. Prophet: This office is a ministry for building up the church through speaking messages and revelations from God for the purpose of revealing Jesus Christ. "His word is in my heart like a burning fire, shut up in my bones. I am weary of holding it in; indeed, I cannot" (Jeremiah 20:9).

We also see this ministry at work among the elders who served as presbyters in 1 Timothy 4:14, imparting a spiritual gift to Timothy by laying hands on him accompanied by a prophetic utterance. (Note: There is a distinct difference between the office of prophet and ministering in the spiritual gift of prophecy in that the office carries a greater responsibility to care for, nurture, and build up the "flock" and is often a formal position of leadership.)

Just like the first prophets, God has called those who hold the

---

[51] We must be careful to note that there is no further revelation that will supersede, add to, or contradict the canon of Scripture.

office of prophet in a local church or parish to reveal the mysteries of Jesus Christ and the cross of Christ. They may also reveal God's hand in current events and in the lives of people. If this is to be considered an "office" within the local church it ought to be one of leading, encouraging, guiding, and teaching others. It is the duty of one holding the office of prophet to oversee the ministries of the spiritual gift of prophecy and to provide loving guidance and discipline for all who are gifted and empowered by the Spirit of Jesus to minister in this gift.[52]

The ministries of this office carry a great responsibility because in speaking and proclaiming, "he should do it as one speaking the very words[53] of God" (1 Peter 4:11). It is impossible to truly speak the oracles of God if you should attempt to minister according to your natural insights, intuition, or abilities.

3. Evangelist: This is one who proclaims the good news gospel either by preaching or by other means of communication. Beginning in the early church and to this day there are evangelists and preachers who are not stationed in any local church and preach in whatever place the Holy Spirit leads. This is similar to the ministries of some missionaries today (Ephesians 4:11). Timothy was exhorted to do the work of an evangelist. Matthew, Mark, Luke, John, and Philip (Acts 21:8) are some of the examples of Evangelists in Scripture. Without question, the greatest evangelist of all was our Lord Jesus as He, in fact, fulfilled all of the offices and all of the gifts of the Spirit, ministering with "delight in the fear of the Lord" (Isaiah 11:3). We see here an example of evangelistic work: "But when they believed Philip as he preached the good news of the kingdom of God and the name of Jesus Christ, they were baptized, both men and women" (Acts 8:12). All of us are called to evangelize and are gifted as God sees fit, but this office of evangelist is an exceptional gift.

---

[52] One who fills the office of prophet, providing leadership, etc. for those who prophesy in the church is not commanded by Scripture to fulfill each of these tasks, but it seems wise and prudent for them to do so.
[53] KJV uses the word "oracle" which translates, "a brief utterance, a divine oracle." What does "brief" mean? Possibly three to five minutes, but Scripture does not clarify this for us. I've heard many sermons and few are brief.

4. Pastor: A pastor is a shepherd within a local flock of believers who prepares "God's people for 'works of service,' so that the body of Christ may be built up..." (Ephesians 4:12). A pastor's work is to feed, tend, and care for the "sheep" of His pasture. This is one of the offices given to a local church. The word for pastor comes from its use in the Scripture. In the Old Testament, the Hebrew word רעה (ra'ah) is used to describe the feeding of sheep as in Genesis 29:7 or, as the prophet Jeremiah writes, the spiritual feeding of God's people: "And I will give you shepherds *(pastors KJV)* after my own heart, who will lead *(feed)* you with knowledge and understanding" (Jeremiah 3:15, notes added). Another part of a pastor's calling is to search for the sheep that have wandered away. Too many of the flock have skipped out the back door of the church, and no one shepherds them back home (Matthew 18:12-14).

In the New Testament, the Greek word ποιμήν (poimēn) is translated as "pastor" or "shepherd." For example, "And He gave some, apostles; and some, prophets; and some, evangelists; and some, pastor(s) and teachers" (Ephesians 4:11). Jesus rightfully called himself the "Good Shepherd" in John 10:11. He is the first and greatest of all who minister pastoral care.

"Pastor" was also used in the New Testament to refer to elders and presbyters; but it's used primarily as a title for Bishops (*episkopos*). For example, in Acts 20:17, the Apostle Paul calls together the elders of the church in Ephesus to give his final words to them. In Acts 20:28, he tells them that the Holy Spirit has made them overseers, and that their job is to shepherd the local church. Peter uses similar language in 1 Peter 5:1-2, writing to the elders that they are to shepherd and not "lord over" the flock in their care, acting as willing servants. Paul gives a list of character traits that to establish a standard for those who serve in this capacity. 1 Timothy 3:1-7 and Titus 1:5-9 contain similar lists written for elders.

No one should ever assume authority as a shepherd over God's people. The effects are devastating as the prophet warns: "A horrible and shocking thing has happened in the land: The prophets prophesy lies, the priests rule by their own authority and my people love it this way. But what will you do in the end?" (Jeremiah 5:30-31).

Shepherds have a great responsibility to the "sheep of God's pasture." They are clearly warned: "You have not strengthened the weak or healed the sick or bound up the injured. You have not brought back the strays or searched for the lost. You have ruled them harshly and brutally" (Ezekiel 34:4). We see an even greater indictment of pastors who betray their calling: "Must my flock feed on what you have trampled and drink what you have muddied with your feet?" (Ezekiel 34:19).

The pastor or elder's pulpit ministry is threefold. 1) They are teachers of the Word. 2) They serve at times in the capacity of prophet, opening the words of God from Scripture for the hearer. 3) They minister as preachers, proclaiming and revealing Christ to the congregation.

5. Teacher: This is the last of the five offices. A teacher opens the Word of God to the hearer, revealing Christ and the cross of Jesus Christ so that hearts are brought to repentance, out of darkness into spiritual maturity and to good works (Ephesians 2:10). Pastors often operate in this gift. Although this office is listed last, it is vital for the strengthening of the church.

There is a great need for all five offices of the church "until we all reach unity in the faith and in the knowledge of the Son of God and become mature, attaining to the whole measure of the fullness of Christ" (Ephesians 4:13). Has the church come to unity in the faith? Are we mature in the knowledge of the Son of God? Have we attained the whole measure of the fullness of Christ? We have not! The church is still in great need of the offices of apostles, prophets, evangelists, pastors and teachers.

Spiritual Gifts for the Church

There is a clear difference between the offices of the church and spiritual gifts. The ministry gifts of the "offices" provide a more formal order within a local church (typically positions of leadership and responsibility) while spiritual gifts fulfill the need for the everyday, hands-on ministries of the church and are intended for all Christians. Gifts of the Spirit are not the exclusive territory of the men of the church, but intended for men, women, boys, and girls. The inclusiveness of Christ becomes more and more clear as we explore each spiritual gift. Creating an exhaustive list of spiritual gifts is not possible because the Scriptures don't give us one. As you read through the various gifts, take time to pray and meditate upon each one and allow the Spirit of Jesus to put in your heart a desire for the spiritual gift He has ordained for you.

As you consider the following spiritual gifts, think how they are witnesses and confirmations of Christ's saving grace at work among His people. This truth is especially evident in the ministries of the spiritual gift of prophecy and also in the spiritual gifts that are ordained for each Christian. Going back to our example of a natural gift of teaching, natural gifts are a witness of God's provisional graces to all mankind (Matthew 5:45). But spiritual gifts are so much more powerful and the result is like a treasure of gold that will stand the test of fire and accomplish an eternal purpose.

Spiritual gifts typically fall within three categories: ministry gifts, utterance gifts, and service gifts. The Bible doesn't categorize them for us, so the classifications vary, depending on the teacher. We will start with ministry gifts, but not because they are greater or lesser than other spiritual gifts. Always remember, they are given as the Spirit determines.

Ministry Gifts

Preacher: A preacher opens a person's eyes to his violation of the law (sin) to bring him to repentance and to see his need of Christ, so the Word may effect faith in the saving grace of our Lord Jesus Christ. By the power and anointing of the Holy Spirit working through a preacher of the gospel, Christ reveals Himself to all those who will hear, to justify them by faith in a Holy God.

<u>Presbyter</u>: Apostles, Elders, Preachers, Teachers, Pastors, Deacons, and Deaconesses who are gifted in the Spirit to call Christians to the ministries of spiritual gifts within a local congregation for the strengthening of the whole church. Paul shows us this spiritual gift at work: "Do not neglect your gift, which was given you through a prophetic message when the body of elders (*Presbytery*) laid their hands on you" (1 Timothy 4:14, note added). This is the same gift at work here: "While they were worshiping the Lord and fasting, the Holy Spirit said, 'Set apart for me Barnabas and Saul for the work to which I have called them.' So after they fasted and prayed, they placed their hands on them and sent them off" (Acts 13:2-3). This ministry is typically administered by the laying on of hands, at times accompanied with prophecies.

The most common and broadest definition of the word Presbyter is "priest;" but clearly the specific gift of presbytery — imparting gifts, ordaining ministers, and calling a Christian to serve in a mission of the church — is included as we focus in on the scriptural application of this gift.

Because the spiritual gift of presbytery is uncommon in Evangelical churches, there is a need to understand the use of this gift. A form of this ministry exists in the Presbyterian and Catholic Churches today. In the Presbyterian Church, it is a governing body of elders who are given the added responsibility of calling and ordaining pastors. In the Catholic Church it is referred to as the Presbyterium, which is a "college of priests" who are responsible to conduct a Mass of Chrism, to anoint with oil to ordain new priests and bishops. Evangelical Christians do the church a great disservice when they ignore this purposeful gift or change it to serve a lesser function than to impart spiritual gifts to all those who are a part of the priesthood of the believers. The church becomes imbalanced and top heavy when pastors, priests, and bishops are the only ones to benefit from this ministry gift of imparting spiritual gifts and calling men and women to the service and ministries of the church.

The Apostle Paul gives us a great insight into the historical work of a presbyter, imparting spiritual gifts to the saints.[54] "I long to see you so that I may impart to you some spiritual gift to make you strong" (Romans 1:11). This Scripture shows us one means for spiritual gifts being imparted and how they may be given to believers within a local church body. Paul imparts the gifts, ministering as presbyter, by the power and authority of Christ. Today, in the same way, an elder or pastor who has the gift of Presbytery obeys the Holy Spirit and imparts the gifts for the strengthening of the local church body. It is important to remember that the variety of spiritual gifts given within a local church body are like the weaving of a fabric that becomes stronger as each thread is woven into the fabric.

Scripture does not state or even imply that all the spiritual gifts you will ever have are given to you upon justification or in water baptism. Clearly the Apostle Paul did not say that he would help them discover or find their spiritual gift. Imparting gifts of the Spirit is the work of a presbyter. And yet, God is not limited to one means of imparting spiritual gifts to believers.[55]

---

[54] Some scholars teach that Paul is not imparting spiritual gifts, but only referring to the gift of mutual strengthening and encouragement between believers. If that is true, why does Paul specifically state, "...that I may impart to you some spiritual gift to make you strong." This is a one-way impartation of spiritual gifts; from the Spirit of Christ through Apostle/Presbyter to the believer that leads to a mutual encouragement of each other's faith. The gifts of the Spirit are for the strengthening and encouragement of all who are in the faith — the church. It is unlikely that Paul was only interested in a "Camp Meeting" temporary shot in the arm or a blessing for the saints. Spiritual gifts are another means by which Christ continually strengthens and encourages His church. To diminish what Paul is saying, reducing it to mean a lesser, generic gifting by which they are a blessing to each other is to miss an important element of his message.

[55] The ministry of a gifted presbyter is an ideal way for spiritual gifts to be imparted. But for those who worship within many Evangelical Churches, the ministry of presbytery may not be available. This doesn't mean spiritual gifts are not available to you. God is faithful to impart His promised gifts even when the church is not faithful. Ask God to give you wisdom to know the spiritual gift He has for you. Ask God to put His desire in your heart and then ask for the gift you desire. Prayerfully consider having a trusted Christian friend pray with you in agreement, wait upon the Lord with fasting and prayer, and then have him/her lay hands on you, anointing you with oil while praying for you to receive the spiritual gift you desire. (Any kitchen oil will do to represent the "oil of the Spirit" who will gift and empower you.)

Spiritual Gift of Healing: This is an extraordinary ministry gift the Holy Spirit gives to those He chooses. Its purpose is to heal the sting of death and its effects on body, soul, and spirit. Jesus gives us a great example of this when He told the paralyzed man, "Son, your sins are forgiven" (Mark 2:5). He breaks the power that death and our sin nature have over us, giving us new life and strength in Jesus Christ, to overcome by the blood of the Lamb. This is the ultimate healing, yet God includes even more blessings for His children. God's very name is "The God who heals." He heals the whole person, spirit, body, soul — yes, this includes healing of the physical body. "He forgives all my sins and heals *all* my diseases" (Psalm 103:3). And, "The Lord will guide you always; he will satisfy your needs in a sun-scorched land and will strengthen your frame" (Isaiah 58:11; see also James 5:14, Mark 2:5-12, Jeremiah 30:17).

Elders and those gifted and empowered to minister Christ's healing touch are under the call, command, and authority of Christ to serve in His Name. Laying hands on the sick is the typical means of carrying out this ministry of God's love and compassion. But this ministry requires an intentional, earnestly persistent commitment and constant refreshing, dwelling in God's council, to gain a scriptural understanding of this reality. In the healing of body, soul, and spirit, we see the very heart and nature of God at work in a lost and dying world.[56] Ministering in this gift requires knowledge of the elementary doctrine of laying on of hands (Hebrews 6:2).

Those who minister in this spiritual gift are on the front line, advancing the kingdom of God in the battle against the kingdom of darkness. Critical to victory in this ministry are earnest, persistent, and supportive intercessors. Watchman Nee wrote, "The need today

---

[56] Recommended reading on this topic: *Authority to Heal* by Ken Blue. On page 62-63, Ken Blue reveals the challenges of ministering in the spiritual gift of healing in our American culture: "It may well be that the whole fellowship of the church needs to be raised to a higher spiritual level today before individual healers in it can repeat the healing activities of the Son of God, and that until the groups within the church today are willing to pass through the same kind of discipline, the healing ministry of the church will be restricted."

is for a company of overcoming saints who know how to wage war for the release of those under the enemy's deception." [57]

Acts 4:8-12 makes clear that God's healing through His gifted people is complete healing. In verse 10, Peter declares that the man is "completely healed." In verse 11, he declares the resurrected Christ, and in verse 12, he proclaims salvation in "no other name under heaven given to men by which we must be saved." Here we see, once again, healing and salvation bound together. Healing of the body and salvation for the soul. Healing and salvation are like hand and glove. This is the ministry for which the Holy Spirit empowers and gifts His people (Isaiah 33:24).

The Holy Spirit may lead those who minister healing to pray with understanding, or pray in the Spirit and lay hands on those who are ill, or to speak to the cause of the illness, or to send a prayer cloth (Acts 19:11-12). It would be futile to attempt a list of all the ways the Holy Spirit may employ in a ministry of healing.

As you serve in this gift, you will find, as in all spiritual gifts, it will increase in strength and effectiveness until the day you mistakenly claim this work as your own, receiving the glory that belongs to our Lord God. When you are faithful in a little, you will be given much more. "Whoever can be trusted with very little can also be trusted with much" (Luke 16:10; see also Luke 19:17).

Exegetical gifts: This is the gift of reading, understanding and interpreting God's Word, especially in the original Hebrew, Aramaic, and Greek languages. Also examining the context of Scripture through historic, geographic, and archaeological study, all under the revealing work of the Holy Spirit.

Discerning of spirits: This gift is especially important and sorely needed in today's church. As we approach the end of the age we are seeing an increase in spiritual activity coming from the kingdom of darkness. We misjudge some disorders that may have a demonic cause because our Western culture requires a scientific label and

---

[57] Watchman Nee. *The Spiritual Man*, pg 60.

medically explainable causes for every malady. And if we can label it, we medicate it.

A Christian operating in the gift of discerning spirits will be given witness by the Holy Spirit whether a message, a messenger, or anyone making claims in the name of God Almighty is doing so by the Holy Spirit, an evil spirit, or to promote their selfish ambitions. If this spiritual gift of discernment is seldom exercised, the church may unknowingly allow false prophecy, false tongues, and false interpretations. While all Christians must exercise godly discernment, this gift operates beyond common godly discernment or intuition.

An example of common discernment occurred for me when the author of a popular book about angelic visitations came to speak at our church. As the preacher spoke, my spirit was disturbed. When I read his book, my spirit was constantly distressed and I put aside his message in spite of all the general excitement about his claims of angelic visitations from the angel Gabriel and other angels. The source of this common godly discernment is the Holy Spirit, and yet it is not categorized as a spiritual gift.

"Dear friends, do not believe every spirit, but test the spirits to see whether they are from God, because many false prophets have gone out into the world" (1 John 4:1). John gives us a means of common discernment, a test for us to use in verse 2 & 3. Because of the exceptionally deceptive nature of ungodly spirits, it is so important for someone in our Christian gatherings to be "gifted" in this, because the spiritual gift of discerning goes beyond being disturbed in spirit, and in fact identifies the spirit at work. This is especially important because too often we mistakenly think that God is the source of everything that seems spiritual.

The most obvious example of the ministries of this gift would be after a prophetic message is given in a gathering of believers. This gift offers a "fire wall" against false prophecies, spiritually discerning the heart of the person speaking and the source of their words. Without this gift at work it could take years to see whether a message or ministry is the fruit of a "choice vine" or "wild vine" (Jeremiah 2:21). The spiritual gift of discerning of spirits offers an immediate test.

Words of wisdom: This is a revelatory gift and may be akin to prophecy. It is speaking out what can only be known by the Holy Spirit, to build up, admonish, and encourage the saints.[58] The ability to give wise and godly counsel may be included in this gift (1 Corinthians 12:8).

Words of knowledge: This is also a revelatory gift made possible by the power of the Holy Spirit and always ministered in love and selfless humility. This gift may at times operate within the spiritual gift of prophecy. This is also a useful gift to work with those who minister, laying hands on the sick and praying. At the hearing of God's Word, spoken by means of this gift, faith to be healed is given to those in need. A word of knowledge may identify an unknown need or even warn of sin in a gathering of believers, but rarely, if ever, publicly singles out an individual by name. "To one there is given through the Spirit a message of wisdom, to another a message of knowledge by means of the same Spirit (1 Corinthians 12:8).

The Spiritual Gift of Miracles: This spiritual gift is to know the heart and desire of God, or to be obedient to His command and to be His hand extended, accomplishing supernatural acts that reveal His power, in the authority of His Name and through the power of His Holy Spirit. People with the spiritual gift of miracles will see God manifesting His power and glory in extraordinary ways, according to His will, purpose, and plan. The miraculous works God performs through His servants may range from simple daily events to notable "signs" confirming God's ever present might and power to save, and proving that God is truly present, indwelling His people.

This gift is truly needed in today's post-Christian, "everything is spiritual" American culture. Paul makes it clear that this gift is included among all that the Holy Spirit desires to give His people: "to another miraculous powers" (1 Corinthians 12:10). The Apostle Paul speaks of the good this gift will accomplish:

---

[58] The spiritual gifts of "Words of Wisdom" and "Words of knowledge" are easily imitated and abused, but the church must not "bury" these gifts out of fear of imitation or abuse. We must accompany these gifts with the spiritual gift of discernment. These gifts are at times difficult to distinguish from the gift of prophecy.

"Therefore I glory in Christ Jesus in my service to God. I will not venture to speak of anything except what Christ has accomplished through me in leading the Gentiles to obey God by what I have said and done — by the power of signs and miracles, through the power of the Spirit." (Romans 15:17-19)

Recorded Church history makes exceedingly clear that this gift is still at work within the church and was not only for the Apostles in times long past; but we must now also "stand in the flow."

Spiritual gift of Encouragement: The Apostle Paul writes of this spiritual gift: "if it is encouraging, let him encourage" (Romans 12:8). The Biblical meaning is to take someone "under your arm" to console, comfort, exhort, and pray with the one being ministered to. Although the outcome of this gift is comfort, motivation, and giving reason for hope, there is also the element of exhortation, pointing to a future hope. The goal is to encourage fellow believers to be all that they are called to be in Christ, to fully participate in Christ. The Holy Spirit directs a person with this gift, opening their eyes to someone who is struggling, leading them to comfort him or her and motivate. They share hope for the future. The nature of this gift is to dispense the healing oil of the Holy Spirit. It is a singular act of grace used in the present moment to bring about an eternal effect.

Spiritual gift of Teaching: The Spiritual gift of Teaching is included as a ministry gift because there are many anointed teachers that do not fill the "office" of teacher in the church. This spiritual gift is of significant importance to the church in many capacities. All facets of Christian Education and training require gifted and empowered instructors to accomplish the eternal work of the kingdom. (See "Teaching" in the chapter "Natural Gifts.")

Teaching in the church is for an eternal purpose and can only be accomplished by the gifting and empowering work of the Holy Spirit. It is also important to know that when you teach, you are not alone in this ministry — it's an effort by a team of three. Look at Acts 8:31-40, where Philip was instructed to travel down the road from Jerusalem to Gaza where he came across an Ethiopian eunuch who was reading the Scriptures in his chariot. He asked Philip how it was possible to understand what he was reading unless someone guided him. We see in this Scripture that three things were necessary for the gospel to take root in the Ethiopian eunuch or any who seek Christ. The team of three includes: 1) The inspired Scripture; 2) an anointed messenger or teacher; 3) the Holy Spirit who teaches in our very heart of hearts. The eunuch's response is proof in verse 36, "See, here is water! What prevents me from being baptized?"

This was a heart response that was made possible through a threefold work of God: the Word, an anointed teacher under authority, and the Holy Spirit.

Utterance Gifts

Utterance gifts are at times called "sign" gifts or confirmatory gifts because they often follow the outpouring, gifting, or empowering work of the Holy Spirit. "When Paul placed his hands on them, the Holy Spirit came on them, and they spoke in tongues and prophesied" (Acts 19:6). We see here the work of the Holy Spirit giving and empowering spiritual gifts and anointing them for a purpose.

Because there is so much misinformation and fear of utterance gifts, we must have a clear understanding of what Scripture teaches (look up 1 Corinthians 14:29-33): 1) The Holy Spirit does not force anyone to speak or act against his or her will. People do not suddenly burst into an utterance that is out of their control. 2) The person operating in an utterance gift does not lose his/her self-control. 3) The speaker will be clearly understood by those who hear what they are saying. When tongues are used, others will understand after an interpretation is given. 4) The person operating in an utterance gift will be totally aware of their surroundings and what is happening around them. They are not in a trance. Typically they will not have an ecstatic experience, although they may well feel as if a flood has just washed through them. 5) The Holy Spirit gives the utterance, which is subject to the person to whom it is given. They can wait their turn or speak the message at an appropriate time. This is entirely consistent with God's nature as a covenant making God, giving His people specific charges, authority, and promises and then empowering them to carry out their charge responsibly.

The book of James in chapter three sheds some light on the reason our mouths are affected by the work of the Spirit in us. James says that the flames of hell have more to do in fanning the fire of the tongue than we are generally aware of. Satan's diabolical schemes inflame men's tongues for destruction. He is a liar, a murderer, an accuser of the brethren, and whenever men's tongues are used in any of these ways, they are certainly fueled by the fires of hell against the kingdom of heaven. But we see in Acts chapter two that the Holy Spirit descended as tongues of fire.[59] The Holy Spirit's fire guides anointed men and women's tongues from within them and leads them to speak truth, to do deeds of holiness, and to act with godly devotion. Here we see clearly that the kingdom of darkness twists, tangles, and enflames the tongue of men to defile and destroy God's creation, while the Holy Spirit affects our mouths to advance the kingdom of God throughout all the earth: "The good man brings good things out of the good stored up in his heart, and the evil man brings evil things out of the evil stored up in his heart. For out of the overflow of his heart his mouth speaks" (Luke 6:45).

The Gift of Spiritual Language:

"O for a thousand tongues to sing
my great Redeemer's praise,
The glories of my God and King,
the triumphs of His grace!"

The gift of spiritual languages deserves extra attention because of pervasive misunderstanding and fear surrounding the ministries of this gift. These are gifts the Scripture refers to as tongues, i.e.

---

[59] In all of Scripture, fire is often symbolic of judgment. When Christians speak God's Word by the power of the Holy Spirit, their words speak judgment to the unrepentant and healing to the contrite.

speaking in the languages of heaven and earth that a person has never learned. Often, this gift is manifested as a spiritual language for the purpose of declaring the wonderful works of God (Acts 2:11) in prayer, thanksgiving, worship, and praise in words or phrases the speaker doesn't typically understand with his mind (1 Corinthians 14:2, 14-15). This gift is a sign for unbelievers when used in public worship because an unknown or foreign tongue that the unbeliever cannot understand may be a sign of God's coming judgment if the unrepentant does not turn from sin (Deuteronomy 28:49). For the believer it is for spiritual strengthening and builds up the whole church when used with interpretation (1 Corinthians 14:26). When used in this manner it is considered a variation of prophecy, but not equal to prophecy. Not everyone is blessed with this gift, because it is given "just as the Holy Spirit determines" (1 Corinthians 12:11). This is a most useful gift that must never be forbidden, marginalized, minimized, or relegated to a time long past (1 Corinthians 14:39).

The Apostle Paul gave two very specific "Do Not" commands regarding spiritual gifts, and both concern utterance gifts: 1) "Therefore, my brothers and sisters, be eager to prophesy, and **do not** forbid speaking in tongues" (1 Corinthians 14:39, emphasis added). 2) "**Do not** quench the Spirit. **Do not** treat prophecies with contempt" (1 Thessalonians 5:19-20). We must not be like the teachers of the Law and the Pharisees who kept their flocks from receiving God's blessings. Jesus also warned against an attitude of exclusiveness: "Woe to you, teachers of the Law and Pharisees, you hypocrites! You shut the kingdom of heaven in men's faces. You yourselves do not enter, nor will you let those enter who are trying to" (Matthew 23:13). Church leadership must not deny any gift or blessing of the kingdom to anyone who is a part of the body of Christ.

Some present day churches forbid this gift. Others don't outright forbid it but downplay it or ignore it as unimportant, refusing to teach and encourage the saints regarding the ministries of tongues. The Bible is clear: the use of tongues in a public time of worship is a sign for unbelievers given by the power of the Holy Spirit just as it was on the day of Pentecost and numerous other times throughout church history. When an unbeliever hears God exalted in his native language from someone who has never learned it, he or she will be cut to the heart and respond, "Varones hermanos, ¿qué haremos?" Or "What shall we do?" (Acts 2:37).

When someone hears the interpretation of a spiritual language, it is a most powerful witness of the power of God.

When did tongues begin in the church? "The church began speaking with tongues the same day it came into being!"[60] (Please remember, in public worship the use of the gift of tongues must be accompanied with **interpretation** — also a spiritual gift.)

When a believer prays in his spirit with tongues in a private prayer closet, this is a most extraordinary gift and is pleasing to God who gives the gift. To pray in a heavenly language is a most excellent prayer that emanates from our spirit, inspired in the Holy Spirit. As long as we have unbelievers among us and as long as there is a need for spiritual strengthening for the church, we have need of this wonderful gift from the Holy Spirit.

Do you desire to speak to God who reveals mysteries in your spirit (1 Corinthians 14:2)? Are you in need of spiritual edification (1 Corinthians 14:4)? Do you desire to pray as the Apostle Paul prayed (1 Corinthians 14:14)? Do you need to be built up in the faith (Jude 20)? Do you want to pray, joined together with God in the Holy Spirit (Romans 8:26)? Do you yearn to pray in your private prayer closet in the languages of angels (1 Corinthians 13:1)? Do you want to be more effective in spiritual warfare (2 Corinthians 10:4)? Do you have a desire for the Bridegroom's bridal adornments? The spiritual gifts of tongues can answer the longing of your heart.[61]

This is a time for boldness. We must not cower in fear. We must not give in to our anxious thoughts. Be encouraged to earnestly pray and ask for this most precious and powerful gift of the Holy Spirit and He will answer you according to His promise. In seeking, you do not seek the gift alone or a personal experience but the Giver of the gift. We must never value the gift more than the One who gives the gift. This may sound simplistic, but it is a common error. Another frequent

---

[60] Jack Hayford. *The Beauty of Spiritual Language*, pg 100.
[61] Song of Songs 1:10-11, Isaiah 61:10, Ezekiel 16:11-12

error is to think of tongues as a cure-all for any and all challenges we face; the gift *does* strengthen and help us, but it's not the only means God has provided.

My personal faltering encounter with tongues may be helpful to our understanding of this gift. During my first year in a Charismatic Church they taught, as many still do, that the gift of tongues was "the sign" always given with the baptism of the Holy Spirit.

When God's empowering work washed through me like a flood — I knew the Holy Spirit had refreshed and empowered me.[62] I knew He did a powerful work in me, but I didn't speak in tongues. I prayed for a several months asking for the gift of tongues after which I received this wonderful gift as a private prayer and praise language. Later I asked for the gift of interpreting what I prayed, and graciously, I was given this gift also. Over the years as I've continued to pray and praise in tongues, God has strengthened my faith, refreshed me in His Holy Spirit, empowered me to serve, and helped me in my weaknesses. At times I've prayed in the spirit and I was only able to grasp the general content of my prayers, not knowing the exact meaning of each word.

---

[62] The truth of Scripture, when examined carefully, teaches us that when we repent, believe, are forgiven, and are baptized in water, we receive the promised Holy Spirit (Acts 2:38 is one example). The baptism I refer to is a baptism in the Holy Spirit, empowering a believer for works of ministry. This is not a one time, once-and-for-all-time event like water baptism. We must continually be filled, saturated in, and refilled with a baptism in the Holy Spirit. We need to have the fire stirred up and rekindled for as long as we serve and minister in the church. The evidence of this baptism is obvious and unquestionable. Would you know if you were out hiking in a desert wash and a flash flood overcame you? Of course! The evidence of the gifting and empowering work of the Holy Spirit is powerfully evident, and then becomes evident again and again as the person ministers in the gift. If the gift is tongues, he will speak in tongues. If prophecy, she will speak out the oracles of God. If singing in the Spirit, a beautiful overflowing of songs revealing Christ and glorifying God. If administration, she will work with a special anointing for organization. God is not limited to work in a specific manner for each and every person's empowering baptism. We see this in Numbers 11:26b, "When the Spirit rested on them, they prophesied, but they did not do so again." God will give sure and unquestionable evidence of the Holy Spirit's baptism and very often the evidence of this baptism pours from the mouth first. This outpouring from the mouth will not be an out of control, no-volume-control kind of outpouring unless the baptized person is attempting to emulate or imitate the work of the Spirit in the strength of the flesh. Any attempt to imitate the Spirit's outpouring becomes a soulish, "look at me" event.

But this kind of prayer is prayed with great confidence. As I continue in the use of this precious gift, I find greater strength and purpose in it.

Our Prayer: "Forgive all our sins and receive us graciously, that we may offer the fruit of our lips" (Hosea 14:2).

The Spiritual Gift of Prophecy: This gift is a most useful and powerful ministry within the Christian church today and must not be excluded. "Do not quench the Spirit. Do not treat prophecies with contempt but test them all; hold on to what is good, reject every kind of evil" (1 Thessalonians 5:19-22). This spiritual gift, at work in the church, is in addition to messages from God's Word given as a part of a pulpit ministry or a teaching ministry. "Two or three prophets should speak, and the others should weigh carefully what is said" (1 Corinthians 14:29). Preaching from the pulpit may include the spiritual gift of prophecy when a message is received and spoken out spontaneously during the sermon.

In worship services that encourage ministries of this gift, many excellent benefits are provided. The church is strengthened, encouraged, and comforted. "But the one who prophesies speaks to people for their strengthening, encouraging and comfort" (1 Corinthians 14:3). When unbelief begins to creep into a church the ministries of prophetic gifts will call it back to the right path. "But if an unbeliever or an inquirer comes in while everyone is prophesying, they are convicted of sin and are brought under judgment by all, as the secrets of their hearts are laid bare. So they will fall down and worship God, exclaiming, 'God is really among you!'" (1Corinthians 14:14-25).

Through the ministries of this spiritual gift, other spiritual gifts and calls to ministry are imparted and confirmed. "Do not neglect your gift, which was given you through prophecy when the body of elders laid their hands on you" (1 Timothy 4:14). By means of this gift, disciples are sent out in Jesus' Name to complete the work God has ordained for them to do. "While they were worshiping the Lord and fasting, the Holy Spirit said, 'Set apart for me Barnabas and Saul for the work to which I have called them.' So after they had fasted and prayed, they placed their hands on them and sent them off" (Acts 3:2-3).

This dynamic spiritual gift is defined simply as proclaiming to a gathering of the church what the Holy Spirit has revealed or whispered into your soul and spirit, often spontaneously.[63] This beautiful gift reveals Jesus' living active presence at work in a gathering of believers in the moment. This powerful gift changes the dynamics of a gathering, going from one where people might ask, "Where is their God?" (Psalm 115:2) to exclaiming, "God is truly among you." A great purpose of this spiritual gift is to reveal Jesus Christ to lost souls, to open eyes to a living Redeemer, to open ears to hear God speak, and to open hearts to receive the Word.

Wisdom and understanding are called for. We must obey Scripture and examine all words of prophecy spoken in a gathering of believers. The speaker must submit to the examination of their fellow believers, to be sure the message is consistent with all of Scripture, not adding to, contradicting, or distracting from God's Word in any way. "Two or three prophets should speak, and the others should weigh carefully what is said" (1 Corinthians 14:29).

For a complete teaching on this spiritual gift, see the third book in this series, *A Jewel of the Kingdom.*

Singing in the Spirit:

"Sing to the Lord, for he has done glorious things;
Let this be known to all the world.
Shout aloud and sing for joy, people of Zion,
For great is the Holy One of Israel among you." (Isaiah 12:5-6)

Singing in the spirit is also an utterance gift and is a most beautiful outpouring of the Holy Spirit in times of public and private worship. It's an especially enriching overflow of the Holy Spirit empowering true praise and worship before a Great and Awesome God. "Praise the Lord.

---

[63] This definition does not apply to those who minister in the office of prophet, but only to the spiritual gift. The definition of prophecy ministered within the office is: 1) to foretell, i.e. give a message from God, whether with reference to the past, the present or the future; 2) to foretell, i.e. to tell something, which cannot be known by natural means.

Praise God in his sanctuary; praise him in his mighty heavens" (Psalm 150:1). Christians are blessed and may partake in praise and worship that begins in the heavenly sanctuary and resounds throughout the church.

Examples of spiritual song in the Bible are:

Moses and Miriam lead the people, singing in the spirit — and what a powerful song it was: "Sing to the Lord, for he is highly exalted. The horse and its rider he has hurled into the sea" (Exodus 15:1).

Luke writes of Mary's song (the Magnificat) as the mother of Jesus greets Elizabeth, the mother of John the Baptist. Mary's song flows from her spirit, inspired by the Holy Spirit in praise to God: "My soul praises the Lord and my spirit rejoices in God my Savior, for he has been mindful of the humble state of his servant" (Luke 1:46).

Zechariah, in obedience to God, wrote, "His name is John" (Luke 1:63). When he wrote this, his mouth was opened and he began to speak, praising God. Words flowed forth as he was filled with the Holy Spirit in prophetic verse. In verse 67, Zechariah sings, "Praise be to the Lord, the God of Israel, because he has come and has redeemed his people."

Throughout Scripture we find a record of spiritual songs by many other men and women. Deborah, (Judges 5); Hannah, (1 Samuel 2:1-10); and most prolific in spiritual songs and psalms of worship was David, shepherd and king of Israel. We see a perfect example in this Scripture: "David, together with the army, set apart some of the sons of Asaph, Heman and Jeduthun for the ministry of prophesying, accompanied by harps, lyres and cymbals" (1 Chronicles 25:1-7).

Are spiritual songs for the modern Christian church? Why do we need them? We have gifted contemporary Christian composers who are well educated, have excellent skills and talents, and who write numerous inspired Christian praise and worship songs. We have many great hymns of the church that have been sung for hundreds of years. Why do we need this spiritual gift? The simplest answer is this: because we are encouraged to do so in Scripture. But there is so much more than just simple obedience. We also find many benefits for building up the church. "Speak to one another with psalms, hymns and spiritual songs. Sing and make music in your heart to the Lord, always giving thanks to God the Father for everything, in the name of our Lord Jesus Christ" (Ephesians 5:19). And, "Let the word of Christ dwell in you richly as you teach and admonish one another with all wisdom, and as you sing psalms, hymns and spiritual songs with gratitude in your hearts to God" (Colossians 3:16).

When we worship God in spiritual song, surely we sing in harmony with the angels of heaven. Paul instructs us, "I will sing with my spirit, but I will also sing with my mind" (1 Corinthians 14:15). Most of us have fallen into default mode and sing before the Lord only with our minds. This is excellent and we must continue doing so, but Paul encourages us to do both and it is for our great benefit.

You may object, saying, "But I like the old hymns of the church." Or some might say, "I like the chants the Hebrew people sing in their worship." Maybe there are those who say, "I like the songs of the 60's Jesus people." "I like Maranatha Praise choruses." "I like rapturous pipe organ music." "I like songs when I can clap along." "I like, I like, I like." Do you see where this takes us? The Spirit of our Holy God is the Creator of all heaven and earth and He has a new song to put in our hearts — continually! "Sing to the Lord a new song, his praise in the assembly of the saints" (Psalm 149:1). Do you get the impression that as the sun breaks over the horizon our Lord is ready with a new song for us to sing in harmony with Him? Is there a new song for the children of the King to sing as the sun breaks over the horizon in Nova Scotia, as dawn breaks over Mexico City, as the morning light reflects over the waters around the island of Oahu, and as the daylight breaks the darkness over Qinghai, China?

The Spirit of Jesus will continually refresh us with a "new song." They are songs of repentance, healing, refreshing, praise, worship, adoration, exaltation, and so much more. We sing in harmony with those who are singing in heaven. How can we turn away from His continual refreshing with new songs?

> *"Sing to the Lord a new song, his praise from the ends of the earth, you who go down to the sea, and all that is in it, you islands, and all who live in them. Let the wilderness and its towns raise their voices; let the settlements where Kedar*

lives rejoice. Let the people of Sela sing for joy; let them shout from the mountaintops. Let them give glory to the Lord and proclaim his praise in the islands. The Lord will march out like a champion, like a warrior he will stir up his zeal; with a shout he will raise the battle cry and will triumph over his enemies." (Isaiah 42:10-13)

In the above Scripture we see God's purpose in giving His saints "new songs."

Can it be true that in every new kingdom battle, in each triumph over the enemy our Lord Jesus has a new song of victory to sing with us?

Our prayer: *"Oh, Lord. Lead us to join in with your song of victory — your new song of triumph."*

From a human perspective, the song prompted by the Spirit may not sound anything like songs written by U2's Bono or Natalie Grant and they may not make the Top-Ten on the Pop chart, but this is certainly the music of heaven and will bring eternal fruit. Spiritual songs may be with or without music accompaniment. In fact, the song may at times sound more like a poetic expression. The spiritual song is subject to the singer, meaning that it's in the songster's control. A spiritual song may be given to you during your time of private worship or spontaneously during public worship. Any spiritual song or verse may become the root of inspiration for composed music and words to be used for all to sing during congregational gatherings.[64] Sing to the Lord a new song! This is a song that is fresh and new, often spontaneous — a precious gift of the Holy Spirit (Psalm 33:3, 40:3, 96:1, 98:1-2, 144:9, Isaiah 42:10). "While the king was at his table, my perfume spread its fragrance" (Song of Songs 1:12). Spiritual songs are a sweet smelling fragrance offered to the Lord, for the sake of His Holy Name — to glorify Him in the congregation.

What is the nature of spiritual songs? They may be pensive, repentant, meditative, reflective, possibly a whisper, reserved, reverent, joyful, exuberant, jubilant, and at times accompanied with

---

[64] When the Holy Spirit inspires a message in tongues, prophecy, or spiritual song, the person ministering in these gifts must wait until they are recognized by the pastor or elders and offered the opportunity to minister to the Church.

shouts. They may be sung in a language you know or in a spiritual or foreign language you have not learned. They may burst forth (at the will of the singer). "Shout for joy to the Lord, all the earth, burst into jubilant song with music" (Psalm 98:4). Even though the person ministering in this gift controls the time, place, and manner in which the song is offered, it may well feel like a bursting forth when you minister in spiritual song. It may well feel as if you've uncorked a champagne bottle.

From the second Great Awakening that began in Kentucky, we get a good description of spiritual song from the Cane Ridge camp meeting:

> *"The most unaccountable — and moving — to chief preacher Barton Stone was the 'singing exercise.' With a sublime countenance, the individual 'would sing most melodiously, not from the mouth or nose, but entirely in the breast, the sounds issuing thence... It was most heavenly. None could ever be tired of hearing it."*[65]

The American church loves its music, its professional musicians, and enjoys cultured and skillfully composed music. We delight in singing to our hearts content, singing praise songs, "I love you, Lord. And lift my voice to worship you." We sing together, clapping our hands and raising our hands, but at times it becomes a self-gratifying exercise in soulish entertainment that focuses on "I." The Sunday morning music is too often planned to please the people rather than God (Galatians 1:10). It is rooted in the natural man and not flowing out from our spirit, inspired in the Spirit. We even sing our hymns, delighting in the excellent four-part harmony sung by the choir. We may even imagine ourselves to be like David, the author of so many Psalms. "You strum away on your harps like David and improvise on musical instruments" (Amos 6:5). But if our song service becomes a soulish, self-centered observance, we're skating on thin ice. "Our holy and glorious temple, where our ancestors praised you, has been burned with fire, and all that we treasured lies in ruins" (Isaiah 64:11).

---

[65] Peter Marshall/David Manuel. *From Sea to Shining Sea.*

The proof of our folly is that we do not live out the words we sing on Sunday morning. We sing the verses projected on the screen, we harmonize with the musicians or the choir, we sway to the beat of the drums — and we love it. (It doesn't occur to us that we raised our hands, sang to the beat and danced to the music on Saturday night also. But we were dancing to "Don't Stop the Music," and getting crazy with a couple margaritas at Club Wild Thing.)

My heart is grieved about the great spiritual poverty in the church today. The living, present words of Scripture call us to repent and turn from our soulish, self-gratifying, music loving, and churchy singing ways; for if we do not, God will desecrate His sanctuary (Ezekiel 24:21).

Because there is so much misunderstanding, misinformation, and fear of the utterance gifts among Christians of many denominations, there is a need to spend extra time on these gifts, including tongues, interpretation of tongues, prophecy and singing in the Spirit.

For a reason I don't completely understand, when the Holy Spirit moves on someone, it affects his or her mouth. "As for me, this is my covenant with them," says the Lord. " 'My Spirit, who is on you, and my words that I have put in your **mouth** will not depart from your **mouth**, or from the **mouths** of your children, or from the **mouths** of their descendants from this time on and forever,' says the Lord" (Isaiah 59:21, emphasis added). The best explanation is this Scripture: "For out of the overflow of the heart the mouth speaks" (Matthew 12:34). When the Holy Spirit fills your heart to overflowing, the overflow comes out of your mouth — it is proof of what is in your heart. When there is evil overflowing from a heart, it will overflow and come out of the mouth in foul language, gossip, running people down, and the ugly list goes on and on.

Let's look at some examples. After Samuel anointed Saul to be king of Israel, the Spirit of the Lord came on him and he prophesied. "The Spirit of the Lord will come upon you in power, and you will prophesy with them; and you will be changed into a different person" (1 Samuel 10:6). Again in v 10, "the Spirit of God came upon him in power, and [Saul] joined in their prophesying."

Luke recorded the song of Zechariah as he sang in the Spirit after the birth of his son John: "His father Zechariah was filled with the

Holy Spirit and prophesied: Praise be to the Lord, the God of Israel, because he has come and has redeemed his people" (Luke 1:67). Another instance of this gift occurred in Paul's ministry: "When Paul placed his hands on them, the Holy Spirit came on them, and they spoke in tongues and prophesied. There were about twelve men in all" (Acts 19:6).

A Lament

How long, O Lord, before we lift pure hearts in song before You?
Raise my voice, rejoicing? I cannot. For Your house lies in ruins.
The music is trapped deep within me, held captive by grief.
My song blows away like dry and parched desert sands.
The chord to be struck is not heard, as if
falling on ears without hearing.
My heart is steeled against uniting in
harmonious song, its part left unsung.
I remember songs of joy we would sing,
but now they are barred away.
My soul cries out for the solace of a violin — strings lie broken.
Songs of the congregation have no voice, for
they are scattered to the four winds.
Silence, silence, silence rings like a crashing
gong, a warning in my ears.
Famine, dearth, and depravation scoff at the stillness.
A prison, a cell, bars of iron, the music locked away.
Yet into the darkness of night a glint of light pierces the horizon.

Our prayer: *"Holy Spirit, overflow from our hearts and cause our mouths to speak words of encouragement, words like refreshing water, strengthening and healing to your people, for the sake of your Holy Name."*

Service Gifts

Hospitality: Those blessed with the gift of hospitality bring people into a warm and friendly church or home, joining them with other

Christians in fellowship and helping them gain a sense of belonging together in Christ. Offering food and warm acceptance for people to partake together in the Lord's presence is a precious, powerful, and underestimated gift. When we invite people to gather around our table we are creating a strong bond of Christian fellowship that is of eternal value. We are opening the door to the kingdom of heaven and the Lord's bountiful banqueting table.

Generosity: A man or woman with this gift has a heart to share the blessings that God has given them for the good of the church and God's kingdom. Their giving is at times sacrificial, out of lack, and at other times overflowing from abundance that God pours out unto them (Romans 12:7). The purpose and result is of eternal effect. We are all called to give from what we have gained and to do so with gladness, imparting what God has given to us in an open hand rather than a tight closed fist. But there are those who the Holy Spirit gives a special gift of generosity, and they are blessed to be cheerfully willing and able to do so. Scripture tells us that "we are not our own," and this includes our wallets and bank accounts. "See that you also excel in this grace of giving" (2 Corinthians 8:7). Those who minister in this special gift are blessed indeed.

Caregiver: Ministering in the name and authority of Jesus to those among us who are in need, infirm, weak, or helpless. The purpose in this gift is not only to satisfy immediate temporal needs, but to fulfill an eternal purpose — for an eternal good. This gift is a fountain of blessing to all who are touched by the ministries of a caregiver.

Administration: The person operating in this gift has the ability to organize and facilitate the efficient working of a supporting church office and staff with an eternal perspective (Romans 12:7).

Leading Others to Worship Together: A gifted worship leader will instruct and lead worshipers into a reverential realm to participate in all forms of true and real worship (Hebrews 12:28-29). Unlike spiritual songs that are spontaneously inspired, this spiritual gift brings a gathering of believers together, in unity, in unison, and in melodious harmony as the body of Christ. By means of this gift we are joined together in anthems of worship.

Whether the congregation sings Psalms, hymns, spiritual songs, acts of reverence accompanied with music, praise, adoration, proclamations of God's Word in song, exalting Christ, singing, poetic expressions of praise to our God, or offering up a sacrifice in songs of praise, this is the ministry of leading in group worship (Romans 12:1, Ephesians 5:19, Colossians 3:16). While this gift is not an office in the church, it can become a formal leadership position. Every gathering of believers is enhanced when this gifts is active among them.

A worship leader will find the gift of spiritual discernment useful to know when a congregation's worship is distracted by a "root of bitterness" (Hebrews 12:15), sin, or dissention within a local body of believers.

Music is an integral part of worship and will be for all eternity. It is a powerful means of proclaiming the Good News. This Scripture speaks beautifully of this form of worship.

> *"Sing to the Lord a new song, for he has done marvelous things; his right hand and his holy arm have worked salvation for him. The Lord has made his salvation known and revealed his righteousness to the nations. He has remembered his love and his faithfulness to the house of Israel; all the ends of the earth have seen the salvation of our God." (Psalm 98:1-7)*

A worship leader's purpose is to lead those gathered to glorify God in His Holiness and Majesty, because of who He is, and because He has done wonderful things for us.

Nehemiah 8:9-12 gives us a beautiful picture of people moved by God's Word to worship. The book of the Law of God was read to the people, and as they were instructed they began to mourn and weep because of their sin. But with the encouragement of the priests, their mourning turned to great joy and celebration. This is the gifting and ministry of worship leaders in the church (Also study: Psalm 28:2, 1 Timothy 2:8, Ezra 9:5, Psalm 141:2).

All gifts given by the Holy Spirit, in addition to building and strengthening the church, are witnesses of Christ's living, ever present saving grace at work among His people — a testimony of the power of His Holy Name. To do the work of the Great Commission by human strength alone limits the powerful effect of our testimony. Certainly, living exemplary lives and telling what God has done in for us is an important part of our witness of Christ, but we ought to be fully prepared by the gifting and empowering work of the Holy Spirit to minister the power of the resurrected Christ. Add to this a servant's heart, a willingness to be God's instrument to demonstrate the saving power of our Savior Jesus Christ by ministering in the authority of His Holy Name and through the power of His Holy Spirit, according to the gifts He has given for the strengthening of His church.

Together in community, as one in Christ, we the church will reveal Christ in every tribe, nation, people, and tongue. To accomplish this great purpose, we must be gifted and empowered in the Holy Spirit.

> *"Very truly I tell you, whoever believes in me will do the works I have been doing, and they will do even greater things than these, because I am going to the Father. And I will do whatever you ask in my name, so that the Father may be glorified in the Son. You may ask me for anything in my name, and I will do it." (John 14:12-14)*

NOTE: There are many more gifts of the Spirit at work in the church today than those listed in this chapter — too many to list. One that may be worth exploring is the gift of exorcisms. The need for this gift in our day and in this culture is desperately underestimated, but it is not a topic that is a part of my understanding.

YOUR JOURNEY JOURNAL
Chapter 7: Kingdom Treasures in Spiritual Gifts

1. What are the five "offices" given to the church.

2. Give examples of various spiritual gifts and their purpose.

3. How do you know what gift you will receive?

4. Why is it that when the Holy Spirit is poured into a person, the mouth is often affected?

Your Journal Notes:

BOOK TWO

Ministries of Spiritual Gifts

1

God's Power Revealed in Weakness

All Christians are called to minister and serve with spiritual gifts and function as a working part among the many parts that make up the church body. This working organism is referred to as the priesthood of the believers (1 Peter 2:5). The great challenge is this: there are no perfect parts (individuals) in this priesthood; yet as imperfect as we are, all of us are called to ministries of spiritual gifts. It's a beautiful, reassuring truth that God uses imperfect people to fulfill His perfect plan, because He is faithful even when we are not. He is faithful because He is a God of covenants, fulfilling all He has purposed and planned for His church. Never fear that God cannot or will not use you until you have overcome everything in your life — it's just not true.

Even though we are weak and imperfect, our aim should be to live a life of delighted personal obedience. When we fail, as all of us will, our hearts grieve over our sin and sinfulness and our hearts will turn from the sin, confessing our sin and receiving forgiveness. A repentant heart prepares us for service and ministries in the gifts of the Spirit. We are confident that God will use whom He will use; but a repentant and forgiven servant is most useful. God has made His covenant with weak and imperfect people to fulfill His perfect plan; this is the topic of this chapter. God's purpose is to manifest His power in weak, fallible people so that there can be no doubt that what He accomplished through our flawed vessels is by His hand, by His might and power.

Flawed Heroes of Faith

Jonah is a good example of a flawed vessel that God chose to use. He ran away from God and finally repented in the belly of a whale. Then God made the whale spit Jonah onto the beach and God sent him on his way to Nineveh to preach God's message to the people. Hebrews chapter eleven is a great history of the heroes of faith. As you study their lives, you'll find they had great failings. When God chooses to use weak and sinful people we find a great paradox as Christ's authority is manifested in fallible vessels. Read Noah's life story and you'll see a fallible man who acted in obedience and built an ark of cypress wood. Moses was prideful, doubtful, reluctant, but he obeyed God, delivering Israel out of slavery in Egypt. Abram had a habit of telling self-protective lies, telling people his wife Sarah was his sister (Genesis 20:2); but he obeyed God and uprooted his family and traveled to a "land I will show you." Joshua was stuck with human weaknesses like all of us, yet he obeyed, calling the people to march around Jericho. Daniel was a prisoner of war from a nation that fell away from God, but he obeyed, honoring God's law even as he was brought to a foreign land. For these giants of faith, their trust and love for God drove them to confess sin, turn from their sin, and delight in obedience. Flawed and sinful as they were, God chose to use them. "All who cleanse themselves of the things I have mentioned will become special utensils, dedicated and useful to the owner of the house, ready for every good work" (2 Timothy 2:21 NRSV).

How is it that God can take flawed, fallible people and make them into clean, useful ambassadors of His eternal kingdom? This is what is referred to as the "effects of righteousness," i.e. the effects of the righteousness of Jesus Christ at work in weak vessels. In fact, God's power is manifested in our weakness. We were like wild olive shoots grafted into the true olive tree to bear good fruit. The true olive tree feeds the wild olive branch, changing it inside and out, producing good fruit where useless fruit once grew (Romans 11:17-24).

The Effect of Righteousness

James adds the balance we need to understand the effect of righteousness that comes from being grafted into the true tree: "You see that a person is justified by what he does and not by faith alone" (James 2:24). (He is not saying that deeds justify you apart from faith.) Isaiah the prophet teaches how righteousness affects you: "And the effect of righteousness will be peace, and the result of righteousness, quietness and trust forever" (Isaiah 32:17). The apostle Paul speaks of this truth as well: "obedience accompanies your confession of the gospel of Christ" (2 Corinthians 9:13). Paul isn't saying you must, on your own, be obedient. Obedience is the effect of the righteousness of Jesus Christ at work in you. In Romans 6:17 Paul refers to the effect of righteousness as being "obedient from the heart." True faith in Jesus Christ yields good fruit by means of spiritual gifts that the Holy Spirit gives to you and empowers in you.

The challenge with the service and ministries of spiritual gifts is that there are no sinless people in the church, and Christians are not self-cleaning. We are washed clean by the blood of the Lamb. We are washed in the cleansing waters of baptism, we are made holy in the Holy Spirit's fire, and we need to be continuously cleaned, purified, and washed in God's Holy Word. Our cleansing comes by means of being convicted of our sin and sinfulness, confessing our sin, having a contrite heart and receiving God's forgiveness and mercy. Now, imperfect as you are, you are made into a useful person in God's kingdom.

Yet serving Christ is so much better than just being useful, for God gives us a robe of His making. "Fine linen, bright and clean, was given her to wear" (Revelations 19:8). (Fine linen stands for the righteous acts of the saints.) Even our own "acts" are only possible because of the righteousness of Jesus Christ at work in us. Christ's righteousness effects righteousness in us and makes it possible to serve under the authority of Jesus and by the power, anointing, and gifts given by the Holy Spirit. Christ's righteousness is not a cover-up, but effectively works through us like yeast in the dough, changing our hearts and minds.

When you, by faith, are justified by His eternal grace, He will supernaturally produce good deeds in you, that is, fruit for the kingdom of God, according to His righteousness and by the means of the gifts the Holy Spirit empowered in you. When you are grafted into the "True Vine" and feed on the "True Vine"[66] you will supernaturally produce the fruit of the "True Vine."

> By the grace God has given me, I laid a foundation as a wise builder, and someone else is building on it. But each one should build with care. For no one can lay any foundation other than the one already laid, which is Jesus Christ. If anyone builds on this foundation using gold, silver, costly stones, wood, hay or straw, their work will be shown for what it is, because the Day will bring it to light. It will be revealed with fire, and the fire will test the quality of each person's work. If what has been built survives, the builder will receive a reward. If it is burned up, the builder will suffer loss but yet will be saved — even though only as one escaping through the flames. (1 Corinthians 3:10-15)

The Beauty of Spiritual Gifts

Spiritual and natural gifts are as dissimilar as Wisdom from above and earthbound wisdom. Wisdom that has its roots in this natural realm alone, flowing out of earthly principles, acting upon human motives and depending upon human reasoning, is only good for serving temporal purposes. It is humanistic and is easily conceived in darkness. Wisdom that is from the Spirit is peace loving. Peace and purity walk arm in arm in the path of godly wisdom. "Love and faithfulness meet together; righteousness and peace kiss each other" (Psalm 85:10). The fruit of wisdom is gentleness; it is selfless, encouraging, impartial, and

---

[66] For Christians it is possible to be attached to the "True Vine" and be a dead branch. You must feed, draw life, and draw strength from the "True Vine" where you are grafted.

teachable. What is sown through godly wisdom will reap a harvest of eternal joy. So it is with the Holy Spirit's spiritual gifts.

Jeremiah asks, "Can a man bear children?" The obvious answer is "no." Men can't bear children, and the natural man cannot produce good fruit apart from Christ. In the same way, in the use of natural gifts we cannot bring about what is eternal and spiritual.

We must also consider the Song of Songs, where we see a picture of the bride of Christ adorned with spiritual adornments, gifts from the Bridegroom. "Your cheeks are beautiful with earrings, your neck with strings of jewels. We will make you earrings of gold, studded with silver" (Song of Songs 1:10-11). Receive the precious gifts of the Bridegroom "as a bride adorns herself with her jewels" (Isaiah 61:10).

When you are adorned with God's special gifts and empowered through His Holy Spirit, you are most beautiful in His sight, a magnificent bride made ready for the Bridegroom who is preparing a place for His bride to dwell with Him for all eternity.[67] We must not respond with indifference to the Bridegroom as did the beloved who hesitated to open the door for her love, saying, "I have washed my feet — must I soil them again?" (Song of Songs 5:2-6).

When you desire the "adornments" of the Holy Spirit for the strengthening of the bride of Christ — ASK — and it will be given you. Remember this truth: "Which of you fathers, if your son asks for a fish, will give him a snake instead?" (Luke 11:11).

An Imperfect Church

After careful study and interpretation of all Scriptures related to spiritual gifts, it is clear that we have a long way to get back to what God desires for us. Throughout church history change has come with great turmoil. Can the established church go forward to embrace all spiritual gifts? Will the traditional church encourage spiritual gifts to be manifested in their gatherings within God's established order,

---

[67] It is easy to imagine our names engraved on pure white stones, set above the doorposts of the room he has prepared for each of us to dwell with Him for all eternity (Rev. 2:17).

under the authority of Jesus Christ and by the empowering work of the Holy Spirit? History tells us that great change comes after major conflict. But with God, all things are possible.

As I'm teaching about spiritual gifts, I feel like a travel agent passing out colorful flyers to places I've never been. There are few churches, if any, who accept all that God has for them. No church or denomination has it all together, because the church is made up of flawed, fallible people. And yet, God is faithful to His Word. He will accomplish all that He has said, even through imperfect people who are part of an imperfect congregation.

Our prayer: *"Lord, level the mountains, fill the valleys, straighten out the crooked places, and smooth out the rough spots in the road to make straight the way of the Lord"* (Isaiah 40:3-4).

Many churches and denominations have begun well "in the Spirit," with an out flowing of the gifts of the Spirit, but have fallen back into doing the work of the Church by the strength and power of the flesh rather than by the strength and power of the Holy Spirit. Paul admonished the Galatians because they began in the Spirit and then tried to "attain their goal" (salvation) by human effort (Galatians 3:3). Most of today's churches have a clear understanding that salvation is by faith and not by works, but we have so easily given up the work of serving and ministering in the Spirit and have slipped into serving in the strength of the flesh. God made this truth clear through the prophet Zechariah: "So he said to me, 'This is the word of the Lord to Zerubbabel: "Not by might nor by power, but by my Spirit," says the Lord Almighty'" (Zechariah 4:6). A paraphrase applicable to the use of spiritual gifts in the Church would be like this: *The work of the Church is not accomplished by human might or power, but by the empowering work of the Holy Spirit through fallible people.*

We serve a God of covenants

Key to our understanding of spiritual gifts at work in weak vessels and their importance to the Christian church is knowledge of the nature of God. He is a God of covenants. God's relationship with those created in

His image is defined by His covenant promises. But what is a covenant? How is it defined? Covenants are unalterable promises, given by God between Creator and created man, that lay down relational provisions.

Most studies of God's covenants with man correctly cover 1) The Covenant of works, first given to Adam and Eve in Genesis 1:28-30 and Genesis 2:15-17; 2) The Covenant of Redemption (Psalm 2 and 110, Isaiah 53, Philippians 2:5-11); and 3) The Covenant of Grace (Ephesians 2:11-12, Hebrews 12:24). These covenants are vital to our understanding of God and our relationship with Him. Covenants are foundational knowledge for grasping the reason and purpose for spiritual gifts.

As we study God's covenants from the very beginning of time, we get a clear picture of how spiritual gifts fit into God's Covenant of Grace. God made covenants with Adam and, through Adam, gave mankind responsibility to "rule over the fish of the sea and the birds of the air, over the livestock, over all the earth, and over all the creatures that move along the ground" (Genesis 1:26). God gave Adam, and those who would come after him, a job to do. Could God have managed the fish, birds, and livestock on His own? Absolutely! But He gave this job to Adam, a man God knew would sin, and to all fallible men and women who would come after. Why? Because this is God's nature to involve His people in His work.

In the beginning God established covenants with mankind: "God blessed them and said to them, 'Be fruitful and increase in number; fill the earth and subdue it.'" Could God have subdued[68] the earth without the help of mankind? Absolutely! Why would God give an earth in need of being subdued to mankind, who were formed out of the dust of the ground? Could God have filled the earth with people apart from Adam and Eve, establishing nations and kingdoms to subdue the earth? No doubt about it! But God gave this job to those He made in His image, to men and women He knew would fall.

God continues making covenants with man all the way through to the book of Revelation. Start turning the pages in your Bible and take a little tour to see for yourself. God covenanted with Adam, Cain (Genesis 4:15), Noah, Abraham, Isaac, Jacob, Moses and the people of

---

[68] כָּבַשׁ *kabash,* to subject, subdue, force, keep under, bring into bondage.

Israel, Joshua and all tribes of Israel (Deuteronomy 28 & 29), Samuel, King Saul, King David and his lineage, King Solomon, Isaiah, Jeremiah, Ezekiel, Daniel, Mary and many more of his prophets and servants.

Where does this lead us? Our Lord Jesus Christ, before He ascended to heaven gave us, flawed, mortal, fallible people, a Great Commission, a work to do — a mission. And He also promised, by the authority given to Him, to give us the power to do all that He requires of us. This is an irrevocable promise, an unbreakable covenant given to weak people. There is no doubt about it. "But to each one of us grace has been given as Christ apportioned it. This is why it says: 'When he ascended on high, he led captives in his train and gave gifts to men'" (Ephesians 4:7-8). By the means of grace, through His Holy Spirit, Jesus gives good gifts to His own and empowers those gifts for works of service to build His church. We are the "body of Christ." Indeed, your hand with the hangnails, the chipped fingernail polish, and the aged, bent fingers is the very hand of Christ extended into a dark and dying world. We are not our own, but were bought at a price (1 Corinthians 6:20).

God is faithful even when we are not. God has chosen to spread his kingdom throughout earth through His people, our prayers, our work, and our ministries. He gives good gifts to His people and empowers those gifts in them so His work may be accomplished. Remember what Isaiah prophecies: "Your descendants will dispossess nations and settle in their desolate cities" (Isaiah 54:2). We often misunderstand this, expecting God to go solo to do His good work when He has given us a trust to accomplish all that He desires — the expansion of His kingdom in the age of the church, one person, one soul at a time.

The Powerful Witness of Spiritual Gifts in Flawed People

When spiritual gifts are evident, they give witness to the living, active presence of God the Holy Spirit at work in the church. We should earnestly pray for the day we hear the lost souls in our churches cry out, "What shall we do?" (Acts 2:37). May we yearn to hear people in our worship services exclaim, "God is really among you" (1 Corinthians 14:25). The time has come for the church to stop trying to be strong by means of their God given natural gifts. We must stop burying these precious gifts of the Spirit because of fear and step out in faith to do what our Lord Jesus commissioned and will certainly empower us to do (Matthew 25:25, Romans 8:15).

We must not despair in our weak and sinful state for we have the greatest of all hope. Our God is the God of new beginnings. Surely He invented the phrase, "turning over a new leaf." He is God of grace and mercy. He is God who freely forgives sinners who turn from their sin and repent. He is the God who restores (Joel 2:25). He is God who is faithful to all He has purposed and planned to do through weak and frail people.

Why are the gifts of the Spirit of such importance in today's church? Why is this important to God's people right now? Look at it in this light. Jesus is God manifested in the flesh. He walked among us and revealed the very nature of God. He said, "If you really knew me, you would know my Father as well. From now on, you do know him and have seen him" (John 14:7). How did Jesus reveal the Father? By everything He said and did. He taught with authority. He forgave sins. He healed people — body, soul, and spirit. He showed compassion and mercy to the weak. He fed the hungry. He raised the dead.

Our Lord Jesus, before He ascended to the right hand of the Father, promised us the Holy Spirit. The Spirit of Jesus is TODAY, in this church age, the manifestation of God in all the earth. The Holy Spirit dwells in His temple, God's fallible people, and through us reveals the Father and the Son to all mankind. TODAY!

It's worth repeating until we absorb this into our heart of hearts. Where does the Holy Spirit dwell today? He dwells in His temple. He indwells spirit, soul, and body of each and every Christian, weak as we are. "Do you not know that your body is a temple of the Holy Spirit, who is in you, whom you have received from God? You are not your own; you were bought at a price. Therefore honor God with your body" (1 Corinthians 6:19-20). The Holy Spirit dwells in the redeemed, in those who are called by His name. Therefore, it is through us, servants of the Word, that He reveals Himself to the world. It is through us that He gives witness, solid proof that the truth of the Word is proclaimed and His kingdom advances. This happens one soul at a time until His Name is glorified in every tribe, nation, people and tongue. It is through us that He feeds the hungry — body, soul, and spirit. It is through us that He strengthens the weak. It is through us that He ministers His Word and promises to His people. It is through us that He pushes back the darkness to spread the light of the gospel throughout every island and nation. It is through us that He will become the desire of every nation. "Peace be with you! As the Father has sent me, I am sending you" (John 20:21). We are the conduits for His healing touch.

We are being called to repent of our self-satisfied forms of godliness. We must grieve over our futile attempts to reduce the power of our Lord Jesus Christ, who is seated at the right hand of God the Father Almighty in His position of power and authority. His desire is to empower His people who are powerless vessels on their own, to be His hand extended to invite all who will come to His bountiful banqueting table.

Too often the church has attempted to reduce God's power to the level of our own powerless condition by elevating our God-given natural gifts to the level of spiritual gifts and attempting to fulfill the Great Commission by the use of human might and natural power. We must clearly understand that the kingdom of God is not advanced by human might and natural strength, but by the power of the Holy Spirit, ministered under the authority of Christ through flawed and fallible Christians.

Will you refuse? Are you satisfied where you are? Do the comforts of the status quo and the safety of your religious paradigm keep you from going forward? Does your knowledge prevent you from receiving? Do you look at His precious gifts and disregard them, because you just don't see the value? Will you be like the children of Israel? "Then they despised the pleasant land, having no faith in his promise. They grumbled in their tents, and did not obey the voice of the Lord" (Psalm 106:24-25).

We, the bride of Christ, are given spiritual gifts by the power of the Holy Spirit so that we may do the work of the kingdom, in the Spirit's power; and in doing this work, we reveal the heart of God to a lost and dying world. Jesus' message to us was this: "Wait for the gift my Father promised... You will receive power when the Holy Spirit comes on you; and you will be my witnesses in Jerusalem, and in all Judea and Samaria, and to the ends of the earth" (Acts 1:4, 8). The days are few. We must be about His business, but first we must wait and receive. Abraham waited for the birth of his promised son, Isaac. Moses waited until he was eighty years old before leading the Exodus of God's people. Noah prophesied for many years before rain finally fell in torrents on the earth and the deep waters gushed out just as God had warned.

- **WAIT** ON THE LORD.
- **RECEIVE** POWER BY THE HOLY SPIRIT.
- **GO** INTO ALL THE EARTH!

Our prayer: *"Lord God. So often we are like a man who is engaged to the love of his life and during this season of their lives he knows of her — he knows about her. But until they are wed, he does not truly know her. Help us to know You, live in You and walk according to Your Word that You have taught us."*

As Christians minister in their Holy Spirit-empowered spiritual gifts, they advance the kingdom of heaven in the battle against the kingdom of darkness. "Rise up, O Lord! May your enemies be scattered; may your foes flee before you" (Numbers 10:35; see also Isaiah 54:2-3). The longer the established church and denominations resist the present work of the Holy Spirit, the greater the power of the breakout will be — just as a stream that is barred in its course bursts out in a flood. "For he will come like a pent-up flood that the breath of the LORD drives along" (Isaiah 59:19).

The great words of the hymn "Onward Christian Soldiers"[69] are so applicable to those who are at the forefront of God's advancing kingdom.

1. Onward, Christian soldiers, marching as to war,
   with the cross of Jesus going on before.
   Christ, the royal Master, leads against the foe;
   forward into battle see his banners go!

---

[69] Sabine Baring-Gould. "Onward Christian Soldiers," 1865.

Refrain: Onward, Christian soldiers, marching as to war,
with the cross of Jesus going on before.

2. At the sign of triumph Satan's host doth flee;
   on then, Christian soldiers, on to victory!
   Hell's foundations quiver at the shout of praise;
   brothers, lift your voices, loud your anthems raise.

3. Like a mighty army moves the church of God;
   brothers, we are treading where the saints have trod.
   We are not divided, all one body we,
   one in hope and doctrine, one in charity.

4. Crowns and thrones may perish, kingdoms rise and wane,
   but the church of Jesus constant will remain.
   Gates of hell can never against that church prevail;
   we have Christ's own promise, and that cannot fail.

5. Onward then, ye people, join our happy throng,
   blend with ours your voices in the triumph song.
   Glory, laud, and honor unto Christ the King,
   this through countless ages men and angels sing.

YOUR JOURNEY JOURNAL
Chapter 1: God's Power Revealed in Weakness

1. How is it possible for a weak, fallible person to minister effectively in a spiritual gift?

2. On what foundation will you build?

3. Describe a covenant between God and man.

Your Journal Notes:

2

The Temple of Worship

Part 1: Our Challenge

From the tender age of five, I would stand up on the pew next to my mom while everyone was singing. With my mouth wide open, I belted out my best tune — the louder the better. The words were of no consequence to me and the melody was immaterial. I would sing out loud, even after everyone else stopped and sat down. I've always loved times of praise and worship in song; but through the years I've come to realize something was missing. Over time, God's Word enlightened me, and the Father's call for His people to worship Him in spirit and truth came alive.

At times when I've gathered with other Christians for times of praise, I've had to confront a natural bent toward singing only with my mind, using my natural gift alone. To worship only with the mind is a limitation that is all too common among God's people, and an act of worship too often devolves into a people pleasing exercise. The prophet Jeremiah confronted this human weakness in his time (Jeremiah 2:13). The apostle Paul admonished the Galatian church on the issue of people pleasing: "If I were still trying to please people, I would not be a servant of Christ" (Galatians 1:10). He repeats this warning in Galatians 3:10: "Are you so foolish? After beginning by means of the Spirit, are you now trying to finish by means of the flesh?" The words of Jeremiah and Paul are also a cutting indictment of Christians today. We have forsaken God's precious gifts for worshipping Him, and have chiseled into stone ways to worship only with our minds. And too often we have defaulted to soulish, humanistic means of worship and refuse the greater blessings.

To apply the prophecy of Jeremiah to the modern day church, allow me to paraphrase it like this: "The bride of Christ (the church) has committed two sins: Forsaking the precious gifts, given for worshipping a Holy God, we instead worship in our own way — by human means. And when we worship by man-made means alone, it doesn't hold water." God holds out a great blessing to His people, to all who will turn their hearts to the fullness of heaven-inspired true and real worship. In this chapter, we will first discuss the challenges of spiritual worship that wells up from within our hearts and souls. Then we'll learn of the awesome, worshipful blessings of spiritual and real worship, by using the design of God's temple of worship as a pattern.[70] In this journey through the temple we will come to see that spiritual gifts are given to the church for the purpose of worship, true worship that reveals the living, active presence of our Lord Jesus.

The value of spiritual and real worship

Why is spiritual and real worship a great treasure of the church? Why is our understanding of worship central, foundational, and at the very core of who we are as the bride of Christ? We must begin at the beginning of time to see the answer.

Our prayer: *Lord, open our eyes to see Your beauty and awaken our ears to hear Your songs of worship.*

Recall for a moment the two trees in the Garden of Eden: the Tree of Life and the Tree of the Knowledge of Good and Evil. When Adam and Eve walked with God in obedience to His command, the center of their attention was directed toward the Tree of Life. Every pathway they walked in the garden would lead them to the Tree of Life. But eventually, they desired what was pleasing to the natural eye. They worshipped another. Their desire turned to what was self-satisfying.

---

[70] Moses was commanded to build a holy tabernacle, a copy of the heavenly temple. Ezekiel was given a vision of the temple. Israel's temple was rebuilt using this pattern and stood on the Temple Mount in Jerusalem during the Second Temple period, between 516 BC and 70 AD.

Who was in the Garden of Eden to distract Adam and Eve from the right path?

> *"You were the model of perfection, full of wisdom and perfect in beauty. You were in Eden, the garden of God; every precious stone adorned you: ruby, topaz and emerald, chrysolite, onyx and jasper, sapphire, turquoise and beryl. Your settings and mountings [71] [tabrets in KJV] were made of gold; on the day you were created they were prepared. You were anointed as a guardian cherub, for so I ordained you. You were on the holy mount of God; you walked among the fiery stones. You were blameless in your ways from the day you were created till wickedness was found in you." (Ezekiel 28:12-15, KJV note added)*

We see here a description of the beauty and decorum given to the created angel Lucifer who was appointed as the angel of worship — to lead the angels and those created in God's image to worship their Creator. He was given tabrets of worship (v. 13 above).[72]

Lucifer was guardian of heaven's treasures to be used for worship, the golden articles and precious gemstones of worship. He was created to be like the morning star (Isaiah 14:12, Job 38:7), but he coveted worship for himself. He desired for God's created beings to be subject to him and to worship him alone. He coveted the adoration that belonged only to the triune God. Rather than leading Adam and Eve into true worship and offering them the precious Kingdom treasures for worship, he held back what was entrusted to him, keeping them as his own. He attempted to subvert God's perfect plan.

Jeremiah 31:4 teaches us that the purpose of tabrets in the temple of worship was to build up God's people in worship, and in this there was great joy. The tabrets (mountings) were used to make the priest's

---

[71] Tabrets: תֹּף *toph*; instruments of worship: Exodus 15:20. The hollow or mounting in which a gem is set; as in Ezekiel 28:13. Hebrew word also means "signet" which is a sign of conferred authority.

[72] The Hebrew word תֹּף, *toph* is translated "tabrets" (KJV), and in context, means "settings" or "mountings" (adornments) for worship.

vestments of worship as we see in Exodus 28:2-4. The tabrets were used to set the precious gems in the priest's breastplate as is shown in Exodus 28:17.[73]

The gold filigree, the settings in precious metal, the finely woven breastplate and the priceless stones were all preparations and adornments necessary for the priest to enter the temple sanctuary of God for worship. The tabrets were given as a signet, a symbol of priestly authority to lead God's people in all the ordained elements of worship to exalt a Holy God. They were representations of real articles of worship in heaven (Revelation 21:14-27).

We must not emulate what became of Old Testament temple worship, repeating what the prophets called "the noise of your harps" (Isaiah 14:11). We must avoid becoming like the tribes of Israel with meaningless worship ornaments "jingling on their ankles" (Isaiah 3:16). God's chosen people were using God's ornaments of worship to entice other so-called gods. Malachi laments, "Oh, that one of you would shut the temple doors, so that you would not light useless fires on my altar!" (Malachi 1:10). The church is now charged with the safe keeping of the gifts of the Spirit, i.e. treasures or tabrets of the kingdom of heaven, and we must not desire them to exalt ourselves or we will become nothing but noisemakers.

But we are called to repentance for our self-centered, soulish worship. We are called to be a people set apart to worship a holy God. With contrite hearts, we will be restored to true worship, taking up spiritual instruments for exalting God, and we will worship in spirit and in truth. The Holy Spirit will once again give the church spiritual gifts for genuine worship. It becomes clear as I examine the Scriptures presented in this chapter that spiritual gifts are likened to precious stones set in gold filigree settings (tabrets), and are the precious instruments or means of true and real worship. Elisha made this truth evident. He knew the power of instruments of worship. "'But get me a musician.' And then, while the musician was playing, the power of the Lord came on him" (2 Kings 3:15). King David understood this great gift. "David and the officers of the army also set apart for

---

[73] Study through the end of Ezekiel chapter 28 to get a complete picture.

the service the sons of Asaph, and of Heman, and of Jeduthun, who should prophesy with lyres, harps, and cymbals" (1 Chronicles 25:1).

The challenge of true worship

Above all, we must confront our weaknesses and enter into this true and real worship adorned with precious gemstones of the kingdom. The greatest obstacle to genuine worship is our humanness — our earth suit. The natural part of us is an important participant as we enter into worship, and at the same time our greatest hindrance. We need our feet to dance before the Lord. We need hands to lift before a Holy God. We need a voice to shout out praises in the presence of God Almighty. We need a body to keep us grounded on earth so we may minister and serve. We need knees to bend as we submit ourselves before our Righteous God, Creator of the ever-expanding universe. But this flesh, our humanness, wants to take over and have power over our worship. Especially of whom we worship. Our dancing feet, our lifted hands, our acts of service, our shouts of praise, our harmonious songs, our bent knees must be subject to our soul, and our soul submitted to our spirit, which must be surrendered to the Holy Spirit who provides the "instruments" to truly worship and enter into the fullness of worship. For our whole being to enter into spiritual worship is a matter of the heart. It is a matter of choosing to put aside what your earth suit demands and take up the true instruments of worship. The temple pattern will teach us and put these instruments in our hands.

Part 2: The Temple of Worship

A worshipful pilgrimage

True worship may be likened to a journey with our hearts set upon a sacred purpose. "Blessed are those whose strength is in you, who have set their hearts on pilgrimage" (Psalm 84:5). Worship is like a trek that begins with setting our hearts on an ascent to the Throne of Grace.

Your earth suit is sure to fight against your spirit as you approach the temple. But trust in God Almighty and you will go from strength to strength with each step you take (Psalm 84:6-7). As you journey through the temple you will ascend the steps and enter each new courtyard of temple worship through gates of righteousness — the righteousness of Christ. As you enter with the congregation and go up into each new courtyard of worship your heart will be compelled anew to confess sin, receive forgiveness and be strengthened in the fullness of fellowship. Your sinful stain will be removed and your faith strengthened. The Holy Spirit will keep you from giving in to our human weaknesses as He guides you in this pilgrimage of worship to enter God's dwelling place. "So I say, walk by the Spirit, and you will not gratify the desires of the flesh" (Galatians 5:16).

With a heart set on a wondrous purpose, embark on this ascent in the temple of worship, entering the gates of the temple with heartfelt thanksgiving. You will ascend into the courtyard with praise and with worshipful spiritual songs, accompanied with instruments of worship. You will step up into the priest's court to serve and minister in the Holy Spirit. You will climb the steps of the temple of worship, and come into the Holy Place to minister before God Almighty, and it is here that you will dwell in God's council.

As you stand at the gate to the temple, the Holy Spirit will prepare you to enter and worship. Put on His breastplate of righteousness ornamented with jewels. Receive His treasures for worship — spiritual gifts — precious treasures of the Kingdom, given to beautify the bride of Christ for worship. These gems are tabrets for the breastplate given as a signet; a sign of authority to minister and serve in acts of worship.

What is true and real worship? How do we ascend in the temple to come into the dwelling of the Almighty, Holy, Righteous Creator of all heaven and earth? We will not come empty-handed, but adorned with precious gifts — true spiritual treasures (Exodus 23:15, 34:20, Deuteronomy 16:16).

The courtyard design of Israel's temple will guide us through the various kinds of worship we offer before God Almighty.

For too long Christians have attempted to worship apart from our spirits that are designed to truly worship. Because of this great failing, we're suffering through a long, hot, drought of soulish (people pleasing) worship. And yet, when we turn from this and repent, our worship will be refreshed. A drought of true worship is a drought of hearing God's Word in preaching, prophecy, spiritual songs, and ministries of numerous gifts of the Spirit. (Amos 8:11). But with hearts refreshed in repentance, we come back to true worship.

Please note that our purpose in looking at Israel's temple is not an attempt to go back to Old Testament worship, but to use the pattern of the temple as a template to illustrate worship in spirit and in truth.

Prepare to enter the temple gates

The temple design we use for illustration includes an outer court for common worship, a sacred enclosure that we will enter with thanksgiving and praise, and a courtyard filled with celebrations and offerings of praise. We will ascend to a priest's court to serve before the altar. We will go up to the sanctuary for high worship and to be prepared for temple ministries. And finally, we will enter God's presence to dwell in His council. By ascending a stairway from level to level, we enter each temple court in turn.[74]

Let's go up to worship before a Holy and Awesome God, and we will worship in various ways as He has ordained. Step through the each level's gates of righteousness and you will find that each court's worshipful service and ministry will bring you into a new manner of worship before God. As we worship, we ascend to enter the various courts that bring us closer and closer to the heart of the Father. God has ordained worship that rises up from the spirit and flows from the whole of man, that is, from body, soul, and spirit. We are a people called to worship in a way that is not possible for those who are separated from a Holy God. But we must first enter through the temple gates.

---

[74] In the Old Testament temple, people were given a place according to nationality (Gentile's court), gender (Women's court), ailment (Leper's court), or by class, whether king, priest or common man (Nazarites' court, Israel or men's court, and priest's court). This is not so with the real temple in heaven (Galatians 3:28).

"Enter his gates with thanksgiving and his courts with praise; give thanks to him and praise his name" (Psalm 100:4).

How ought we to worship our Creator God before whom the angels cry, "Holy, Holy, Holy" (Revelation 4:8)? As we consider this truth we hear the Psalmist calling us to praise and worship: "Shout for joy to the Lord, all the earth. Worship the Lord with gladness; come before him with joyful songs" (Psalm 100:1). The courtyard walls of the temple have a gate called Praise: "No longer will violence be heard in your land, nor ruin or destruction within your borders, but you will call your walls Salvation and your gates Praise" (Isaiah 60:18). Now you must choose. Will you enter the holy temple's gates of righteousness?

The outer courtyard of worship

The Outer Courtyard of the temple is the area for common worship. In the ancient temple, people were permitted to buy and sell with honest scales in this place.[75] The outer courtyard represents the first form of worship that glorifies and honors God: "My mouth will speak in praise of the Lord. Let every creature praise his holy name for ever and ever" (Psalm 145:21). The natural man performs tasks for which God has given him the talent, strength, and resources to accomplish. This work is a form of worship when its purpose is to glorify and honor God, working at our occupations and our trades as if we were working unto the Lord. God is pleased when those whom He created in His image do what He has given them to do by means of His common, natural gifts. We are *all* gifted and bestowed with talents to perform a "work of our hands." Idle hands without work are contrary to the very nature of our Creator God. "May the favor of the Lord our God rest on us; establish the work of our hands for us — yes, establish the work of our hands" (Psalm 90:17).

Psalm 148 declares the praise of our Creator God. Even the creatures of the deep praise the Name of the Lord, "for he commanded and they

---

[75] "But you have made it a 'den of robbers'" (Mark 11:17). In Jesus' day this became a marketplace monopoly for the fleecing of the people.

were created" (verse 5). When deep-sea creatures do what God created them to do, God receives this as an act of praise. When the wild stallion races across the open meadow, hoofs thundering, his tail in the air and his mane blowing in the wind, God is pleased and receives it as an act of praise. God created us and gave each of us natural gifts for the good of all mankind on the earth and for His glory.

The work of our calloused hands is good and excellent in every way when performed as unto the Lord. This is building as if with wood, hay, and stubble (1 Corinthians 3:12). These things are good building material for this present world, but it is not an eternal kind of building. All the work of our human hands, while useful and necessary, comes to a final end.

If God has given you a gift for running: RUN! If you have been given the gift of an excellent voice: SING! If you have been given the gift of skilled craftsmanship: BUILD! If you have been given a gift of leadership: LEAD! If you're a skilled medical practitioner: PRACTICE! Honor God with your natural talent and offer it as a sacrifice before the Lord. This is the worship of the outer courtyard.

The sacred enclosure

Our natural strength fails us as we attempt to ascend to the next courtyard in the temple, because it is here that we enter into the spiritual realm of worship. We must leave behind the toils of this world that we carried into the outer courtyard.[76] Entering this courtyard is only made possible by the cross of our Lord Jesus Christ, on whom we cast all of earth's cares (1 Peter 5:7). As we enter the sacred courtyard, we examine ourselves, confess our sin, and receive the forgiveness and cleansing of our Lord Jesus. We are forgiven and the Spirit of Jesus is like a gentle wind to lift us up in worshipful ascent.

We entered with prayers and songs of thanksgiving. "Open for me the gates of righteousness; I will enter and give thanks to the

---

[76] Jeremiah 17:24 presents a "type" or picture for us to learn spiritual truths for today as we learn from Israel's appointed Sabbath day of rest.

Lord. This is the gate of the Lord through which the righteous may enter. I will give you thanks, for you answered me; you have become my salvation" (Psalm 118:19-20). This is a courtyard for us to present offerings of thanksgiving, petitions, intercessions, and meditations, to cast our cares upon Him, to fast and pray, and to humble ourselves as we prepare ourselves to commune with God. Here we pray with our minds and these prayers are a great treasure before the Lord (1 Corinthians 14:15, Revelation 5:8).

The joy in this courtyard is boundless. "Those who sow with tears will reap with songs of joy. Those who go out weeping, carrying seed to sow, will return with songs of joy, carrying sheaves with them" (Psalm 126:5-6). Entering this courtyard of worship is like a dive into pools of refreshing water. We are given a garment of praise — the heaviness is left behind. We entered corrupted with ashes, and we'll ascend clothed in His beauty. Our hearts may have been in mourning as we entered, but we have been given the Oil of Joy instead. In this place we sense something real and our eyes are opened to see the beauty and majesty of our Lord, which then compels us to press on in worship.

Courtyard of celebration

When we enter this gathering place, a new song stirs in our hearts and it's as if we hear a choir of heaven's angels singing in harmony with us. We recognize the voice of our Lord Jesus, calling us to examine ourselves and come before Him with contrite hearts to worship. As we stepped through this gate, we come ever closer to the council of God. Cleansed and forgiven, we are filled with eager anticipation as we discover a courtyard surrounded by colonnades and filled with worshipers' songs of harmonious celebration. We are blessed to offer our prayers of thanksgiving, alms, and the offerings of stewardship as we enter. We join with the congregation and the singing of Psalm, hymns, choruses, and the reading of Holy Scripture greet our ears. Our toes begin to tap and before long we are in the flow of dancing feet, and hands clapping with the music of instruments.[77] Our hearts are lifted as we join in with applause, shouts of praise, resounding clash of cymbals, hymns being sung, choruses flowing forth, and children joining with instruments of praise.

In this place, we enjoy the freedom of celebrative worship, centering our attentions upon the Light of Life. With a song on our lips, we fall at the feet of our Lord Jesus who says: "For my yoke is easy and my burden is light" (Matthew 11:30). Now a hush comes over us as if we are being made to rest in green pastures beside still waters (Psalm 23). We witness those around us kneeling in awe, heads bowed in reverence, and eyes closed in meditation and prayer. In all of this we are brought together in a harmonious spirit, with orderly songs of worship and praise that take place in this courtyard of celebration.

In this joyful manner we are prepared to ascend the steps into another courtyard of worship. We have raised our voices as a choir, our instruments an orchestra making a joyful noise before our Holy and Righteous God. We stand as a congregation in joyous harmony, with singing and offerings of praise overflowing from our hearts (1 Corinthians 14:15). Adorned in garments of praise we are prepared to step up.

Courtyard of priestly ministry

As we continue up steps of the temple, joy fills our hearts as we walk together arm in arm with our Christian brothers and sisters to pass through a magnificent gate. In the Priest's court we tremble with a splendid terror of our Omnipotent God. "Would not his splendor terrify you?" (Job 13:11).

We examine our hearts once again to see what weighs us down. We are reminded of the need to continually confess before God our

---

[77] Please note: Dancing feet, lifting our hands, clapping our hands and great music are not, of themselves, true worship. But when our soul and spirit are stirred in love, the Holy Spirit compels us to worship in a way that is spiritual and real. The effect may be that our feet will dance, our hands will lift up, and our instruments will declare His praise.

sinful, selfish passions and turn to Christ Jesus to be forgiven and washed clean by means of His sacrificial blood. As we draw near to a Holy God, our sins are more clearly evident, and this is a place for further confronting our sin and confessing. Because we are cleansed and forgiven, a reverent awe comes over us. A delight in obedience to God our Father and Jesus Christ the Son washes over us. In this place of worship we find our hearts reveling in His commands — joyfully steadfast and living in agreement with His Word to serve in gifts of administration, generosity, encouragements, admonishing, gifts of helps, and many other service gifts. We come into worship that is manifested as spiritual and real.[78]

The sanctuary of high worship

Now we are called to pass through a high and lofty gate that ushers us into the Holy Sanctuary. Our hearts are contrite, forgiven, and cleansed. We are wrapped in His robe of righteousness. Here we submit ourselves, again offering our bodies as living sacrifices so that we may minister before God by the empowering work of the Holy Spirit. In this courtyard of worship we wait upon the Lord and prepare ourselves to minister as priests by means of gifts offered to the bride. These gifts are given as tabrets for every part of our priestly worship. The word pictures we are given in the Bible for the effect of the outpouring of the Spirit in this worshipful gathering are beautifully vivid and diverse.

You are shown as being prepared as a bride to receive gifts for the work of ministry for which you have been called to serve in the church. You are being armored up as a mighty warrior to stand fast against the attacks of the enemies of the cross. You are being prepared to humbly serve as a priest before the altar of God. The tender beauty

---

[78] In 1 Corinthians 12:31 the Apostle Paul writes: "Now eagerly desire the greater gifts." Paul's teaching on spiritual gifts makes it clear that the "body," the church, is made up of many parts. All gifts of the Spirit are of vital importance and must work together. There is no hierarchy of gifts; they are all necessary, interwoven, and mutually supporting.

of a bride, the strength and power of a warrior, the servant's heart of a priest — this is the work of the Spirit of Jesus (Revelation 21:2, Ephesians 6:10-19, 1 Peter 2:4-5).

You are being prepared to serve and strengthen your brothers and sisters in the Lord, prepared to minister healing, prepared to teach, to preach, to evangelize, to prophesy, to pray in the spirit, to speak in tongues, to interpret tongues, prepared to minister as presbyters, to give generously, and so much more. This preparation is not only for those who are "called" and ordained by a denomination or church organization. This is for the priesthood of **ALL** believers. You are standing in the court of waiting and preparation[79] to be strengthened and prepared for work and for warfare in the Body of Christ.

For all who will listen to the Good Shepherd's call to true and real worship, from this court you continue your ascent into God's dwelling place.

> *"But you have come to Mount Zion, to the heavenly Jerusalem, the city of the living God. You have come to thousands upon thousands of angels in joyful assembly, to the church of the firstborn, whose names are written in heaven. You have come to God, the judge of all men, to the spirits of righteous men made perfect, to Jesus the mediator of a new covenant, and to the sprinkled blood that speaks a better word than the blood of Abel." (Hebrews 12:22-24)*

But who is worthy to ascend God's holy sanctuary? "Who may ascend the hill of the Lord? Who may stand in his holy place? He who has clean hands and a pure heart" (Psalm 24:3). Clean hands? With despair on our faces we look down at our hands, only to see the filth of our sin. But Jesus allays our fears with a touch, saying, "Don't look at your own hands, look at my hands." With our hands in His, we can lift them in worship that is spiritual and real.

---

[79] This waiting and preparation has little to do with time, days or hours. It is a condition of the heart that binds us and conforms us to the very nature of God.

God's dwelling place

Now our Lord Jesus ushers us into God's holy presence: "And God raised us up with Christ and seated us with him in the heavenly realms in Christ Jesus" (Ephesians 2:6). Because we have ascended in Christ Jesus, we have not come empty handed, but with precious treasures (Exodus 34:20). We have come to offer ourselves as bondservants, to hear, to see, to understand, and to be empowered in gifts of the Spirit. This is, more than any other place, where we receive revelation knowledge. "Guard your steps when you go to the house of God. Go near to listen rather than to offer the sacrifice of fools, who do not know that they do wrong" (Ecclesiastes 5:1). [80]

We have reached the highest point in the temple. "He makes my feet like the feet of a deer; he enables me to stand on the heights. He trains my hands for battle; my arms can bend a bow of bronze" (Psalm 18:33-34). This is God's dwelling place, the Council of God. "Put the altar in front of the curtain that shields the Ark of the Covenant law — before the atonement cover that is over the tablets of the covenant law — *where I will meet with you*" (Exodus 30:6, emphasis added). The temple curtain is now torn (Matthew 27:51), and it is here that we come face to face[81] with God Almighty, Creator of all heaven and earth. But we are not consumed by fire, because we have confessed our sin and we have been forgiven and cleansed by the blood of the Lamb.

In the councils of God Almighty, in the Holy of Holies, in the very presence of God, the Holy Spirit is poured out like baptizing oil to saturate every fiber of our being.[82] The gifts of the Spirit, those given or those we will receive, are empowered for our works of ministry in

---

[80] "Who do not know that they do wrong" could be paraphrased in context, "who don't know when to be silent and listen."

[81] This is not a reference to a physical manifestation of God to be seen with natural eyes. We enter God's presence in spirit and in Christ.

[82] Psalm 133:2 shows us the difference between an Old Testament anointing and the New Covenant anointing. In OT the oil of anointing was poured *upon* them. In the NT covenant it saturates every part — body, soul, and spirit. "From him the whole body [people who are the church], joined and held together by every supporting ligament, grows and builds itself up in love, as each part does its work" (Ephesians 4:16).

service to our brothers and sisters in Christ and to a lost and dying world in need of Christ.

"But if they had stood in my council, they would have proclaimed my words to my people" (Jeremiah 23:22). In this Holy Place our ears are refreshed and awakened further to hear the living, present words of a Holy God, spoken to us for the strengthening of God's people.[83] From a distance His voice was heard as thunder. His words flowed like a roaring waterfall of life-giving water. But here we draw near to hear His words as a whisper of wind. Our understanding awakens like the first gleam of dawn, which brightens as we look forward to the full light of day. We sense God speaking within our heart of hearts, words too wonderful for description, words like a consuming fire. We hear Him speak but do not comprehend the glory of His words. The fire of the Spirit of Jesus begins to burn within our hearts and we know in part the message He speaks (1 Corinthians 13:9,12, Ephesians 2:6, Hebrews 1:2). He is offering, through us, words of wisdom, words of knowledge, words of prophecy, words of strengthening, words of encouragement, words of admonishment, words of blessing and so much more. You as a bride, adorned and prepared, now receive the tabrets of worship as a breastplate, a signet giving you the authority of the Name of Jesus Christ our Lord and Savior to minister and serve. You are called as a priest to receive the tabrets as a breastplate of righteousness. You are compelled to raise up His Holy Banner and go forth to do battle in His Holy Name.

This is not a one time, once and for all time visit to the presence of God Almighty. This is the beginning of dwelling in His presence. We may dwell in His presence as we are prepared with the gifts and power of the Holy Spirit to descend in the courtyards of the temple to minister and serve. This is not only a weekly hour out of our Sunday morning thing. This is now and forever. "Surely goodness and mercy shall follow me all the days of my life: and I will dwell in the house of the Lord forever" (Psalm 23:6 KJV).

There is no need to go up to the third heaven or any other part of

---

[83] In the words God speaks to us as we stand in His council, He will never contradict, change, or add to what is written in the cannon of Scripture.

heaven. There is no need for an out of body experience to come face to face with a Holy God. There is no call for a trance-like spiritual moment to enter here. Enter into Christ by faith for He has made a way for you to be ushered in before the Father — Abba. You are covered with Jesus' robe of righteous and He will gently present you to His Father saying, "Here is Your adopted one to whom you have given a new name" (Revelation 2:17).

You can see a picture of what is happening when you look at Moses as he ascended the mountain of God and dwelt in the council of God for forty days and nights (Exodus 24:18). You, too, are given spiritual gifts and power for ministry. God's people are empowered to strengthen, encourage, heal, teach, preach, prophesy, and evangelize. You are empowered by the Holy Spirit for speaking God's words of wisdom and knowledge, for messages in tongues and for interpretation of tongues. You are gifted and given authority as a signet for presbytery, for the miraculous works of God through the saints, for generosity, for building up, and many, many more ministries of worship, serving in the body of Christ.

A worshipful, power-driven descent

You ascended in the rags of sorrow. You descend wearing garments of praise. We came up in weeping and mourning; we descend comforted. You climbed up in the ashes of repentance. You depart wearing a crown of beauty. You trudged your way toward the Father in despair because of your wretched condition. You come away in great splendor. You came before the Father to dwell in His council and hear His precious Word to be gifted and empowered by the Holy Spirit and to be sent out in the authority of the Name of Jesus. You ascended as an observer of worship. You descend to participate in worshipful ministries and services.

God's dwelling place

There is a river flowing from the God's dwelling place in the temple: "Then the angel showed me the river of the water of life, as clear as crystal, flowing from the throne of God and of the Lamb down the middle of the great street of the city" (Revelation 22:1-2). Step into the river and be filled to overflowing with Living Water from the Spirit. You will be overwhelmed as with a flood of blessing. It is through you, the church, that God will manifest Himself as living and actively present among His people, so that a lost and dying world may hear, see, and exclaim, "God is truly among you."

Moses came down the mountain in glory to minister God's law to the tribes of Israel. In the greater glory of Christ Jesus, we go down the temple steps and courtyards in a joyful, empowered descent from the council of God. His presence remains, burning in our hearts as a fire. With this burning in our hearts, we have confidence in the authority of the Name of Jesus; and we hold in our hand the sword of the Spirit, which is the Word of God. We are secure and strengthened, holding out the shield of faith against the fiery darts of the enemy. We are sure and steadfast, standing in the cleansing flow that comes from the throne of God. We are prepared and adorned as a bride, armored as a warrior, and given the servant heart of a priest; we are gifted and empowered for ministries as an act of worship before a Holy God. We have authority to speak out with great boldness. We are empowered to be used by the Spirit, extending the very hand of Jesus to touch and heal. Our hearts burn within us, compelling us to do what the Spirit has instructed. Go as the Spirit has directed. Speak what the Spirit has spoken. Touch as the Spirit has empowered you to touch. Do not shrink back (Isaiah 54:4).

The fire of the Spirit will continue to burn within you as you descend from God's dwelling place. You enter into empowered ministries and service of the kingdom of heaven. As you descend through the courtyards, you are greeted with ministries of the Word, responsive singing, spiritual songs, joyful and triumphant shouts, singing in the spirit, revelations of the Word, praying in the spirit, and prayers of deep groaning. This is a festival of worship that is only possible in the spirit and by the empowering work of the Holy Spirit. This is a feast of joy and strength. It is in the courtyards of worship more than any other place that His eternal beauty is poured into your vessel, the oil of joy. You are clothed with garments of praise, all for the glory of God.

Sanctuary of high worship

We step into this courtyard with a sense that our faces reflect Christ's glory. The Holy Spirit's gifting and empowering work is fresh, quickening our spirit and strengthening our hearts. Our brothers and sisters in Christ are serving shoulder to shoulder with us in the courts of worship. We witness them preaching the Word, evangelizing the lost, and humbly serving in pastoral ministry. Some do the work of reaching out to the lost and establishing churches, spreading the kingdom as the Spirit leads. Others in the gathering serve as presbyters, imparting the gifts of the Spirit for the strengthening of the church. This is worship that is acceptable and true before a holy God.

Courtyard of priestly ministries

Again, the gifts of the Spirit are effectively ministered in this court of worship. You serve as one, working as a team. Because of this, the spiritual gifts powerfully manifest the living, active presence of our Lord Jesus. You witness Jesus' presence as those who extend their hands, the very hand of Christ, to minister healing. Words of wisdom and knowledge strengthen and admonish the people. Beautiful voices sing out in new spiritual songs. Others speak messages in tongues with interpretation. The burning in your heart tells you that your moment of ministry has arrived. You speak out to teach the precious words of Scripture — your gift reveals Christ's presence in the assembly. Joy overwhelms you in this blessed moment as you witness the Spirit's power ministering to those you teach, changing hearts and minds and drawing them to Christ. All these acts of worship are by means of the Spirit, and true to the call of worship.

Courtyard of Celebration

Now step forward in an empowered descent to this festive courtyard. Here we continue our worship and serve as unto the Lord — in the authority of His Name and in the power of the Holy Spirit as never before. Together we offer ministries of renewal, lifting burdens, restoring the soul, and rebuilding lives. We are Jesus' hand extended. We are the visible presence of Jesus Christ manifested in the earth. We are ministering in the authority of His Name, and in the power of His Holy Spirit for the strengthening of His church. We're overjoyed to join in this worship as joyful hearts sing gifts of thanksgiving, alms, offerings, psalms, hymns, and choruses. We clap our hands in unison; we lift our hands, exalting God Almighty together with those who play instruments of praise to worship in reverent awe. Beyond a doubt, with each act of worship, Christ's living, active presence is once again revealed in the assembly. This is worship that is spiritual and real.

The sacred courtyard

It is here that God's people speak out with words of thanksgiving, offerings of generosity, prayers to intercede for all people; eyes look heavenward in meditation, and in blessed union with our Lord and Savior we cast our cares away. God's people quietly fast and pray, seeking the Lord's face — all true and genuine acts of worship before a holy God.

Outer courtyard

Descend again to the blessings of this present life. Gingerly, we step into the daily workings of the world around us to spread the blessings (Exodus 23:25-26, Psalm 122:9). We labor according to the natural gifts God has given, but now more than ever within God's hedge of protection. The work of our hands is blessed, we prosper, and through us the Light of Life touches all the people around us.[84] It is here that we join in a celebrative feast of earth's bountiful harvest.

---

[84] Material prosperity is a supernatural side effect, the result of, and the blessed consequence of seeking first His kingdom. If you are repressed, forcefully impoverished, imprisoned, or even threatened with death for the cause of Christ, cry out to a holy God (Psalm 109). He will hear and answer your heart's cry. Above all, He will assure you of greater blessings stored up for you for all eternity (Matthew 6:19-20).

This is Christ's Jubilee![85]

Look again at the pilgrimage you have just completed. From the outer courtyard, you stepped into the Sacred Enclosure with thanksgiving, offerings, petitions, intercessions, with fasting and prayer. You stepped up into the courtyard of celebration with worship, spiritual song, music, and dancing. You ascended into the courtyard of priestly ministries. You came up into the sanctuary of high worship to minister before God Almighty. You entered into God's dwelling place to dwell in the council of your God and Heavenly Father.

As you entered each courtyard, you observed spiritual and real worship. You were prepared to enter into the spiritual realm for worship. You ascended to worship before a Holy God in a way that is true and real, and according to spirit and truth. You entered into the gates of thanksgiving, and into His courts with praise. Joyful noises were sung out in the gathering of saints. You came to dwell in God's council. You received the gifting and empowering work of the Holy Spirit to be prepared to partake in the highest form of worship, to minister and serve among God's people, the church.

In worship, you are the bride of Christ, putting on the precious jewels of the kingdom of heaven. You are armored as a warrior for kingdom warfare. You serve as a priest, putting on the breastplate embedded with precious stones and wearing His ring as a signet. Receive all that God has promised and adorn yourself for the Bridegroom. Dress yourself in the precious ornaments of gold, silver, and priceless gems to prepare for the wedding feast. Fill your lamps with the Oil of the Holy Spirit. This pilgrimage through the temple of worship makes powerfully evident that spiritual gifts, the treasures of the Spirit, are given to God's people for the purpose of truly worshipping a Holy God.

If you have buried these Kingdom treasures, dig them up. If you lost them, search diligently until you find them. If you left them behind,

---

[85] The Jubilee was proclaimed every fifty years in the nation of Israel. In that year, liberty would be pronounced to all its inhabitants. All property that had been surrendered to pay for unpaid debts was returned to the original families, tribes, or clans. All debtors were released from debt and given a new start as their land was returned to them. Now, in Christ, we are released from the debt of our sins and set free from our bondage of our transgressions. We become heirs of God's promised rest. We are *free* to minister and serve the cross of Jesus Christ.

go back to collect them. If you have never received the Spirit's gifts, earnestly ask for them. Seek the Giver of the gifts. Search as you would for lost treasure. Joyfully receive and ascend in worship. Enter God's council and descend with the glow of His presence radiating from your face.

Have you stepped outside the bounds of God's love? Have you turned your back on what that is right and good to partake of what is pleasing to the eye? Is your body marked and scarred because of your sin? Are you walking on a broad and easy downhill pathway? Have you been driven away from the fold? Have you been plundered by the enemy? Call on Jesus! He is waiting for you with open arms and will forgive, cleanse, and restore you. He has precious Kingdom treasures for you beyond anything you've ever imagined. You, too, are called and will be lifted up onto to the mountain of the Lord, into the courtyard for the priesthood of all believers, to put on His breastplate of righteousness and minister at the altar of God.

"I, Jesus, have sent my angel to give you this testimony for the churches. I am the Root and the Offspring of David, and the bright Morning Star" (Revelation 22:16).[86] How can we do less than to receive these precious treasures of the Kingdom and offer them up in worship, ministering and serving before the Lord God Almighty? We must not reject them, for He is worthy to receive glory and honor and power. He created all things, and by His will all things have their being. Glory be to the Father and to the Son and to the Holy Spirit.

Amen! Maranatha!

Note: For a more complete look at the topic of worshipful ministries, review the following Scripture: Psalms 15:1, 16:11, 27:4-5, 43:3-4, 65:4, 73:28; Isaiah 2:3; Jeremiah 31:6; Hebrews 4:16, 7:18-19, 10:1-25, 11:6; Matthew 6:6; James 4:8; John 10:7-10, John 14:6-7; Romans 5:1-2; Ephesians 3:12.

---

[86] Compare with Isaiah 14:12.

YOUR JOURNEY JOURNAL
Chapter 2: The Temple of Worship

1. What is the significance of the tabrets of worship?

2. Describe the significance of the "courts" as you ascend and descend.

3. How will you begin your worshipful ascent?

4. What is Christ's Jubilee?

Your Journal Notes:

3

Caution and Encouragement

Fortune hunters who search for gold and other lost treasures in shipwrecks at the bottom of the ocean are driven and determined people. Imagine a salvage team with wreckage coordinates in hand. They brave ocean currents and raging sea to find its location, anchor their ship, put on deep-sea diving gear, descend to the bottom, swim through the storm battered wreckage, and finally locate the treasure chest. The divers attempt to lift the chest and realize it is very heavy and must be full of gold. It may be worth millions. So they leave it behind, ascend to the surface, and sail home because it would just be too big a burden, too much trouble to salvage. Besides, there were sharks, eels, stingrays, and stinging jellyfish all around the treasure.

Never happen. Right? Of course not. But as Christians, we do just that. The Head of the church, Jesus Christ, holds out to us in His nail scarred hands gifts of inestimable value. He holds out bridal adornments that are, by grace, given to the church to gift and empower God's people to fulfill the work of the church, His Great Commission. Yet, because it's too heavy a burden, because the gifts have been misunderstood, misinterpreted, or mishandled, we reject all or some of His precious gifts of the Spirit. We are frightened away because of opposition. We neglect the gifts because they fall into the realm of the unknown and ignorance is our undoing.

This must not be! The church will never be more than a fine and beautiful building where we get together to be blessed if we reject or despise the bridal treasures the Bridegroom gives to His betrothed church. Yet we must handle spiritual gifts with godly wisdom, as good stewards of what God has given to gift and empower His people. Too often, spiritual gifts are misused, misapplied, buried, or even faked, and we must be encouraged to ask for, receive, and then use them as wise and godly stewards. Too many of us in the church today are like the slothful servant in Jesus' parable who buried his talent of gold. We do ourselves a great disservice when we dig a hole and bury the Spirit's good gifts. (Read Matthew 25:14-30.)

Desiring Spiritual Gifts for the Wrong Reason

Encouraging caution in handling spiritual gifts is not meant to make you shy away, but to urge you to be a wise steward of your gifts. Caution is called for in that we must not desire the gifts of the Holy Spirit for the wrong reason — to gain some "special" position before God, to curry extra favor in His kingdom, or to become known as super spiritual among our brothers and sisters in Christ. After being blessed with a spiritual gift, you will not be a cut above others or earn any part of your redemption. Spiritual gifts do not create two classes of Christians, the "called" and the "ordinary" — the gifts are for all Christians — for the priesthood of all believers (1 Peter 2:9). Spiritual gifts are unmerited, free, and given as the Spirit sees fit. We do not perform works of service to gain anything for ourselves in this temporal world. By grace, we are given saving faith in our Lord Jesus Christ, and by grace we bear the fruit of the Spirit just as naturally as the grafted branches of a tree, a tree planted by streams of living water. When you are "in Christ," grafted into the true Vine, He will bear fruit through you just as naturally as the branches of a grape vine produce plump clusters of grapes. "He is like a tree planted by streams of water, which yields its fruit in season and whose leaf does not wither. Whatever he does prospers" (Psalm 1:3).

Rejecting Spiritual Gifts

Because God works through the means of grace (Romans 12:6), His people may reject His spiritual gifts (just as Adam and Eve rejected the very best of God's creation), though it grieves Him when we do. Grace comes to us as a gift from the Holy Spirit, freely given but not forced upon those in rebellion. Some people ignore or reject spiritual gifts because they know it means they must humble themselves and apply the gift in kingdom service. "Let the pastor do it," the people say. "Let the elders do it." But Scripture tells us otherwise: "Each one should use whatever gift he has received to serve others, faithfully administering God's grace in its various forms" (1 Peter 4:10). *"Each one"* means all Christian believers. *"Whatever gift"* refers to the gifts given to Christians by the Holy Spirit. *"Serve others"* is just as it says, "faithfully ministering God's grace in every form to those around us."

Other people ignore the gifts because of ignorance (even willing ignorance); they simply don't know what ministry gift the Spirit wills to give to them for the good of the church. "But my people do not know the requirements of the Lord" (Jeremiah 8:7). Their spiritual ears are plugged up and they will not hear, learn, or do what they are called to do. Too many accept the existence of gifts of the Holy Spirit for **other** Christians but say, "That's for them, not for me, thank you." The prophet speaks clearly to this attitude: "Does a maiden forget her jewelry, a bride her wedding ornaments? Yet my people have forgotten me, days without number" (Jeremiah 2:32).

Some denominations put down those who seek all the gifts of the Spirit saying that they are seeking a spiritual experience rather than seeking Christ. I reject this accusation outright because asking for and receiving a precious gift, a bridal adornment from the Spirit of the Bridegroom is what Scripture instructs and encourages us to do. Receiving the Bridegroom's gifts is a significant milestone toward the church's attaining and being filled with the whole measure of Christ (Ephesians 4:13).

Desire, Ask, and you Will Receive: If you have no desire for spiritual gifts, ask God to put **His** desire in your heart. When you are given this desire for spiritual gifts, ask God and He will be faithful to His Word: "Ask and it will be given to you; seek and you will find; knock and the door will be opened to you. For everyone who asks receives; the one who seeks finds; and to the one who knocks, the door will be opened"

(Matthew 7:7). Ask for the Master to give you, His steward, the gold of the kingdom so that you may invest it wisely and offer Him a bountiful return. Ask for the Spirit's gifts to adorn you as His bride. Ask for the spiritual gift or gifts He has ordained for you, and He will be faithful to give what you ask.

Be encouraged to ask for gifts to build up and encourage your brothers and sisters in the Lord to strengthen the whole church. "So it is with you. Since you are eager to have spiritual gifts, try to excel in gifts that build up the church" (1 Corinthians 14:12). A lack of spiritual gifts, or having no knowledge of gifts of the Spirit is easily remedied. Ask, fully aware that you ask according to His perfect will. "Follow the way of love and ***eagerly desire*** spiritual gifts, especially the gift of prophecy" (1 Corinthians 14:1, emphasis added). This Scripture is for you — for all who are in Christ — all who are a part of the priesthood of believers. The spiritual gifts are intended to be common among the people of God's Church. No one is to be left out.

Put Fear Aside: Satan has done a terrible work among believers, giving Christians a fear of being "possessed" by the Holy Spirit and doing things they have no desire to do, or of losing control of themselves and looking foolish. The evil one has also caused us great harm by creating a fear of counterfeit gifts of the Spirit. Ask for what is true and right. Request of the Lord what is pure and holy and He will not give you a poor substitute. "Which of you, if his son asks for bread, will give him a stone" (Matthew 7:9). The Spirit of Jesus will give you good gifts that are entirely within your power to manage and to use according to godly wisdom. "The spirits of the prophets are subject to the control of prophets" (1 Corinthians 14:32). God will not gift us with something we resist, refuse, or despise. He will never force us to say or do what we say "no" to — but He may well lead us, gently as a Shepherd, guiding us with His staff, so we may receive what He desires for us.

Confront the Challenges: The challenges we must face are two extremes at work in today's churches. At one end of the spectrum are churches and denominations that believe, for example, that speaking in a tongue is not for today or worse yet, is of the Devil. (They didn't get this teaching from the Scriptures.) On the opposite end of the scale are the churches that allow almost anything and everything that appears to be "spiritual" without testing it by the Word and without using any spiritual discernment. They embrace *any* prophetic utterance, any experience, any interpretation, any supernatural manifestation, any message — all are acceptable, taught, and even encouraged for fear of quenching the Holy Spirit. (This is a misapplication of 1 Thessalonians 5:19, which is saying that we put out the Spirit's fire when we treat prophesies with contempt.) Both extremes serve the enemy's purpose of creating fear, anxiety, and misunderstanding among Christians about the Holy Spirit and the gifts of the Spirit.

Somewhere in between these extremes we have those people who say, "Yes, I believe in the gifts of the Spirit and I will not deny them, but I see that the fruit of exercising these gifts is chaos and disorder." We cannot throw out a portion of the Bible because we don't think it works for us. Indeed, Paul had the same problem with the Corinthian church and he disciplined them accordingly.[87] The church at Corinth was moving away from exercising their gifts in the Spirit to a soulish, fleshly exercise of spiritual gifts.[88] I can only guess that after they were comfortable in their spiritual gifts, they got an attitude that would say, "Move over Holy Spirit, I can handle this from here. Thanks for getting me started."

Repeating the Sin of Corinth

The early church in Corinth began with the manifest power of the Spirit of Jesus present and active among God's people by means of

---

[87] This is a part of the work originally assigned to the office of apostle. It is at times difficult for a local pastor who must live with his congregation every day to properly discipline his sheep. Sometimes sin, selfish ambition, disorder, and many other evils creep in so slowly that local leaders don't see it happening. The church still needs this kind of ministry today because we are fallible beings who have not completely overcome our weaknesses. We have not yet attained to the whole measure of the fullness of Christ (Ephesians 4:13).

[88] For the Corinthians, the natural man was gradually taking precedence over the spiritual.

spiritual gifts empowering His people. But like them we have slipped into complacency, ignorance, and confusion. Too many of today's churches have not separated what is holy from what is common and have come to rely on education, training, and great organizations to accomplish the work of the church. Is it possible that today's churches have rejected spiritual gifts (what is holy), such as the spiritual gift of prophecy, because too often prophetic messages have challenged pet doctrines, dogmas, and theologies? God forbid! Oh, the pride of man. *"Lord God, forgive us and cleanse us! Change our hearts."*

In Jesus' teaching from Matthew 25:31-46 regarding the separation of the "sheep and goats," i.e. the righteous and the wicked, we see a clear picture of "works" and the judgment of works. Jesus specifically mentions works of charity. This included feeding the hungry, giving water to the thirsty, offering hospitality to strangers, giving clothes to those who are naked, caring for the sick, and visiting those in prison. The wicked claimed to be doing these works of charity while the godly didn't know when they did these things "unto the Lord." The difference is like light and darkness. The righteous served and ministered by the gifting and empowering of the Spirit in their work. What they did was just as natural to them as a healthy fig tree bearing figs in season. It was the fruit of their faith — the fruit of being grafted into the Vine. The charity was not done as a work of the flesh nor was it accomplished by the power of the flesh. But on the Day it is tested by fire, the work will be proven to be like pure, eternal gold.

Why do Christians depend on what is common to accomplish what is holy? The prophet laments, "But my people do not know the requirements of the Lord" (Jeremiah 8:7). We have not been taught what the Lord requires of us. Because of our ignorance, we are blinded to the treasures the Lord holds out to us. Jeremiah warns of the consequences of ignoring God's requirements. "There will be no figs on the tree, and their leaves will wither. What I have given them will be taken from them" (Jeremiah 8:13; see also Matthew 21:18-19). The Bridegroom has given His bride precious treasures, gifts of great splendor and beauty. If we forbid, despise, or bury them out of fear, we stand to lose them. "Take the talent from him and give it to the one who has ten talents" (Matthew 25:28).

Instead of receiving the gifts of the Spirit with gladness, what do we do? We despise, forbid, or ignore what is good, what is right, and what is pure. But Paul says, "do not forbid speaking in tongues" (1 Corinthians 14:39). In forbidding these good gifts, the church has suffered a great loss. Isaiah gives us a picture of God's people in their state of depravity: "But this is a people plundered and looted, all of them trapped in pits or hidden away in prisons. They have become plunder with no one to rescue them; they have been made loot, with no one to say, 'Send them back'" (Isaiah 42:22).

But you say, "I have been grafted into the True Vine. I confess my faith every Sunday in church. I profess my faith in many ways every day." Our protests are similar to what the Israelites told the prophet Malachi. Listen to his response: "You have wearied the Lord with your words" (Malachi 2:17). Why? Because the professions and the deeds of God's people did not agree. What they said and did was as far apart as heaven and hell.

Wouldn't a newlywed husband grieve if he gave his bride a beautiful diamond ring, gold bracelets engraved with his messages of love and a diamond studded locket with his picture — and his bride continually proclaimed her love to him with her words, but refused to wear his ring and expensive gifts any time she was out of his sight?

We must not reject so great a gift that came at such a high price and thus grieve the Holy Spirit. Put aside fear. Cast your doubts upon the Lord. Don't allow yourself to continue apart from knowledge of what God requires of you. Search for the "key" by committing yourself to knowledge and understanding in the fear of the Lord. Allow God's Word to be light to your eyes to see the precious treasures our Lord Jesus holds out to you in His nail scarred hands. Receive all God has ordained for you, so that you may accomplish all He has purposed and planned for you as your part in fulfilling His Great Commission.

YOUR JOURNEY JOURNAL
Chapter 3: Caution & Encouragement

1. What special position or stature will you attain in your church when you minister in your spiritual gift?

2. In what ways might a Christian reject his or her spiritual gift?

3. How do spiritual gifts play a part in the church's attaining the whole measure of Christ?

Your Journal Notes:

4

Laying on of Hands

The writer of Hebrews teaches us that the church's doctrine of prayerfully laying hands on people is an elementary and foundational truth. This practice remains important for the church even today. We must first get a clear picture of the foundation before we can build toward maturity in Christ: "Therefore let us leave the elementary teachings about Christ and go on to maturity, not laying again the foundation of repentance from acts that lead to death, and of faith in God, instruction about baptisms, the laying on of hands, the resurrection of the dead, and eternal judgment" (Hebrews 6:1-2). Unless Christians build on this foundational doctrine revealed in Scripture, we are in danger of building on shifting sand. The need for ministries of laying on of hands as a vital work of the church is straightforward, clear, and of great importance.

In ministering with our spiritual gifts, some go to extremes and lay hands on anybody without any serious prayer or thought of what they are doing. The apostle Paul warns against this. "Do not be hasty in the laying on of hands, and do not share in the sins of others. Keep yourself pure" (1 Timothy 5:22). Paul shows us a better way: "Paul went in to see him and, after prayer, placed his hands on him and healed him" (Acts 28:8). Others go to the opposite extreme and neglect this truth, beating a hasty retreat away from this practice. A Biblical understanding of this doctrine will help us to find the balance in teaching as well as in the practice of the laying on of hands. But balance is not the goal; it is to be God's instruments, to extend our hands where God is extending His hand and to practice this ministry just as the apostle Paul demonstrated in Acts chapter 28. This immensely important, foundational spiritual practice cannot be diminished, set on the shelf, or used only for ordaining pastors, bishops, and priests. God has given the laying on of hands to all who will receive. We hold back God's blessings, compassion, and mercies when we limit the use of this means of ministry that comes from the hand of God.

What Is the Meaning of Laying on of Hands?

This is a ministry of allowing your hands to be the very hands of Christ, and by the leading of the Holy Spirit, placing your hands on someone for a specific spiritual purpose. It is most often accompanied with prayer and at times a confirming prophetic message. Because too few of us understand the meaning of "laying on of hands," some try things like pushing or shaking a person's head and some make their own hands shake while laying hands on others. We should not give importance to our physical movements while practicing this ministry. (But if the Holy Spirit is shaking you, don't fight it.)

Laying hands on people is found throughout all of Scripture, beginning with the patriarch Jacob (also called Israel) in the first book of the Bible: "But Israel reached out his right hand and put it on Ephraim's head" (Genesis 48:14). Jesus used this powerful ministry as He showed compassion for the people. "Then people brought little children to Jesus for him to place his hands on them and pray for them" (Matthew 19:13). The apostles followed Jesus' pattern of ministry. "They presented these men to the apostles, who prayed and laid their hands on them" (Acts 6:6).

We find great spiritual significance, power, and purpose in laying on of hands in the Old and New Testaments. We are called to extend the hand of God to impart His blessings upon His people. These may include blessings: to set apart for ministry, to impart authority for a purpose, and to impart the Spirit's wisdom to those who are called to lead. The ministry of hands was used to transfer sins of the people upon the cleansing sacrifice. This practice is used in ordination of those called to serve, and to heal the infirm, the weak, and the downcast. It is often a means for conferring the gifting and empowering work of the Holy Spirit.

The Purpose of Laying on of Hands in Old Testament

1. The Transfer of sins:

> *"He is to lay both hands on the head of the live goat and confess over it all the wickedness and rebellion of the Israelites — all their sins — and put them on the goats head. He shall send the goat away into the desert in the care of a man appointed for the task."* (Leviticus 16:21,22)

By laying their hands on the animals, their sins were transferred to the animal and those animals were slain as their substitute (Leviticus 1:4). This is a picture of Jesus taking our sins upon Himself and then offering Himself as a sacrifice in our place, for our sins (Romans 6:23).

2. To impart God's blessings:

> *"But Israel reached out his right hand and put it on Ephraim's head, though he was the younger and crossing his arms, he put his left hand on Manasseh's head, even though Manasseh was the firstborn... He blessed them that day."* (Genesis 48:14, 20)

3. To impart spiritual authority:

> *"So the Lord said to Moses "Take Joshua son of Nun, a man in whom is the spirit, and lay your hand on him. Have him stand before Eleazar the priest and the entire assembly and commission him in their presence. Give him some of your authority so the whole Israelite community will obey him... Then he laid his hands on him and commissioned him, as The Lord instructed through Moses."* (Numbers 27:18-20, 23)

Moses transferred his anointing for leadership by laying his hands on Joshua. Joshua received a part of the spiritual authority God had given to Moses, because Moses laid his hand on him as the Lord commanded. We read in Luke 24:50 that Jesus lifted up His hands to bless His disciples as He ascended into heaven. By raising His hands over them, He commissioned His disciples and gave them authority to fulfill the Great Commission.

4. To impart spiritual wisdom:

> *"Now Joshua son of Nun was filled with the spirit of wisdom because Moses had laid his hands on him." (Deuteronomy 34:9)*

Moses imparted the spiritual wisdom to Joshua through "laying on of hands."

5. To set apart for ministry:

> *"You are to bring the Levites before the Lord, and the Israelites are to lay their hands on them." (Numbers 8:10)*

God accepted the Levites in place of all the firstborn sons in Israel (Numbers 3:12). They represented the whole community of Israel.

Purpose of Laying on of Hands in New Testament

1. To minister God's healing touch:

Lord Jesus and His disciples practiced the laying on of hands again and again to heal the sick (Luke 4:40, 13:13, Acts 9:17, 28:8,9); "and these signs will accompany those who believe" (Mark 16:17). Verse 18 shows us that one of the signs is that "they will place their hands on sick people and they will get well."

Ministering prayer by the laying on of hands is used in healing of sinners. Prayer and anointing with oil is a common way to pray for believers to be healed (James 5:14, 15). However the laying on of hands is practiced to impart the healing as a blessing to the saved and unsaved alike.

All believers have the privilege and call to lay hands on the sick.

This practice is not limited to spiritually gifted people, elders, deacons or ordained ministers (Mark 16:17,18). As an example, Ananias, an ordinary disciple, placed his hands on Paul for his healing (Acts 9:17,18).

Without having a special healing gift, any believer can lay his hands on the sick and with a prayer offered in faith, be the conduit for healing from God. Let's be clear, healing is not in the hand of man; it is in God's Mighty Hand. God chooses to extend His hand using our hands, because that's His nature.

2. To empower people for specific mission:

> *"So after they had fasted and prayed, they placed their hands on them and sent them off" (Acts 13:3).*

As shown in the above verse, teachers and prophets laid hands on Barnabas and Saul to send them out from the Antioch church to minister in their apostolic calling.

Barnabas and Saul were called to be apostles (Acts 13:2) and their calling was confirmed in a prophetic message. All of this was accomplished by the leading of the Holy Spirit, by the power of the Spirit and with fasting prayer.

Local churches are called to practice this even today while sending people out for specific work. This is the means the Spirit uses to gift and empower them to complete what God has commended them to do (Acts 14:26,27).

3. To appoint elders, deacons/esses and other leaders in the local churches:

Apostles fasted, prayed, and then laid their hands on chosen men to appoint them as elders and deacons in each local church. Paul instructed Timothy not to lay hands on anyone in haste, while appointing elders (1 Timothy 5:22). Before the laying on of hands and thereby appointing elders, we must be sure that the person meets the Biblical standards laid out in 1 Timothy 3:1-12 and Titus 1:5-11.

In the local church at Jerusalem, apostles laid their hands on seven selected men to appoint them as deacons (Acts 6:3). "They presented these men to the apostles, who prayed and laid their hands on them" (Acts 6:6). It is an affront to Scripture and the work of the Spirit when a church appoints anyone as an elder or a deacon who is not first chosen by God. It is crucial that we search out the mind of the Holy Spirit regarding the appointment of elders and deacons, and all others who minister and serve in the church, accompanied by prayer and fasting.

4. To impart the Holy Spirit upon the believer:

The Apostles, at times, laid their hands on new believers, for them to receive the baptism of the Holy Spirit (Acts 8:14-24, 9:10-17). Apostle Peter, in rebuking Simon, refers this as a gift of God (Acts 8:20). Whoever is born of faith will receive the Holy Spirit to dwell within him (Romans 8:15, Galatians 4:6, Ephesians 1:13). And yet, our Lord Jesus has even greater blessings of the Spirit for those who will receive. This is all the work of the Holy Spirit of our Lord Jesus Christ (Acts 1:5).

5. To impart and empower spiritual gifts:

> "Do not neglect your gift, which was given you through prophecy when the body of elders laid their hands on you." (1 Timothy 4:14)

> "Therefore I remind you to stir up the gift of God which is in you through the laying on of my hands." (2 Timothy 1:6)

> "For I long to see you that I may impart to you some spiritual gift, so that you may be established." (Romans 1:11)

These verses clearly prove that spiritual gifts can be imparted by the laying on of hands. We must be very clear: even though spiritual gifts can be imparted through laying on of hands, they are given according to the will of the Holy Spirit and not by our own purpose or plan (1 Corinthians 12:11, Hebrews 2:4).

God has given us a great, beautiful, and powerful way to minister His blessings upon the sheep of His pasture. Our heavenly Father is reaching out His hand to touch, bless, heal, and comfort all who will receive. God has sent His Holy Spirit to gift and empower His disciples for the ministries and service of the church to all who will come. Those who are called to go out, to plant churches, to evangelize, to speak out God's message of the gospel must first receive the touch of Spirit of Jesus, through your hand extended, as He gifts and empowers those willing to be sent out.

Why would we do anything less than to be what that God has called us to be — His instruments; vessels to release His power and might? This practice ought to be common in the church, extended with wisdom and ministered according to the historic, orthodox practices of the Christian church from the very foundations of the church.

YOUR JOURNEY JOURNAL
Chapter 4: Laying on of Hands

1. Create a word picture to explain the meaning and purpose of the ministries of laying on hands.

2. What are some of God's purposes He desires to accomplish in His people through the laying on of hands?

3. Why is this ministry important for the church today?

Your Journal Notes:

5

In the Fear of God, We are Fearless

When I was the wise old age of thirteen, my older brother and I decided to climb Haystack Rock at Cannon Beach, Oregon. My family, all seven of us, were enjoying the sand and surf of the Oregon coast on a summer camping trip. When we tired of searching for starfish in the tide pools, we got the wild idea to climb this two hundred thirty-five foot tall volcanic monolith. What we didn't understand is the power of the tide and the force of the surf. We climbed up the craggy cliff, littered with greasy bird droppings, unaware of what was happening below us. We were about seventy feet up when we heard a bullhorn blast a warning from below. The beach patrol was demanding that we come down immediately. When I looked down, I could see why. The incoming tide had surrounded the base of the monolith and we would soon be stranded. Haystack Rock was becoming an offshore island.

We had fearlessly embarked on our mission. Our daring adventure was made possible by our lack of understanding the laws of nature and the need to surrender ourselves to these more powerful forces. But unlike the fearlessness of charging up cliffs in ignorance, the fear of the Lord keeps us within the bounds of love that makes the ministries and service of spiritual gifts most powerfully effective. We must start at the beginning of knowledge and wisdom — the fear of the Lord. This foundation of knowledge — it is the bedrock of learning, it is the wellspring of understanding, it is the hub of the wheel, it is the alpha and omega of knowledge; it is the basic ingredient in the recipe and must not be overlooked as we minister and serve in our spiritual gifts. Scripture by Scripture this chapter reveals essential truths from Genesis to Revelation to encourage in each of us a heart that delights in obedience, and a reverent, worshipful awe of God, thereby freeing us from that dreaded, servile fear of God.

Today's American Christians are so much like those adventurous brothers, having so little fear of God, not knowing Him or the power of His mighty arm. But God is to be feared, exalted, reverenced, diligently served, and truly worshipped; and each of these things is part of the fear of the Lord. Job calls this the "fear of his splendor" (Job 31:23). This fear (reverent awe and delighted obedience of God) is so important as we begin to seek revelation of God, because if we neglect this truth the spiritual gifts go astray. If you should hear a thousand sermons, hang your confirmation certificate on your wall, go to a hundred Harvest crusades, get a doctorate of theology, attend every Bible class possible — if you have not built a foundation in the Fear of the Lord, you will not have what you need to build your "house" by the knowledge of God.

Because of fearless ignorance, we do not know that Christians hold the key to something of incredible value. "He will be the sure foundation for your times, a rich store of salvation and wisdom and knowledge; the fear of the Lord is the key to this treasure" (Isaiah 33:6). The worth of this treasure is enhanced by the fact that its value is eternal, never to be corrupted by moths or rust. Just as important as its value is the miracle within this treasure. You are part of that miracle because you hold one key to knowledge of this treasure, but when you pass on the knowledge, the treasure multiplies like the flame of a candle used to light another's candle.

Use your key that unlocks knowledge and take a journey with me. Ride with me on an excursion through the Scripture, in much the same way that the Lord led me through this process of discovery. Our journey begins in Matthew 25 with Jesus' parable of the Bridegroom and the ten bridesmaids. Five foolish bridesmaids were caught without oil for their lamps when the bridegroom arrived. Five were wise and brought oil for their lamps. Jesus uses this parable to teach us an important truth about being prepared for the day of His return, and yet it becomes painfully obvious that five of the bridesmaids had little fear of the Lord. Their laissez-faire attitude let them sit back and relax while waiting. This parable reveals God's grace — continually coming before the throne of grace to be refilled and refreshed in mercy, cleansing, and forgiveness. This parable is also about oil as a symbol of the Holy Spirit and the need to be continually filled. But the point is, Christians do well to fear a holy God and this godly fear compels us to be ready with oil for our lamps. A healthy fear of having an empty vessel ought to drive us to the Spirit of Jesus who will fill us up with oil for our lamps.

But how does this happen?

There are few books on the topic of the fear of the Lord.[89] I've never found a seminar on this subject, and I've never noticed this sermon title announced on a church marquis. But let's go back a few years. Do you recall the old expression, "He's a God-fearing man?" Why don't we hear ourselves referred to in those terms today? Underline or highlight this Scripture in your Bible. "Fear of the Lord is the beginning of knowledge. Only fools despise wisdom and discipline" (Proverbs 1:7). This is a _beginning_, a foundational truth that we often neglect.[90] Here is another good verse to help us understand the full dimensions of the fear of the Lord. "The fear of the Lord is pure, enduring forever" (Psalm 19:9).

The fear of the Lord is so important that the teacher in Proverbs says the same thing again: "Fear of the Lord is the beginning of wisdom. Knowledge of the Holy One results in understanding" (Proverbs 9:10). James' letter offers a great perspective on this topic:

> *"If any of you lacks wisdom, you should ask God, who gives generously to all without finding fault, and it will be given to you. But when you ask, you must believe and not doubt, because the one who doubts is like a wave of the sea, blown and tossed by the wind." (James 1:5-6)*

Why are we driven and tossed about by the wind? Because there is no foundation. Who is the foundation? The Rock, our Lord Jesus Christ. And the Fear of the Lord is the foundation of knowledge, of

---

[89] Finally found a book on the subject and I give it 2 ½ out of 5 stars. *The Two Fears* by Chris Poblete.
[90] "To fear the Lord is to hate evil [especially my own sin]; I [wisdom] hate pride and arrogance, evil behavior and perverse speech." (Proverbs 8:13)

knowing God, of knowing His very nature, and of knowing the desire of God's heart.

This is the way Bible commentator Matthew Henry describes the "fear of the Lord":

> *It is not only the Lord and his greatness that we are to fear, but the Lord and his goodness, not only his majesty, but his mercy. They shall flee for fear **to** the Lord and his goodness (so some take it), shall flee to it as their city of refuge. We must fear God's goodness, that is, we must admire it, and stand amazed at it, must adore it, and worship as Moses did at the proclaiming of this name, Ex. 34:6. We must be afraid of offending his goodness, of making any ungrateful returns for it, and so forfeiting it. There is forgiveness with God, that he may be feared, Ps. 130:4. We must rejoice with trembling in the goodness of God, must not be high-minded, but fear.*[91]

Methodist circuit riding preacher, Bishop Francis Asbury, put it this way; "I am afraid of losing the sweetness I feel."[92]

Chuck Swindoll speaks from the perspective of the fear of shattering his testimony of Christ, offending a holy God and thereby suffering the consequences of severed fellowship:

> *"What we sow, the Scriptures warn, we will also reap. This is a sobering reminder to me that life on earth is really nothing more than a string of moments, one after another. And I do not want my testimony for Jesus Christ to be shattered by a single moment of indulging my flesh. I don't want one moment of rage or pride or arrogance to cast a shadow over a lifetime of walking with my Lord. Frankly, I fear that possibility. And do you know what? I want to fear that possibility. When I stop fearing it, I am in grave danger."*[93]

---

[91] *Matthew Henry's Commentary on the Whole Bible, New Modern Edition.*
[92] Peter Marshall/David Manuel. *From Sea to Shining Sea.*
[93] Charles R. Swindoll. *Moses.*

Today's Christians are building their spiritual houses on sand without having constructed a solid footing on which to build. "But everyone who hears these words of mine and does not put them into practice is like a foolish man who built his house on sand. The rain came down, the streams rose, and the winds blew and beat against that house, and it fell with a great crash" (Matthew 7:26-27). Why do we have no dread of God's wrath or the consequences of our sin? Why don't we seek his favor? The history of Israel in the book of Judges shows us what happens when God's people become self-satisfied, content with their place in life and pleased with their circumstances. Like them, we do not walk in the fear of the Lord, and we do not walk according to knowledge. Each time this happened with them, the nation was conquered and oppressed until they once again cried out to God. We can learn from their example, turn back to Christ and once again seek to know this foundational truth — the fear of the Lord.

Are you hearing the message that pursuing knowledge by the fear of the Lord is a very foolish thing to neglect? Will you side with the five foolish bridesmaids, who in ignorant contentment did not continually seek God's grace and the Spirit's anointing; or will you join hands with the wise and search out knowledge in the fear of the Lord?

As Moses came down from Mount Sinai, "Moses said to the people, 'Do not be afraid. God has come to test you, so that the fear of God will be with you to keep you from sinning.'" Moses' statement amazes me. For us in our human weakness, it's an impossible dichotomy. Don't be afraid, but fear God. How do we resolve this clash of fear? Simply, when we fear God, we have nothing else to fear; and this is only possible in Christ.

The answer to this next question amazes me. Did our Lord Jesus walk in the "fear of the Lord?" He is God, manifested in the flesh. He is God revealed among men. Does he even need to fear of the Lord? We find the answer in Isaiah's prophetic message about our Messiah: "The Spirit of the Lord will rest on him — the Spirit of wisdom and understanding, the Spirit of counsel and of power, the Spirit of knowledge and the fear of the Lord — and he will delight in the fear of the Lord" (Isaiah 11:1-3). This is delighted obedience! Jesus did indeed have the fear of the Lord and He delighted in it. This is a sure truth:

"Blessed is the man who fears the Lord, who finds great delight in his commands" (Psalm 112:1). The fear of the Lord and delighting in His commands are one and the same. They walk together hand in hand.

Did the apostle Paul walk in the "fear of the Lord"? He wrote: "It is because we know this solemn fear of the Lord that we work so hard to persuade others" (2 Corinthians 4:11 NLT). If it's good enough for our Lord Jesus and good enough for the Apostle Paul, shouldn't we be crying out for more of it?

I need the fear of the Lord when my finger is poised over my remote. I need the fear of the Lord when my hand is on the computer mouse, making choices. I need the fear of the Lord when someone cuts me off in traffic. I need the fear of the Lord when I'm struggling with my greatest weaknesses. And this blessed fear is what I enter into as I lift my hands, worshipping in reverent awe; this reverent awe leads me into delighted obedience.

Consider how deep our need is for this special fear. My flesh needs this fear, my soul desires it, and my spirit delights in it. How does our Lord Jesus lead us into this delighted fear? He leads us along a narrow pathway so we come to dwell in the council of a Holy God. In God's council we come into a reverent awe. "In the council of the holy ones God is greatly feared; he is more awesome than all who surround him" (Psalm 89:7).

But this holy, awe-inspired reverence and delighted obedience is only one aspect of the fear of the Lord.[94] We must also look at the terror-filled dread of a just and righteous God.

Fear of God is a two-sided coin. This becomes clear in the examples we see throughout the Bible. First, we see this in Adam and Eve. At first they walked and fellowshipped with God in reverence, awe, and delighted obedience. But that all changed when they rebelled and the "Fear of the Lord" turned into a dreaded fear of God, and they hid themselves from God.

---

[94] This is not a fear-based morality. "Honesty born of fear does nothing to root out the fundamental cause of evil in the world — the radical self-centeredness of the human heart. If anything, fear-based morality strengthens it, since ultimately elder brothers are being moral only for their own benefit." Timothy Keller. *Prodigal God*, pg. 60.

Next, we see the two sides of the coin played out with Cain and Abel. Abel made a sacrifice to God in reverence, awe, and delighted obedience. He knew what God desired of him and he honored God accordingly. Cain did not fear God. He did not delight in obedience and he ended up living in a dreadful fear of God because of the consequences of his sin. "My punishment is more than I can bear" (Genesis 4:13).

In Deuteronomy 27, we see two sides of the coin revealed when the tribes of Israel were divided into two groups. Some tribes were instructed to stand on Mount Gerizim and other tribes were told to stand on Mount Ebal. They were told of the blessings that come with serving God in reverence, awe, and delighted obedience, symbolized by Mount Gerizim. They were also told of the curses that come with disobedience, symbolized by Mount Ebal. But thanks be to God, an altar of sacrifice for sin was built on Mount Ebal — a demonstration of God's mercy and forgiveness and pointing forward to Christ. This demonstration was a picture of God's mercy, shown in the sacrifice of Jesus, His only Son, who took upon Himself the penalty for our sin and for our rebellion.

Mount Gerizim is one of the two mountains in the immediate vicinity of the West Bank city of Nablus and forms the southern side of the valley in which Nablus is located, the northern side being formed by Mount Ebal. The mountain of blessing is higher than the mountain of the curse. In the Jewish culture, a mountain is a symbol of power. Hebrew symbolism tells us the higher the mountain, the greater the power. Grace and mercy are greater than judgment, but they are like two sides of the same coin.

Again, we see the two sides of fear of the Lord when King David moved the Ark of the Covenant. The first time, they did not do so in reverence, awe, and delighted obedience. They did it in ignorance and it ended in a fearful dread of the Lord when one of David's men touched the ark and died (2 Samuel 6:1-9). The second time they moved the ark, they did so in reverence, awe, and delighted obedience. They searched the Law and found out what the Lord required of them and it turned into a victorious occasion.

Please understand — this is important. One side of the coin is reverence, awe, and delighted obedience. The other side of the coin is a servile fear, and it is not what God desires for us because it is contrary to the spirit of adoption (Romans 8:15). We saw it first when Adam and Eve hid from God in the Garden. It is our fear of what God will ask or require of us if we surrender to Him and do His will. It is a misguided fear that is rooted in ignorance and _must have no part_ in our walk with the Lord. It's a fear that lies to you and tells you that if you surrender to God's will, He will grab you by the collar and drag you off to Africa where you will have to eat bugs and drink polluted water to survive as a missionary to some strange people you can't even talk to. It is a servile, cowering, and self-centered fear. This fear is best defined as the fear of paying the full price or penalty for your offenses, especially those imposed upon you by a Just, Holy, and Righteous God.

If you have this kind of servile fear of God, you will want to hide from God and cover up your sin with fig leaves like Adam and Eve in the garden

Join me in this prayer. _"Lord, put Your love in our hearts to compel us to diligently search Scripture to learn what You desire. Overcome our fear of what You, Lord, will require of us if we know the truth."_

Willing ignorance will rob you of the benefits of wisdom and steal away the joy of knowledge that brings you to delightfully obey a Holy God. Apart from delighted obedience, you may come to feel like you're groping in the dark: "Then they will call to me but I will not answer; they will look for me but will not find me, since they hated knowledge and did not choose to fear the Lord" (Proverbs 1:27). Whom do you fear?

Every Christian I have ever known who will admit it, has weaknesses to overcome. "Sin is crouching at your door; it desires to have you, _but you must master it_" (Genesis. 4:7, emphasis added). "All have sinned, all fall short of the glory of God" (Romans 3:23). Everyone who is born of the flesh has something to overcome.

What keeps you from entertaining your weaknesses? What keeps you from allowing evil to camp on your doorstep? We all fight these things, but what keeps you from allowing them to entrap you like a net? Are you allowing your weaknesses to rule over you because you are not aware of the indwelling presence of the Spirit of the Lord? Is it because you see God from afar? Is it because you do not see His loving, watchful eye upon you? Is it because you only experience God in the moments of ritual worship and not in every word and action of your workday? The beginning of turning from our errant ways is a delighted fear of the very living presence of the Lord Almighty.

You have a great hope above and beyond God's watchful care. Christ has overcome all of these weaknesses on our behalf.[95] And then He does an even greater work for your good. He imparts righteousness upon you, declaring you to have right standing before God.[96] And then His righteousness works in you, resulting in works of righteousness in your life. Because of all Christ has done on your behalf, because of His abundant grace and mercy, you have cause to delight in the fear of the Lord.

Let's look at the benefits of having a heart that delights in obedience and in awe of God — the fear of the Lord. When you applied for your job, you asked the employer about the benefits. Medical, dental, life insurance, paid time off, and so on. Did you know there are benefits that come with the "fear of the Lord?" The Psalmist tells of this truth: "He will have **NO FEAR** of bad news; his heart is steadfast, trusting in the Lord" (Psalm 112:7). You need fear no man, no nation, no weapon, no terrorist, no economic downturn, no natural disaster, no war, no boss, no news, not even the phone ringing at three am — there is no need to fear any of these, when you delight in the fear the Lord. (Read Psalm 103.)

Have you ever found a job with benefits as good as what you just read? If you were hired on a new job and given this list of benefits, you would race home, show them to your family and you'd all be shouting "Woohoo," and doing a hallelujah dance with your wife and kids right in middle of the living room.

So how do you begin to walk in the fear of the Lord? When we come across the kind of Scripture that instructs you about what to do, we do well to ask, "Okay, Lord. I want to do this because I'm reading it right here in Your Word, so *how* do I do it? Lord, show me what to do." By the leading of the Holy Spirit, and by allowing your natural man to be subject to the Spirit and to the Word you can walk in this delightful fear.

How do you build a solid foundation for wisdom and knowledge?

---

[95] "I have told you these things, so that in me you may have peace. In this world you will have trouble. But take heart! I have overcome the world." (John 16:33)
[96] "God made him who had no sin to be sin for us, so that in him we might become the righteousness of God." (1 Corinthians 5:21)

Here's an example. When mom wheels her three-year-old down the aisle in the toy department, what does the child do when he sees something he wants? He cries out. When you've misplaced your wallet with all your cash in it, what do you do? You search for it until you find it. "Cry out for insight and understanding. Search for them as you would for lost money or hidden treasure" (Proverbs 2:3 NLT).

Is the Lord your first love? Will you fear the Lord? Will you love the Lord and build a solid house on the Rock, Christ Jesus? Will you become a strong and useful vessel, woven with threads of godly fear and love? These are threads of pure, refined gold and silver.

Why is there no fear of the Lord? "Is it not because I have long been silent that you do not fear me?" (Isaiah 57:11). We put God on mute when we stay away from the proclamation of God's Word from the pulpit, when we avoid the teaching of the Word, and when we run away from Christian brothers and sisters who hold us accountable, when we leave a church to avoid discipline. We are subject to silence when our Bible collects dust on the shelf. (Making the sign of a cross in the dust doesn't fix anything.) Also, we are deaf to the voice of God when we spurn the ministries of prophecy.

Build knowledge and wisdom on **this** foundation: "Wisdom has built her house; she has hewn out its seven pillars" (Proverbs 9:1). You can build on the seven pillars of wisdom's house starting today. Will you do it? Will you begin today?

> *"How happy are those who fear the Lord — all who follow his ways! You will enjoy the fruit of your labor. How happy you will be! How rich your life! Your wife will be like a fruitful vine, flourishing within your home. And look at all those children! There they sit around your table as vigorous and healthy as young olive trees. That is the Lord's reward for those who fear him." (Psalm 128:1-4 NLT)*

What a promise. What an incredibly valuable treasure. A treasure that you can have **now** and it will last forever. Psalm 118:4 says, "Let those who fear the Lord say: 'His love endures forever.'"

What does the fear of the Lord have to do with **spiritual gifts**? We have already learned that it is the foundation of knowledge and wisdom. When there is no fear of the Lord, it becomes painfully obvious that the power in the ministry of spiritual gifts is diminished in our gatherings because we don't know what God desires for us, "for they do not know the way of the Lord, the requirements of their God" (Jeremiah 5:4). If we do not know the requirements of the Lord, do not know what God desires for us, what He promises us, holds in store for us, even holds out to us in his open hand — we cannot be effective in the powerful ministries and service of spiritual gifts. We step out from under His blessed showers.

Here is the second part of this equation regarding spiritual gifts. As we minister in our spiritual gift, the fear of the Lord keeps us on the right pathway. For example, the fear of the Lord in the use of the spiritual gift of prophecy is what keeps us from adding to what God has revealed to us, and we avoid thinking, "Well, I have a few things to say about that too." Our delighted obedience keeps us from adding to what God is making known to us.

The fear of the Lord helps to keep us from using our spiritual gifts for self-advancement. It keeps us within the bounds of God's love as we serve in our gift. It keeps us from reducing the gift — regressing from spiritual to soulish.[97]

God's love at work in your heart will elevate your ministry in spiritual gifts to a form of worship and the fear of the Lord keeps you ministering according to His grace, love, and mercy. You will not, and cannot, rightly fear what you do not know. In your ignorance you are like the two brothers who climbed Haystack Rock not knowing the nature of the powerful tide, rip currents, and surf below them. You cannot approach a Holy God with reverence, awe, and trembling fear unless you see His Holiness. A reverent awe and a fall-on-our-knees kind of fear are only possible when the Spirit of Jesus reveals the Holiness of God to you. Revelation knowledge of God is essential to gaining this blessed gift, the fear of the Lord; and in this reverent fear we can minister and serve fearlessly. You have been given the key to revelation knowledge; use your key to enter into the blessings of the fear of the Lord.

---

[97] Soulish: This is a reference to the soul part of man being bound to the natural man, which cannot receive spiritual gifts apart from a regenerated spirit.

Our prayer: *Lord God. Reveal your holiness to Your people, open our eyes to see, and lead us to come trembling in awe before You. Give us clean hearts to receive Your good gifts in these last days, so Your church may be prepared, presentable, a beautiful bride adorned for the Bridegroom (Hosea 3:5). In the ministries of our gifts, help us to serve in the fear of the Lord to keep us from reducing what is holy to what is common.*

YOUR JOURNEY JOURNAL
Chapter 5: In the Fear of God, We are Fearless

1. What is at the root of having little or no fear of the Lord?

2. How is it that we come to delight in the fear of the Lord?

3. What is the difference between a fear-based morality and a shame-based culture versus a love-driven obedience?

4. What does the fear of the Lord have to do with spiritual gifts?

Your Journal Notes:

6

A Call to Repentance

A grievous sin of the American Church is that we have regressed, trying to accomplish the work of the church, advancing the kingdom of heaven, by the power and strength of the natural man alone. We have abandoned the Springs of Living Water and dug our own well (Jeremiah 2:13). We have deceived ourselves, because this work of ministering the grace of our Lord Jesus Christ to a lost and dying world is not to be accomplished by human might nor by natural strength, but by the gifting and empowering work of the Holy Spirit in the saints (Zechariah 4:6). Instead of putting on God's armor, we put on the armor of education, the armor of great organizations, and the armor of human reasoning. These are good things in their place, but they must not supplant the empowering work of the Holy Spirit. We must not be like an altar made of well-polished stones without fire burning at the top.

When we, the church, endeavor to serve the Kingdom's purpose by our own wisdom and strength alone, it is detestable before the Lord, because in doing this we fail to separate the common from the Holy (Ezekiel 22:26). Please understand this: when Christians attempt to do in the strength of the flesh what can only be done by the power of the Spirit, they steal away the power of the cross, the power of the Resurrected Christ. The apostle Paul spoke of the power of the cross being stolen away: "For Christ did not send me to baptize but to preach the gospel, *and not with words of eloquent wisdom, lest the cross of Christ be emptied of its power*" (1 Corinthians 1:17, emphasis added).

Too many "shepherds" of the church deny *spiritual* gifts to God's people, reducing them to ministries and service by means of natural gifts alone.

> *"Is it not enough for you to feed on the good pasture, that you must tread down with your feet the rest of your pasture; and to drink of clear water, that you must muddy the rest of the water with your feet? And must my sheep eat what you have trodden with your feet, and drink what you have muddied with your feet." (Ezekiel 34:18-19)*

When Christian leaders deny good gifts to God's people, the power of the Spirit is forfeited in the church and we are left with "having a form of godliness but denying its power" (2 Timothy 3:5).

Some may scoff at the thought of "Paul the Plumber" or "Bob the Butcher," who barely graduated from High School, saying anything useful in a church service, even under the power and anointing of the Holy Spirit. We may think, "What could they possibly say that we need to hear?" After all, we have excellent pastors in the American Church who spend precious hours in preparation and preach outstanding sermons, so why do we need to hear some plumber spouting off in church? "For it is written: 'I will destroy the wisdom of the wise; the intelligence of the intelligent I will frustrate'" (1 Corinthians 1:19). We take pride in our intelligent, wise, and polished three-point Sunday morning messages; but when we deny any other word to be spoken we are in danger of despising the true oracles of God, given through whomever He chooses. Our arrogance is our undoing and it is detestable. Jesus condemned the teachers of the Law in His day for this same prideful selfishness. "Woe to you, teachers of the law and Pharisees, you hypocrites! You shut the door of the kingdom of heaven in people's faces. You yourselves do not enter, nor will you let those enter who are trying to" (Matthew 23:13).

The book of Revelation is written to reveal our returning Messiah, Yahshua HaMashiach. The letters to the churches in Revelation chapters two and three are a call to prepare the bride of Christ (the church) through repentance. Reading these words compels us to weep with great sorrow. "Repent" (Revelation 2:5). "Repent" (Revelation 2:15). "Repent" (Revelation 2:22). "Repent" (Revelation 3:3). "Repent" (Revelation 3:19). Remember that John the Baptist called the people to repentance to prepare the way for Christ Jesus to walk among his people. In the same way, the apostle John's letter to the churches call us to repentance to prepare us for the Bridegroom, who is our Lord Jesus Christ.

The apostle John's words call us to repent of the sin of doing God's work in our own strength: "Repent and do the things you did at first" (Revelation 2:5). Paul warned the church in Galatia as he watched their downhill slide into human effort. "Are you so foolish? After beginning by means of the Spirit, are you now trying to finish by means of the flesh" (Galatians 3:3). Jesus warned us of doing the work of the kingdom by human means: "Flesh gives birth to flesh, but the Spirit gives birth to spirit" (John 3:6). We are called to turn from the hypocrisy of human strength because the end result of human effort is like wood, straw, and chaff.

Again and again the Scriptures call us to receive all that God desires for us — to strengthen us, to empower us, to gift us, to send us out to be the very hands of Jesus held out to a lost and dying world. But before repentance comes, revelation must wash over us — the realization that before a Holy God we are miserable and depraved. We are still not ready to repent until we see clearly our depravity before a Holy God, and then we will see Christ as the resolution for our corrupt condition. "Come, let us return to the Lord. He has torn us to pieces[98] but he will heal us; he has injured us but he will bind up our wounds" (Hosea 6:1).

God desires that we minister in His Name, in His power and authority, and by means of Holy Spirit empowered gifts. "Our sufficiency is from God, who has made us sufficient to be ministers of a new covenant, not of the letter but of the Spirit. For the letter kills, but the Spirit gives life" (2 Corinthians 2:5-6). Only then will we be able to accomplish His Great Commission, His command to go into all the world (Matthew 28:18-20). But we have refused His precious gifts, His beautiful bridal adornments. We have not separated what is holy from what is common, by confusing God-given natural gifts with spiritual gifts empowered by the Holy Spirit. Lord have mercy. Lord, change our hearts.

---

[98] "He has torn us to pieces" refers to God's Word tearing at our hearts as our sin is revealed to us.

My hope is that the Holy Spirit has used this study to put a new and burning desire in your heart. May the Spirit of Jesus cause you to hunger and thirst. Do you desire the precious gifts the Bridegroom holds out to the bride? Are you eager to uncover what you've buried and put to work the gifts the Spirit has for you? Ask! Seek! Pursue Christ with all diligence, for the Spirit has put His burning desire in you. God is faithful and will give you His heart's desire, just as He promised.

Our Prayer: *"May our Lord give us eyes to see our depravity and turn our hearts to our Lord Jesus who binds up our wounds. Give us repentant hearts, contrite hearts that turn away from what is detestable. Gracious God, convince us of our sin, convict us of our sin, and give us hearts that grieve. Forgive us for our complacency, for our self-satisfied ways, and for thinking that we are so spiritually rich, when we are 'wretched, pitiable, poor, blind and naked' (Revelation 3:17). Forgive us for despising and even forbidding your good gifts, given for the good of your people, the Church. Forgive us for our empty forms of godliness, our hollow man-made traditions, and the powerless ministries of our churches (Ezekiel 24:21). Forgive us for confusing what is common with what is holy (Ezekiel 44:23).*

"Lord, if our hearts reject Your call to repentance and will not turn away from our grievous sin, yes, amen, take away the delight of our eyes, the stronghold in which we take pride, the object of our affection. But in wrath, remember mercy. And then in Your time, may Your church be rebuilt, Lord God Almighty. Let its foundations be restored (Isaiah 44:28). Oh Lord Jesus Christ, refresh Your people with the most excellent fruit of the Spirit by pouring out on Your people the gifts of the Spirit (Joel 2:29). Oh Lord, rebuild what we have abandoned. Lord God Almighty, restore what we have torn down. Gather the lame and the weak, assemble those who have been cast away and brought to grief. Blessed Redeemer, renew a right spirit in us. Holy Spirit, refresh those who are weary and faint, washing them in Your Holy Fountain (Jeremiah 31:25). Melt us, mold us, shape us into useful vessels into whom you can pour the oil of your Holy Spirit — full to overflowing so that we may be your instruments to call those bound in darkness into your glorious light, and to invite the lame, the weak, the blind, those in the streets, the byways, the alleys, and those without a place to lay their heads to Your bountiful banqueting table in the kingdom of God. Lord, pour out your rain on your people — Your autumn rains

to produce a bountiful harvest.[99] *Renew, restore, rebuild, refresh, and revive Your church (Isaiah 61:4, Psalm 85:1,6), for all who will come to celebrate Your Great Wedding Feast.*

"Yes, Lord, Amen!

"May your will be done on earth as it is in heaven. We pray in the Mighty Name of Jesus. YOUR KINGDOM COME!"

YOUR JOURNEY JOURNAL
Chapter 6: Call to Repentance

1. Consider the Great Commission: What is the consequence if we do not clearly distinguish between what is holy and what is common?

2. What is at the root of our arrogance regarding manifestations of the Spirit of Jesus through spiritual gifts ministered in the church?

3. What is God's purpose in calling us to repent for the sins of the whole church?

Your Journal Notes:

---

[99] The autumn rains are symbolic of the "first rains" of the Jewish New Year and are given to refresh the earth after the long, dry summer. Jesus' words, as He taught the people, refreshed them after over four hundred years of drought from not hearing God's prophets speak the oracles of God. God sends the autumn rains to prepare the earth to produce a bountiful harvest in season (Psalm 84:6, Joel 2:23, Jeremiah 5:24, James 5:7).

The Great Banquet

"He Sets a Feast Before Me"

I dug deep into my pocket to get some rattling loose change as I passed by a beggar who held out a cardboard sign saying, "I was born blind. Spare some change?" His bony shoulders were wrapped with a dirty, ragged coat held together with duct tape. Weeks of stubble poked from his gaunt cheeks, and he smelled of neglect. He stumbled in oversized shoes as he paced about. I stepped back as someone approached and grasped the beggar's arm with a gentle hand.

His words were as tender as his touch. "Follow me," he said. Then he guided the beggar, urging him forward. I'm not sure why, but I followed them. They entered a room filled with sunlight, and I saw a banqueting table overflowing with a bountiful feast. I wanted to help the blind man stretch out his hand, for he would find a cornucopia of plump red, purple, and green grapes, melons, and squash of every variety, fresh ripe mangoes, pears, oranges and apples, bright yellow bananas, roasted turkey, fresh baked bread, fancy pastries, and so much more.

The beggar stood there, grasping his tin cup as if desperate to hear the clink of a coin. He could not comprehend what had been prepared for him. In his dark world he must be imagining that today would be like all other days. He reached out his dented, stained tin cup in trembling hands hoping for a little something; maybe even some warm, watered down beggar's broth to still his growling stomach. He could not grasp what had been set before him — for his good — and he suffered for want in the midst of bounty.

The blind beggar suddenly leaned forward and breathed deep as if his senses were awakened. A puzzled look and a glimmer of hope displaced the sadness in the wrinkled lines of his face. Then, as if something burst open from depths of agony in his soul, his head went back, his mouth opened wide, his lungs filled with air. He screamed, "No more of this!" With a look of disgust he tossed away his tin cup. His soiled hands and bent fingers groped in the air for what he could not see. What he found was the One who had guided him, still standing close by. "Oh, please. Open my eyes to see. Please, help me to see." His cry became urgent. "If only I could see."

The beggar man felt a warm touch to his eyes. The loving warmth electrified him to the depth of his impoverished soul. His eyelids began to flutter with anticipation as he leaned forward and took a step toward the banqueting table and spread out his hands. "This is for me? This is all for me?"

-------------------------------- ††† --------------------------------------

Are you that blind beggar? Do you know *about* the feast at the banqueting table set before you but cannot see it? The Holy Scripture tells of it. "You prepare a table before me in the presence of my enemies" (Psalm 23:5). Do you know *about* the bounty of His table, but your hands grope without taking hold of all that is set before you? God's Word reveals it. "Let him lead me to the banquet hall, and let his banner over me be love" (Song of Songs 2:4). The Good Shepherd is waiting for you to partake in His great blessing and bounty given to you through the sacrifice of Jesus Christ, our Lord and Savior.

The abundance of Christ is available to all who will come — from blind beggars to presidents and princes. No matter your place in life, come to the table with a repentant heart. Put aside the cares of this world and make yourself ready to partake of the kingdom's treasures set before you — an abundance of spiritual gifts for the purpose of worshipful service and ministry. Gifted and empowered with instruments of true worship, you are now ready to fearlessly minister Jesus' living, active presence in the world today. In receiving these precious gifts, you are prepared to lead those who Jesus has called to His bountiful table.

Please pray with me: *Lord, open my eyes that I may see wonderful things you have set before me. Submerge me, bury me, saturate me, wash me, envelope me, permeate me, fill me to overflowing with the oil of Your Holy Spirit. Make me a useful instrument of worship in your kingdom. Yes, Lord. With delighted heart I receive the joys of Your salvation, and bountiful gifts of the Spirit set before me.*

Yes, Lord. Amen!

Appendix

Recommended resources for study and reading:

Every serious student of Scripture would do well to make time for earnest prayer, seeking the Lord, interceding for the church and our shepherds. It is also beneficial acquire the following study resources, as your budget allows:

1. The Holy Bible in reliable versions (NIV, NLT, ESV, NRSV)
2. Personal notebook or journal
3. Topical Bible: *The Zondervan NIV Nave's Topical Bible.*
4. A written systematic theology: *Systematic Theology* by Wayne Grudem
5. *Book of Concord*, Translated by Theodore G. Tappert.
6. Bible Dictionary: *Vine's Expository Dictionary*, by W.E. Vine.
7. Concordance: *Strong's Exhaustive Concordance of the Bible*, by James Strong.
8. Bible commentary: *Matthew Henry's Commentary:* and *Jamieson, Fausset and Brown Commentary.*

Many of these resources are available online (www.blueletterbible.org and www.bible.cc/).

Additional reading:
The Beauty of Spiritual Language by Jack Hayford
Authority to Heal by Ken Blue
The Spiritual Man by Watchman Nee
The Pursuit of God by A. W. Tozer

Notes, Quotes & Credits

Cover Art:
Microscopic photo. Copyright ©Reuben Birkholz 2015, Calcite on other minerals, Pima County, AZ. Used by permission.
Cover Design: Ian Loudon

Preface:
Pg. 11. *The Shack* by William Paul Young. © 2007, Windblown Media, 4680 Calle Norte, Newbury Park, CA 91320.

Book 1

Chapter 1:
Image by "Thinkstock." Used by permission.

Chapter 2:
Pg. 42. *Pursuit of God, with Study Guide* by A. W. Tozer. © 1982, 1993 by Zur Ltd. Wing Spread Publishers, Camp Hill, PA. Used within approved guidelines.
Pg. 62. *Screwtape Letters* by C. S. Lewis. Signature Classics published by Harper Collins. 1942. Used within guidelines.

Chapter 3:
Pg. 68. Illustration by: Ian Loudon.
Pg. 69, 70. *The Spiritual Man* by Watchman Nee. © 1968. Christian Fellowship Publishers, Inc. 11515 Allecinglie Parkway, Richmond, VA 23235. 804.794.5333. Used by permission.
Note: Research material used: 1) *The Gift of Prophecy in the New Testament and Today, Revised Edition* by Wayne Grudem. © 1988, 2000 by Wayne A. Grudem. Published by Crossway, Wheaton, Ill. 2) *Systematic Theology* by Wayne Grudem. © 1994. Inter-Varsity Press and Zondervan, Grand Rapids, MI.

Chapter 5:

Pg. 96. *The Works of John Adams, Second President of the United States* by John Adams. Edited by Charles Francis Adams. (Boston: Little, Brown and Co., 1856). 10 volumes. Vol. 6. November 16, 2015. Quote from pg. 416.

Chapter 6:

Pg. 106. *The Communion of the Holy Spirit* by Watchman Nee. © 1994. Christian Fellowship Publishers, Inc. 11515 Allecinglie Parkway, Richmond, VA 23235. 804.794.5333. Used by permission.

Pg. 109. *Spirit Rising: Tapping into the Power of the Holy Spirit* by Jim Cymbala. © 2012 by Jim Cymbala. Used by permission of Zondervan Publishing.

Pg. 115. *Called to Believe Teach and Confess: Introduction to Doctrinal Theology* by Steven P. Mueller. Used by permission of Wipf and Stock Publishers.

Pg. 115. *Elijah* by Charles Swindoll. © 2000 by Charles R. Swindoll, Inc. Published by Thomas Nelson Inc., PO Box 141000, Nashville, TN 37214. Used by permission.

Pg. 117. *The Spiritual Man* by Watchman Nee. © 1968. Christian Fellowship Publishers, Inc. 11515 Allecinglie Parkway, Richmond, VA 23235. 804.794.5333. Used by permission.

Pg. 126. *Authority to Heal* by Ken Blue. © 1987 Ken Blue. Used by permission of InterVarsity Press, PO Box 1400, Downers Grove, IL 60515. Used by permission.

Pg. 127. *Baptism in the Early Church: History, Theology, and Liturgy in the First Five Centuries* by Everett Ferguson. © 2009, Wm. B. Eerdmans Publishing Co. 2140 Oak Industrial Drive N.E., Grand Rapids, Michigan 49505. Used by permission.

Chapter 7:

Pg. 158. *The Spiritual Man* by Watchman Nee. © 1968. Christian Fellowship Publishers, Inc. 11515 Allecinglie Parkway, Richmond, VA 23235. 804.794.5333. Used by permission.

Pg. 167. *The Beauty of Spiritual Language: My Journey Toward the Heart of God* by Jack Hayford. © 1992 Jack Hayford. Used by permission.

Pg. 176. *From Sea to Shining Sea.* © 1986, by Peter J. Marshall and David Manuel, Published by Fleming H. Revell Co, Old Tappan, New Jersey. Used by permission.

Book 2

Chapter 1:
Pg. 198. "Onward Christian Soldiers," Sabine Baring-Gould, 1865.

Chapter 5:
Pg. 229. *Matthew Henry's Commentary on the Whole Bible. New Modern Edition.* © 1991 by Hendrickson Publishers, Inc., Peabody, Mass. Used by permission.
Pg. 248. *Moses* by Charles Swindoll. © 1999 by Charles R. Swindoll, Inc. Published by Thomas Nelson Inc., PO Box 141000, Nashville, TN 37214. Used by permission.
Pg. 248. *From Sea to Shining Sea* by Peter J. Marshall and David Manuel. © 1986. Published by Fleming H. Revell Co, Old Tappan, New Jersey. Used by permission.
Pg. 251. *The Prodigal God: Recovering the Heart of the Christian Faith* by Timothy Keller. © 2008 by Timothy Keller. Published by Dutton, a member of Penguin Group (USA) inc. Used by permission.

Glossary

The purpose of this glossary is not to repeat definitions available in a Bible Dictionary, but to offer dimensions of the original words and relate how these meanings apply to the study of *Treasures of the Kingdom*. Also listed are terms used in this study that are not in common use today.

- **Adorned, Adornments, עָדָה** *(`adah),* κοσμέω *(kosmeō):* The bride of Christ is given bridal adornments, or ornaments of worship for the glory and honor of the Bridegroom. These are not only for the time when the Bridegroom returns for His bride, but for the age of the church — the bride in waiting. Ezekiel beautifully creates a complete picture of this word, showing the blight washed away and beauty given in its place (Ezekiel 15:11-13). Revelation 21:2 reveals another dimension, "as a bride adorned for her husband."

- **Autumn rains, מוֹרֶה** *(mowreh):* The rains of autumn, the first rains to come in the Jewish new year, are promised in Deuteronomy 11:14. The rains are referred to in Psalm 84:6: "As they pass through the Valley of Baka, they make it a place of springs; the *autumn rains* also cover it with pools." God promises to refresh His people again in Joel 2:23: "Be glad, people of Zion, rejoice in the Lord your God, for he has given you the *autumn rains* because he is faithful. He sends you abundant showers, both autumn and spring rains, as before." The autumn rains became symbolic of rains sent to refresh the earth after the drought of summer. As Jesus began His earthly ministry, His words to the people were like the autumn rain, refreshing them after four hundred years of silence, a drought of hearing God's Word.

- **Authority, Authority of the Believer,** ἐξουσία *(exousia)*: God is Authority. His Name is Authority. Christ's position at the right hand of the Father is Authority. Christ Jesus confers His authority on whomever he pleases. For the believer, submission is the key to all authority. Christians have *NO* authority apart from Christ, the Head of the church, and what He commands us to do. All authority in Christ comes by virtue of our submission to His authority and the Word. God has established an order of authority for the church and for the family. This authority has a heart of love, the heart of a servant, a foot-washing mindset. As an example: Jesus had authority to lay His life down because of His reverent submission to the Authority of His Father.

- **Body of Man, Natural,** σῶμα *(sōma)*: Scripture refers to our earthly body as earthen vessels, jars of clay, perishable, a tent, or a house. In this study it is, at times, referred to as our earth suit. We can't mistake what it is. We can pinch it, poke it, walk about in it, feel pain, experience pleasure, laugh, shed tears, break a bone, and the list goes on. This body is our means for remaining here on earth to accomplish all that God has ordained for us to do.

- **Cessation, Cessationist:** Those within the Christian church who believe that many of the spiritual gifts have ceased, especially utterance gifts, are considered to be cessationists. Their belief system is promoted in many different ways. Some don't outright deny prophecy, but instead redefine it as preaching — pulpit ministry. Others simply overlook these spiritual gifts and refuse to acknowledge them or teach truthfully about them. Still others claim that these gifts were only needed for the establishment of the church in the beginning of the church age. Still others teach that God only speaks to His people today in the written, canonical Scripture. In addition, some claim that spiritual gifts are nothing more than God-given natural gifts, applied for spiritual purposes within the church.

- **Church,** ἐκκλησία *(ekklēsia):* The universal body of all Christian believers who are called by Jesus' Name and gather together in Jesus' Name. The church is Christ. It is the means by which Christ is manifested to a lost and dying world. A church gathering will consist of three parts: Christ, the Head; Leaders (under authority) who establish order, i.e. pastors, elders, deacons, deaconesses, etc.; and congregants (under authority) who also minister and serve in the church. It is a gathering for worship, for serving, for singing praises before the Lord, and for the preparation of the saints to minister the saving grace of our Lord and Savior, Jesus Christ. To be a church, order must be established; an order of authority, just as there is order in God's created universe. Note: This is not one person in authority, but an order of authority (1 Corinthians 14:40).

- **Civil or Civic Righteousness:** The distinction between righteousness of saving faith and the righteousness of works became blurred in the 15th century Christian church. Martin Luther served to make this distinction clear. Civic righteousness is that in which humans work for the good of the community — the betterment of the whole. Civic righteousness does not lead to the salvation of the soul, but brings about the improvement of cultures and societies. When we confuse civil righteousness and the righteousness of saving faith, we are not discerning between what is common and what is holy.

- **Commission,** οἰκονομία *(oikonomia):* The Great Commission of the Christian Church came through a command from our Lord Jesus. He instructed his disciples, then and throughout the age of the church, to make disciples, baptize them, and teach them to obey, revealing and ministering the resurrected, living Jesus Christ to every tribe, nation, people, and tongue in all the earth (Matthew 28:18-20). A church, in submission to Christ, may, under the authority of the Great Commission, appoint one of their people to a specific calling, duty, ministry, or mission through fasting, prayer, and the laying on of hands.

- **Common Grace:** This refers to the grace of God that is common to all mankind. The benefits of God's common grace are for all humans for the purpose of giving them the means to earn their way and to provide for their families. These common gifts and talents are for the good of societies and cultures. "For he makes his sun rise on the evil and on the good, and sends rain on the righteous and on the unrighteous" (Matthew 5:45 NRSV).

- **Covenant** ברית *(berith)*, διαθηκη *(diatheke)*: God made a covenant with Abram, Noah, King David and many more. God is a God of covenants. This is His very nature. In His covenants with people, He promises His goodness and His blessings, each revealing and fulfilling His purpose and plan for all eternity. God's covenants are one-sided grants, and at times give conditions (if you..., then I...) and establish requirements as in the Mosaic covenant and in His covenant with King David: "*If* your sons keep my covenant and the statutes I teach them, *then* their sons will sit on your throne forever and ever" (Psalm 132:12, emphasis added). As New Testament Christians, we have a covenant sealed by the blood of a risen Savior who has satisfied the "If you" requirements of the covenant.

- **Covenant, Sign of:** God gave "signs" along with His covenants. To Abram He gave a new name (Abraham), to Noah he gave a rainbow, to King David a kingdom and lineage eternally blessed. Jesus is the Mediator of a covenant for the New Testament church, and He gives a sign: His Holy Spirit. He confirmed this covenant and gives all who are His disciples His robe of righteousness.

- **Eleazar Effect:** Eleazar was one of David's three mighty men (2 Samuel 23:9-10). The "Eleazar Effect," as used in this study, is descriptive of moments when Christians see God doing through them what they could not possibly do themselves, in their own strength or by any other human means. The Eleazar effect is what we do by spiritual "might and power and by the Spirit" (Zechariah 4:6).

- **Empowering of Spiritual Gifts:** From ages past God has ordained for _all_ who are called by His Name, a work, service, or ministry (Ephesians 2:10). For this work, God gifts His people to accomplish what He has called them to do. Whether these gifts are given when a soul receives the gift of saving faith or in a subsequent outpouring of the Spirit of Grace, these spiritual gifts must be empowered by the Holy Spirit. Apart from an empowering work of the Spirit and without continual, ongoing, refreshing anointing from the Holy Spirit, these gifts are like a sailing ship with no wind, or a lamp without oil, or a car without fuel.

- **Ecstatic Experience:** There are many examples of ecstatic experiences throughout Scripture. Abram's is recorded in Genesis 15:12: "As the sun was setting, Abram fell into a deep sleep, and a thick and dreadful darkness came over him." Ezekiel says in Ezekiel 1:1, "the heavens were opened and I saw visions of God." The Apostle Paul was "caught up into the third heaven" (2 Corinthians 12:2). John the Apostle writes in Revelation 1:10, "On the Lord's Day I was in the Spirit, and I heard behind me a loud voice like a trumpet." Ministries within the church in a spiritual gift, whether prophecies, spiritual languages and interpretations, or singing in the spirit, typically do not involve any kind of ecstatic experience. Ecstatic experiences as listed above are uncommon in everyday Christian life. Yet they must not be relegated to a time long past.

- **Fallibility:** The word "fallible" is not found in Scripture. But we find similar words that make its meaning clear: Fall, Fallen, Falling and Fell. In essence, we ought to always keep in mind that we are all fallible, i.e. subject to false steps, blunders, trespasses, moral failings, offenses, lapses of judgment, and the list goes on. Often it's a daily process of acknowledging our weaknesses, praying for strength to overcome them and then confessing our failings to receive forgiveness of our sin and God's cleansing flow.

- **Filled with the Spirit, πίμπλημι (pimplēmi):** Some would refer to this as the Baptism of the Holy Spirit. Others believe that we receive all that the Holy Spirit has for us as we come to saving faith. The controversies are not worth the trouble. In searching Scripture, this is what I see: When saving faith is given to a soul, the Holy Spirit indwells them. The Spirit of God washes over them and through them, cleansing them and sealing them against God's just wrath. The believer is "born of the Spirit." But the Holy Spirit isn't finished in His ministries to the new disciple. This adopted child must continually be filled and refilled in the Holy Spirit. There are also subsequent, powerful infillings or empowering of the Holy Spirit when the spiritual gifts are empowered for the good of the whole church, for deeds of service, worship, and ministry to the body of believers. The Old and New Testaments reveal a clear demarcation in the ministries of the Holy Spirit. In the Old, the Holy Spirit washes over or comes upon people, and in the New, the Holy Spirit indwells His people, filling them from within like springs of Living Water.

- **Five-fold Ministry Gifts:** In Ephesians 4:11-13, the Apostle Paul lists five ministries that are considered the five-fold ministries of leadership for the church. Paul lists apostles, prophets, evangelists, pastors, and teachers. At times these leadership gifts may be blended or combined, but typically, these gifts are for five different leaders within a body of believers.

- **Foretell:** To foretell is to tell something which cannot be known by natural means, intuition, investigation, scientific methods, or through any other human enterprise, especially to predict events before they occur. Foretelling prophecies are centered on the coming Messiah, focused upon Jesus Christ. These future events are known only to the mind of God and are made known to whom God chooses by the revelation power of the Holy Spirit.

- **Forthtell:** To deliver a message from God, whether with reference to the past, the present, or future. This ministry in the church is speaking forth the mind and counsel of God through prophetic utterance. Through "forthtelling," Jesus Christ is revealed by revelation power of the Holy Spirit. In this prophetic ministry there will be godly counsel, correction, admonition, exposed sins, encouragement, enlightenment, direction, and building up of the saints. Prophetic messages for the purpose of forthtelling proclaim a clear, specific, and authoritative message. They are not expressed in broad and general terms that are subject to various interpretations.

- **Infallibility:** Incapable of failing or failure, unerring in doctrine. Old Testament prophets were held to a standard of infallibility. Should they utter a prophetic message, whether foretelling or forthtelling, the message must prove true or they were marked as false prophets. Those who minister in the spiritual gift of prophecy are not held to this standard of infallibility for the words they choose to express the message they offer. But they must submit to the gathering of believers and church leaders for examination of the content of their messages, using Scripture as the standard.

- **Kingdom of heaven/God:** The church is not the kingdom of God, but is a part of God's kingdom. The kingdom of God is principally the sovereign rule of God (where God's will is done), manifested in Christ to bring all things to be subject to Him (under His feet). Thus, the kingdom of God is the reign of God, and the church is a community or fellowship given to God's people within the Kingdom. These Scriptures are key to our understanding: Mark 9:1, Matthew 3:2, 4:17, 10:7, Luke 21:31.

Note: Jesus and His disciples preached, taught, and healed, as they proclaimed, "The kingdom of heaven has come near to you."

- **Natural Gifts:** These God-given talents, skills, and special abilities are exercised through human might, power, skill, and effort. In the world of commerce, in a person's profession, a man or woman is apprenticed, trained, schooled, or mentored, and thereby gains experience, knowledge and skill, in a trade or profession. This work exercises and provides for the nourishment of the body, with daily bread that God provides, so they will have the strength and energy to perform their daily tasks. Working at these daily tasks requires various levels of reasoning ability, motor skills, strength, and dexterity. These natural gifts, when enhanced through training and education, are applied for the good of families and communities and may be distinguished by referring to them as "civil righteousness." When we do our work with skill and excellence using our gifts and talents, we honor God who created us and gave us the abilities to do our work.

- **Pastors, Shepherds,** ποιμήν *(poimēn):* Numerous references are made throughout Scripture regarding Pastor-Shepherds. The clearest charge to the ministries of a Pastor is what Jesus spoke to Peter: "Do you love me?" Because of your love for me above all else, feed the lambs, search for them and care for them, provide pleasant pastures and still waters for them to be fed and refreshed. Call them to lie down and rest in the Good Shepherd. To Pastor-Shepherds of the church, the Good Shepherd has entrusted His greatest treasure. This is not a position of lordship, but serving "shoulder to shoulder (Zephaniah 3:9) with the priesthood of believers. A pastor is not the first link in the chain of command. He is not the top boss on the organizational chart, but is a part of the order of leadership, placed within a circle of order for the church. This does not mean that the pastor-shepherd is subject to a democratic system of church government, answering to everyone who has a vote, but he is accountable to those who are serving "shoulder to shoulder" with him.

- **Preaching, Teaching,** κηρύσσω *(kēryssō),* διδασκαλία *(didaskalia):* May be accomplished by any who are called to serve the church. Often, elders, deacons and deaconesses are called on to teach. Preaching is not teaching, even though these gifts often blend together. Typically, preaching is not prophecy. They are distinctly different, especially in that teaching and sermons are prepared in advance using various preparation methods, special tools, and by the inspiration and anointing of the Holy Spirit. It is the preacher's work to reveal Jesus Christ by proclaiming the Scripture to the hearer, to exhort, to correct, to encourage, to build up, to strengthen and prepare the saints, and to declare the message of God's saving grace to the unbeliever.

- **Presbyter,** πρεσβύτερος *(presbuteros):* Apostles, Elders, Preachers, Teachers, Pastors, Deacons, Deaconesses, and others who are gifted in the Spirit to call Christians to minister and serve in spiritual gifts within a local congregation for the strengthening of the church. We see this gift working in 1 Timothy 4:14: "Do not neglect your gift, which was given you through a prophetic message when the body of elders (Presbytery) laid their hands on you." This is the same gift at work in Acts 13:2-3, "While they were worshiping the Lord and fasting, the Holy Spirit said, 'Set apart for me Barnabas and Saul for the work to which I have called them.' So after they fasted and prayed, they placed their hands on them and sent them off." This ministry is typically administered by the laying on of hands, at times accompanied by prophecy. In churches today, the practice of presbytery is a council of pastors or elders who are charged with calling and ordaining pastors to fill a pulpit and serve in a local church. The word "presbyter" is used as an alternative to "priest." In this study the term is used in the earliest sense of the word. In Acts 14:23, the apostle Paul, with prayer and fasting, ordained presbyters in the local church. This ministry in the church is not limited to calling and ordaining pastors, but for the good of the whole church, for all who are called to serve and minister in the church — for the benefit of the universal Priesthood of all believers.

- **Signet, Signet Ring,** חוֹתָם *(chowtham):* A symbol of authority and conferred authority. An emblem for a person's title or name. Several references are made throughout Scripture to signet rings. Genesis 41:42 says, "Then Pharaoh took his signet ring from his finger and put it on Joseph's finger." The priestly vestments of worship were adorned with precious stones as a signet (Exodus 28). Esther 3:10 says, "So the king took the signet ring off his finger and gave it to Haman son of Hammedatha." Haggai 2:23 says, "'I will take you, my servant Zerubbabel son of Shealtiel,' declares the Lord, 'and I will make you like my signet ring, for I have chosen you,' declares the Lord Almighty." Each reference shows us authority being conveyed to someone who would rule in his name, in his stead, in submission to his authority, and according to his commands.

- **Soul of Man,** ψυχή *(psychē):* The immortal, non-material part of humans. May be referred to as the "heart" of man. The soul is the source of our intellect, will, emotions, personality, and our uniqueness. As God brought together the body and breath of life in Adam, he became a living soul — a tripartite being made in the image of God. All of Adam's progeny are of the same nature.

- **Soulish,** ψυχικός *(psychikos):* When body and spirit (the breath of life) are brought together, man becomes a living soul — tripartite beings. All Christians face a daily struggle between fleshly weaknesses and our spirit, which is born of God. Our flesh wars against our spirit to rule over the whole person. When we walk in the Spirit and are led by the Spirit, our spirit will be strengthen and will rule over the soul and the flesh. When the flesh rules over the soul, this is soulish. Another word that is similar, but not as descriptive or useful is carnal, (σάρξ, sarx) which means "of or related to the flesh." "Soulish" is the best translation of the Greek word psychikos, but it is common to translate the word psychikos as "natural" or "sensual." It is the adjective of the noun "soul" which ought to be translated from psyche.

- **Spirit of Man,** πνεῦμα (pneuma): The Greek means, "breath, wind." The writer of this study holds to the "trichotomist" view of man, which he finds to be consistent with the nature of all God's creation. The spirit of man is the eternal, immaterial part of man bestowed upon man by the breath of the Holy Spirit. Romans 8:15-16 is descriptive of the nature of man's spirit: "When we cry, 'Abba! Father!' it is that very Spirit bearing witness with our spirit that we are children of God." It is our spirit that is the connecting point with the Spirit of a Holy God. It is our spirit that the Holy Spirit indwells as a temple. The application to our study is that spiritual gifts are for the reborn spirit of man while natural gifts are for the well being of the natural man — the body. See 1 Thess. 5:23, Hebrews 4:12, 1 Cor. 14:14.

- **Spirit Filled,** πίμπλημι (pimplēmi): The term is not used specifically, but implied throughout this study. The study writer holds to the belief that the Holy Spirit indwells and seals those who are justified in Christ. Also, the Holy Spirit desires to work continuously in the lives of Christian disciples, gifting, empowering, refreshing, and anointing for works and ministries for the good of the church.

- **Spiritual Gifts,** χάρισμα (charisma): Gifts for ministries to the church, or within the church, given and empowered by the Holy Spirit are "spiritual gifts." In this study, we find it necessary to distinguish the common from the holy by separating the spiritual and natural gifts, even when those natural gifts are used for work and service in the church.

- **Spiritual Language,** γλῶσσα *(glōssa):* This is a gift the Scripture refers to as tongues, i.e. speaking in the languages of heaven and earth that a person has never learned. Often, this gift is manifested as a spiritual language for the purpose of declaring the wonderful works of God (Acts 2:11) in prayer, thanksgiving, worship, and praise in words or phrases the speaker doesn't typically understand with his mind (1 Corinthians 14:2, 14, 15). This gift is a sign for unbelievers when used in public worship because an unknown or foreign tongue that the unbeliever cannot understand may be a sign of God's coming judgment if the unrepentant does not turn from sin (Deuteronomy 28:49). For the believer it is for spiritual strengthening and builds up the whole church when used with interpretation (1 Corinthians 14:26). When used in this manner it is considered a variation of the spiritual gift of prophecy, but not equal to. Not everyone enjoys this gift, because it is given, "just as He determines" (1 Corinthians 12:11). This is a most useful gift that must never be forbidden, marginalized, minimized, or relegated to a time long past (1 Corinthians 14:39). In a gathering of believers, ministering in the gift of spiritual language must always be accompanied with the gift of interpretation.

- **Submission,** ὑποτάσσω *(hypotassō):* See Authority above. Submission is key to the exercise of all authority within the church that is to be exercised in submission Christ's authority. Submission takes us from working in our own strength to serving in the power and might of God Almighty.

- **Tripartite:** In three parts. We are created in God's image, one person consisting of three parts. We are not three persons, but one person consisting of three distinct parts. Because it is difficult to discern the dividing line between soul and spirit, some teach that they are one and the same, but this teaching is not consistent with Scripture or with the very nature of God's creation.

- **Vestments, לָבַשׁ** *(labash):* Liturgical garments, adornments, and robes for leading worship. Often worn by priests, pastors, ministers, or bishops as they lead the congregation in worship. For the purpose of this study, vestments are not visible outward garments, but adornments, ornaments of worship, spiritual gifts, given by the Bridegroom to beautify the bride in preparation for His return.

- **Worship, προσκυνέω** *(proskyneō):* Giving glory and honor to God in His presence, whether in private or in a gathering of believers. We worship a Holy God in acts of lifting up our voices, ministering the Word, ministering or serving others in our spiritual gift, lifting holy hands, making music before the Lord. Worshipping in spirit and in truth, true and real worship flows from our spirit in unison with the Holy Spirit.

- **Yeshua HaMashiach** (ye-SHOO-ah ha-mah-SHEE-akh): This Hebrew name is used for the coming, promised Messiah. Jesus the Messiah, Jesus the Christ, Jesus the Anointed One.